A SECOND BIOLOGY COURSE

Also from Stanley Thornes (Publishers) Ltd

A FIRST CHEMISTRY COURSE by E N Ramsden

A FIRST PHYSICS COURSE by R B Arnold

A FIRST BIOLOGY COURSE by P T Bunyan

A FIRST ELECTRONICS COURSE by R B Arnold (forthcoming)

A SECOND BIOLOGY COURSE

P T Bunyan BSc MIBiol

Roade Comprehensive School, Northants

Stanley Thornes (Publishers) Ltd

First published in 1985 by Stanley Thornes (Publishers) Ltd
Old Station Drive
Leckhampton
Cheltenham
GL53 0DN

British Library Cataloguing in Publication Data

Bunyan, P.T.
    A second biology course
    1. Biology
    I. Title
    574   QH308.7

ISBN 0-85950-190-6

Phototypeset by Tech-Set, 15 Enterprise House, Team Valley, Gateshead
Printed in Great Britain at the Bath Press Ltd., Bath

Contents

Preface

This book is a sequel to *A First Biology Course*. It aims to provide sufficient information to take average pupils through to the 16+ examination.

Like its predecessor, this book is intended to be read and enjoyed by the pupils themselves. I have tried to keep both the language and the style simple to encourage the pupils to read. The range of information provided has been limited in order that the essential information is more easily accessible.

The chapters in the book can be used in any order. However, when writing it I was conscious of a developing theme, both within and between chapters. It very much reflects the way I teach, and there is a certain progression within the book. Teachers may find that, because of this, some chapters fall more logically into the sequence I have used.

It is not necessary to have used *A First Biology Course* to make sense of this book. Some topics which were treated in depth in the first book do not receive such a detailed treatment here. I have tried, however, to ensure that no topic is omitted entirely.

Bearing in mind the rigours of examination, there are summaries within each chapter. These can be used as a framework for revision.

I hope that pupils reading this book will come to appreciate some of the complexity and elegance of nature. In doing so may they derive as much pleasure at the wonder of it as I do.

P T Bunyan
Northampton 1985

Acknowledgements

I would like to thank the following, who have kindly supplied photographs for inclusion in this book:

All-Sport Photographic Ltd, for Figure 1.12

Heather Angel, for Figure 11.11

Barnaby's Picture Library, for Figures 3.20, 13.7, 14.7 and 14.19

Biofoto Associates, for Figures 3.2, 3.5, 3.24 and 9.7

British Museum (National History), for Figure 9.2

Bruce Coleman Ltd, for Figure 2.16

Phillip Harris Biological Ltd, for Figures 10.20 and 11.4

ICI Plant Protection, for Figure 6.12

Opdebeeck M-Edegem, for Figure 3.18

Natural History Photographic Agency, for Figure 10.5

Claude Nuridsany and Marie Pérennou, for Figure 12.8

Science Photo Library, for Figure 2.19

Teaching Aids at Low Cost (TALC), a teaching activity of the Tropical Child Health Unit, Institute of Child Health, London, for Figures 9.12 and 9.13

C G Vosa, Botany School, Oxford for Figure 9.6

I would like to thank the following people for all the help they have given me during the preparation of this book: The staff of Stanley Thornes (Publishers), without whom the book could never have come to fruition; Mr K C Plant, who read the original manuscript and made some very valuable criticisms and suggestions; Mr Don Manley, who prepared the word puzzles; and finally my wife, Terry, who once again devoted many summer weeks to the typewriter rather than to her garden.

P T BUNYAN

Section 1

HOW ORGANISMS
STAY ALIVE

1. The energy supply

1.1 The basic needs of organisms

An organism is something which is alive — for example, a plant or an animal (Figure 1.1). Being alive means being able to grow and reproduce.

Figure 1.1   Living organisms

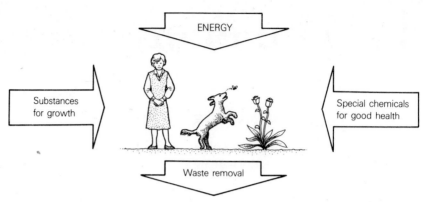

Figure 1.2   What organisms need to stay alive

Now look at Figure 1.2. To stay alive *all* organisms need:

(a) energy, usually obtained from food.
(b) substances to make and repair cells.
(c) certain special chemicals to keep healthy — for example, vitamins.
(d) to be able to get rid of any waste substances which they make during
      the processes of living and growing, for example carbon dioxide and
      urea.

Since *every* cell in an organism has these four needs, then large, complex
organisms like humans have special organs and structures to make sure
each cell gets what it needs. (See Figure 1.3.)

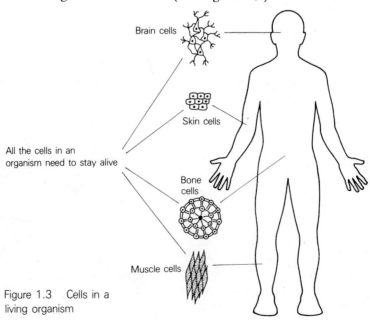

Figure 1.3   Cells in a
living organism

In addition, an organism must be able to *respond* to its environment. Animals need to be able to find food and mates and to avoid harmful conditions. Plants need to grow towards light. (See Figure 1.4.)

In this book we will study living organisms to see how they are *organised*. That is, we shall study how each cell is supplied with its needs. To do this we must study how organisms are made and what each part does.

If animals and plants are to survive they must respond to the environment in ways which help them. The responses above do not do this, but the ones below do. The way an organism responds will depend on what sort of organism it is.

Figure 1.4

1.2 Respiration

Living organisms need energy for growth and for many of the chemical reactions which take place inside the cell. Animals need more energy than plants because animals use energy for movement. Animals like humans are 'warm-blooded' (more correctly called *homeothermic*), and they need more energy to keep their temperature constant.

Figure 1.5   Food provides energy for all animals

Organisms get their energy from food substances (Figure 1.5). Foods which can provide lots of energy are *carbohydrates* (like starch and glucose) and *fats*.

Most living organisms, both plants and animals, get most of their energy from the simple sugar, glucose (Figure 1.6). The energy is stored inside the molecules of glucose and is released when the glucose is broken down into simpler substances.

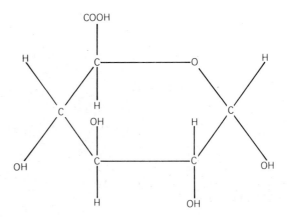

A molecule of glucose is made of 6 carbon atoms (C). 12 hydrogen atoms (H) and 6 oxygen atoms (O). The energy that holds the atoms together is released by respiration and is used by plants and animals.

Figure 1.6   Glucose molecule

Releasing energy from food substances is a chemical process called *respiration*. It takes place inside all cells. There are two sorts of respiration. One needs oxygen to release the energy and is called *aerobic respiration*. The other does not need oxygen and is called *anaerobic respiration*. Most living organisms use aerobic respiration most of the time because it releases more energy than anaerobic respiration.

Do not be confused by the word respiration. To a biologist it means getting energy from food. This is *not* the same as breathing, which is simply the way air is moved in and out of the body.

Aerobic respiration

The chemical reaction for aerobic respiration can be summarised as

$$\text{Glucose} + \text{Oxygen} \longrightarrow \text{Energy} + \text{Carbon dioxide} + \text{Water}$$

A chemist would write this as

$$C_6H_{12}O_6 + 6O_2 \longrightarrow \text{Energy} + 6CO_2 + 6H_2O$$

To be able to respire aerobically a cell needs oxygen and glucose. It also needs to get rid of carbon dioxide and water. We can be certain that any cell or organism which is using oxygen and producing carbon dioxide must be respiring aerobically. (See Figure 1.7.)

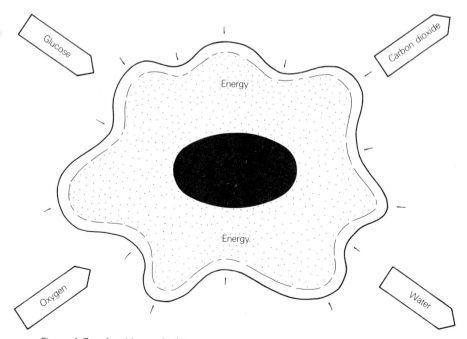

Figure 1.7   Aerobic respiration

Experiment 1.1

Experiment to show that we use oxygen

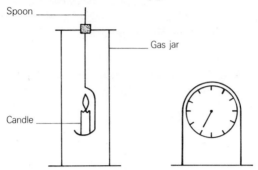

Figure 1.8   Apparatus to compare the amount of oxygen in air and breath

1. Take a gas jar, a clock and a candle on a long spoon with a lid (a deflagrating spoon) (Figure 1.8).

2. Light the candle with a splint.

3. Quickly, but steadily, put the candle into the gas jar. Time how long the candle takes to go out from the moment the lid touches the gas jar.

4. Repeat this four more times. Record all your results in a chart like the one opposite.

5. Now fill the gas jar with your breath. You need a bowl ¾ full of water, a plastic tube and a gas jar lid with Vaseline on it.

6. Fill the gas jar with water and hold it in the bowl as shown in Figure 1.9.

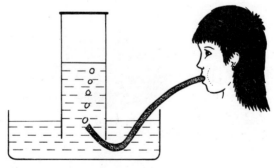

Figure 1.9   Filling the gas jar with your breath

7. Put one end of the plastic tube under the mouth of the gas jar and gently blow so that the jar becomes filled with your breath.

8. Slide the Vaselined gas jar lid on to the jar before you take it out of the water.

9. Remove the jar of breath and burn the candle in it as you did before. Remember: do not take the lid off until the candle is ready to be put into the jar, or you will lose the breath.

10. Repeat this four more times and record your results.

11. Work out the average time the candle took to go out for both ordinary air and breathed-out air.

	Time recorded in seconds (s)	Average time
Ordinary air		
Breathed-out air		

12. What gas does the candle need to burn?

13. Which does it burn longest in?

14. Which has most oxygen?

15. What does this experiment show?

16. Why is it important to work out the average times?

Experiment 1.2

Experiment to investigate breath and carbon dioxide

1. Assemble the apparatus as shown in Figure 1.10. Note carefully which is tube 1 and which is tube 2.

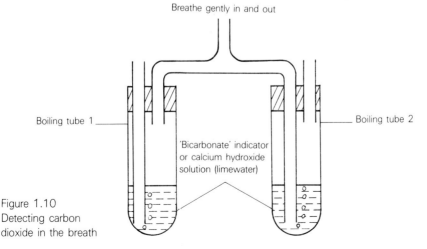

Breathe gently in and out

Boiling tube 1

Boiling tube 2

'Bicarbonate' indicator or calcium hydroxide solution (limewater)

Figure 1.10
Detecting carbon dioxide in the breath

2. Pour enough 'bicarbonate' indicator or calcium hydroxide solution (lime-water) so that the long glass tube in each boiling tube is covered by about 1 cm of liquid. (When carbon dioxide is present 'bicarbonate' indicator turns from red to orange/yellow and limewater turns cloudy.)

3. Copy out and fill in a results chart to show the appearance of the liquid in each tube.

4. Gently breathe in and out through the central tube as shown.

5. After 30–60 seconds, stop and compare the liquid in the tubes. Fill in the results chart.

Appearance of indicator			
Before experiment		*After experiment*	
Tube 1	Tube 2	Tube 1	Tube 2

6. Which boiling tube did you inhale through?

7. Which boiling tube did you exhale through?

8. Which tube showed carbon dioxide present?

Anaerobic respiration in animals

Almost all living organisms can respire without oxygen for a certain amount of time. People who do a lot of exercise will often use more energy than they can obtain by aerobic respiration. They cannot breathe fast enough to supply the oxygen they need. At such times their muscle cells will respire anaerobically for short periods (Figure 1.11).

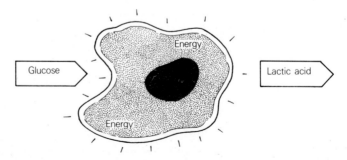

Figure 1.11   Anaerobic respiration

This reaction can be summarised as

Glucose $\longrightarrow$ Energy + Lactic acid

A chemist would write this as

$C_6H_{12}O_6 \longrightarrow$ Energy + $2C_3H_6O_3$

Unfortunately, animals cannot respire anaerobically for very long because lactic acid is a muscle poison. It causes the muscle to seize up with cramp. The only way to get rid of the lactic acid is to break it down further by using oxygen or to build it back into glucose, which needs energy. After exercise, most people will puff and pant quite heavily (Figure 1.12). The extra oxygen they are taking in is being used to get rid of lactic acid.

Figure 1.12   The athelete is getting rid of lactic acid by breathing extra oxygen

Anaerobic respiration in yeast

Yeasts are one-celled fungi (Figure 1.13).

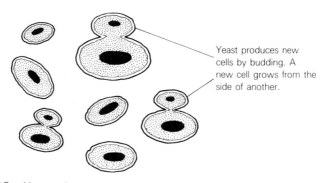

Yeast produces new cells by budding. A new cell grows from the side of another.

Figure 1.13   Yeast cells

They often get the energy they need to grow by respiring anaerobically. Although there are many different varieties of yeast, the chemistry of anaerobic respiration is the same for many of them (Figure 1.14). The reaction is

$$Glucose \longrightarrow Energy + Carbon\ dioxide + Alcohol$$

A chemist would write this as

$$C_6H_{12}O_6 \longrightarrow Energy + 2CO_2 + 2C_2H_5OH$$

This reaction can be demonstrated by Experiment 1.3.

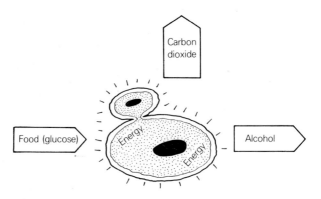

Figure 1.14   Anaerobic respiration in yeast

Experiment 1.3

Experiment to show anaerobic respiration in yeast

1. Boil a little water for a few minutes and pour about a 2 cm depth into a boiling tube. Boiling will drive all the oxygen out of the water.

2. Cool the water to about room temperature.

3. Add a spatula of glucose (or ordinary white sugar) and a few drops of an actively growing yeast suspension.

4. Pour a thin layer of liquid paraffin on to this mixture. (This will stop any oxygen from dissolving in the water.)

5. Pour a little limewater or bicarbonate indicator into a *clean* test-tube and then assemble the apparatus as shown in Figure 1.15.

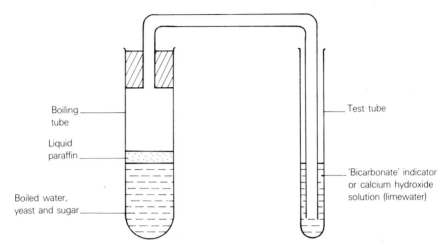

Boiling tube

Liquid paraffin

Boiled water, yeast and sugar

Test tube

'Bicarbonate' indicator or calcium hydroxide solution (limewater)

Figure 1.15   Demonstrating anaerobic respiration in yeast

6. Watch for changes in the calcium hydroxide solution or 'bicarbonate' indicator which will show that the yeast is producing carbon dioxide gas. If the yeast is respiring only slowly, then you may have to wait several hours.

7. What changes in the indicator will show carbon dioxide gas? Is this experiment a valid demonstration of anaerobic respiration?

The baking and brewing industries both make use of anaerobic respiration by yeast. In baking, the yeast is mixed in the dough and the bubbles of carbon dioxide given off make the bread rise. Any ethanol (alcohol) produced is evaporated off when the bread is baked.

Brewing produces alcoholic drinks, and so it is the alcohol which is important. Drinks like beer and sparkling wines are fizzy because not all the carbon dioxide is allowed to escape. The brewer's name for anaerobic respiration by yeast is *fermentation.*

In Brazil, sugar cane is grown. It is fermented by yeast and the alcohol produced is used in cars in Brazil as a substitute for petrol.

Summary

1. Obtaining energy from food is called respiration.

2. Aerobic respiration uses oxygen.

3. Anaerobic respiration does not use oxygen.

4. Carbohydrates (very often glucose) and fats are energy foods.

Questions on Chapter 1

1. Respiration means obtaining energy from food.
    (a) What sorts of food provide lots of energy?
    (b) What things have you eaten today which are providing you with energy?

2. What is the difference between aerobic and anaerobic respiration?

3. Why do most living organisms respire aerobically?

4. (a) Look back at the equation for aerobic respiration on page 5 for 10 seconds. Then close the book and write the equation down.
    (b) Now explain as simply as you can what the equation means.

5. Why can people not respire anaerobically for long periods of time?

6. Why is anaerobic respiration in yeast a very important process?

7. A pupil burnt a candle in a jar of air three times. The candle was then burnt in a jar of breath three times. Here are the results:

    Time the candle burned in air: 15 seconds, 14 seconds, 16 seconds.
    Time the candle burned in breathed-out air: 11 seconds, 14 seconds, 11 seconds.

    (a) What is the average time the candle burned in air?
    (b) What is the average time the candle burned in breathed-out air?
    (c) What fraction of the oxygen had been used up between breathing in and breathing out again?

Wordfinder on Chapter 1

(Teacher, please see special note in front of book.)

Copy or photocopy the wordfinder, then solve the clues and put a ring around the answers. Answers go in any direction backwards and forwards, up and down, and diagonally (the first one has been done for you). Do not write on this page.

R	A	F	E	P	L	A	N	T	F	E
R	E	F	M	S	E	A	A	N	U	S
C	R	S	O	T	O	F	C	E	N	L
I	U	A	P	O	T	C	N	T	G	L
B	H	A	C	I	D	E	U	I	I	E
O	C	I	B	O	R	E	A	L	O	C
R	R	C	N	G	C	A	A	R	G	B
E	A	R	Y	E	A	S	T	O	N	D
A	T	A	I	O	L	A	M	I	N	A
N	S	M	S	I	N	A	G	R	O	X
A	I	P	O	I	S	O	N	D	E	N

1   Something which is alive is called a living _____ (8)

2   All living things need _____ (4)

3   2 can provide 1 with _____ (6)

4   The basic units in 1 are called _____ (5)

5   One sort of living thing (6)

6   Another sort of living thing (5)

7   A food which can provide energy (3)

8   A common carbohydrate (6)

9   A chemical process releasing energy from 2 (11)

10   9 which needs oxygen is called _____ (7)

11   Its formula is $C_6H_{12}O_6$ (7)

12, 13   Its formula is $C_3H_6O_3$ (6, 4: two words in separate places)

14   12, 13 is a muscle _____ (6)

15   9 which does not need oxygen is called _____ (9)

16   It is used in baking and brewing (5)

17   16s are one-celled _____ (5)

18   12, 13 can cause _____ in the muscles (5)

19   A waste substance (4)

20   _____ (12)

21, 22   _____ (6, 7)

The answers to 20 and 21, 22 may be formed from the unused letters taken from left to right row by row top to bottom. Please write your own clues for these.

2. How animal cells obtain energy

Large animals, like ourselves, are organised in such a way that all the cells are able to produce energy (Figure 2.1).

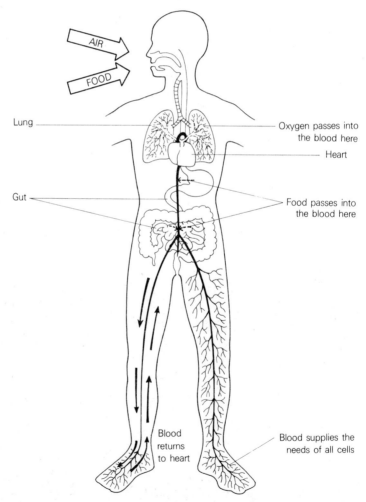

Figure 2.1   The organisation of the human body

Each cell gets its food and oxygen from the blood. Blood collects food from the digestive system (gut) and oxygen from the lungs. The blood is then pumped by the heart so that it can reach every cell in the body. Waste carbon dioxide and water are removed by the blood to places where they can be got rid of. The job of the digestive system, the lungs and the blood system is to make sure that the body cells get all the substances they need to live and grow. We can see how this works by looking at the systems separately.

2.1 The digestive system

Feeding All animals feed. Some feed on plants and are called *herbivores*. Some feed on other animals and are called *carnivores*. Some feed on both, as most people do, and are called *omnivores*. Whatever they feed on, animals have mouths which are *adapted* to their food.

We have teeth to bite and chew. In our mouth we have biting teeth — the incisors and canines — and chewing teeth — the premolars and molars (Figure 2.2).

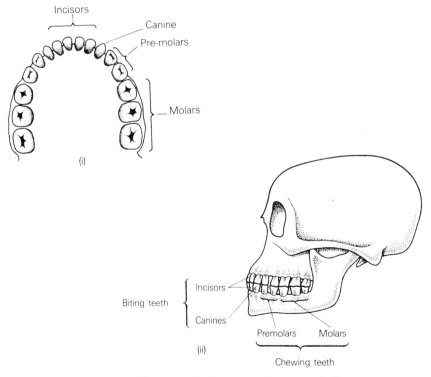

Figure 2.2   A dental plan (i); Side view of skull showing the teeth (ii)

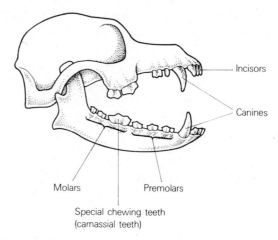

Figure 2.3   Side view of a dog skull showing the teeth

A carnivore, like the dog, has teeth which are different from ours. It has very long canines to rip flesh and sharp pointed molars and premolars to slice through meat and crunch bones (Figure 2.3).

A herbivore, like the sheep, has rows of ridged molars and premolars which it uses to grind grass. To get any food substances from plants it is necessary to crush the cells completely. By chewing from side to side, sheep and other herbivores use their molars and premolars like grindstones. Sheep have small incisors and canines at the front of the lower jaw only (Figure 2.4). These chop grass by pressing against a hard pad of skin on the top jaw, rather like an upside-down chopping board.

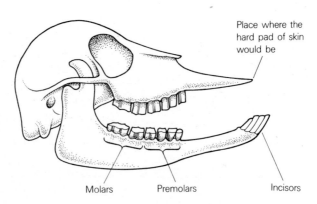

Figure 2.4   Side view of a sheep skull showing the teeth

The fly and the mosquito both feed on liquid foods. The fly 'spits' saliva which dissolves a little food and the fly sucks this back up again. The mosquito has long needle-like mouthparts which it sticks into the skin to suck blood. The mosquito, too, produces saliva but this is used to stop the blood from clotting. (See Figure 2.5.)

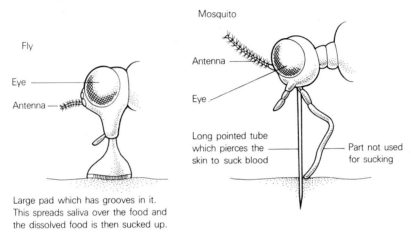

Figure 2.5   Mouthparts of a fly (left) and a mosquito

The earthworm does not have a very specialised mouth (Figure 2.6). It simply sucks in rotting, semi-liquid food and particles of soil. Any food on the soil is digested as it passes through the worm's gut and the soil particles are dumped in the form of worm casts above the ground.

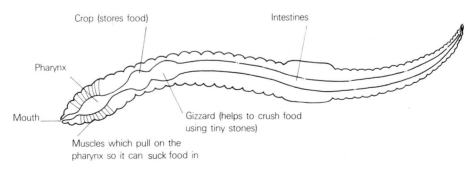

Figure 2.6   The digestive system of an earthworm

Digestion

Digestion means breaking down food into pieces small enough to dissolve and pass through the gut into the blood and be used by the body. Digestion begins with chewing the food. Once it has been swallowed, however, the food is broken down further by very special chemicals called *enzymes*. It is hard to imagine enzymes working, but look at Figure 2.7. The enzymes in your gut break down food substances which have large *molecules* and do not usually dissolve easily, into food substances which have small molecules and do dissolve. For example, enzymes digest proteins into amino acids and starch into glucose.

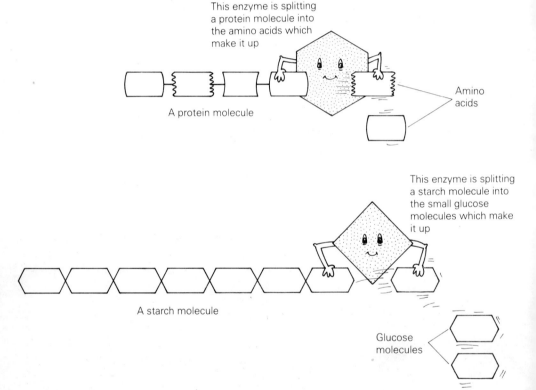

Figure 2.7   How enzymes work

Here are a few facts you need to know about enzymes:

(a) All the chemical reactions in your body are controlled by enzymes — not only digestion but also respiration and the reactions which make new body cells. There are thousands of different enzymes in the body.

(b) An enzyme can only work one sort of chemical reaction. For example, the enzymes which digest proteins cannot digest starch and vice versa.

(c) Enzymes work more quickly if they are warm. If they get too hot, they are destroyed. 'Too hot' generally means above 45 °C. The enzymes in our bodies work best at 37 °C, which is the temperature our bodies are kept at. Enzymes hardly work at all at 0 °C, but the cold does not destroy them — it only stops them from working.

(d) Enzymes work best with the correct acid or alkaline conditions. The ones in our small intestine will not work if they are too acid, they must be neutral.

(e) Enzymes are not changed or worn out by the reactions they control. They can be used over and over again.

You can investigate enzymes in the following experiments.

Experiment 2.1

To investigate the effect of temperature on an enzyme

The enzyme for this experiment is *amylase,* found in saliva. It controls the digestion of *starch* to *maltose* and *glucose*.

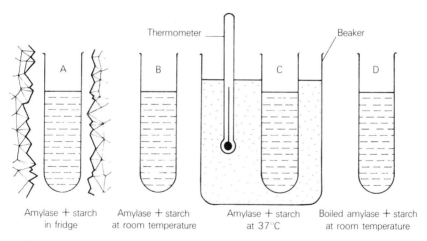

Figure 2.8   Investigating the activity of amylase at different temperatures

1.   Take four clean test-tubes labelled A, B, C, D and a clean boiling tube. You will also need a glass rod, a white tile and a bunsen burner.

2. Collect about 8 cm³ of saliva in the boiling tube. You may find it easier to make saliva if you chew a clean rubber band.

3. Now treat the test-tubes in the following way:
    Tube A. Pour in about 2 cm³ of saliva and place the tube in the fridge.
    Tube B. Pour in about 2 cm³ of saliva and place it in the lab in a test-tube rack.
    Tube C. Pour in about 2 cm³ of saliva and place it in a beaker of water at 37 °C. (Try to keep this as near to 37 °C as you can.)
    Tube D. Boil the remaining saliva in the boiling tube for about a minute. Then pour about 2 cm³ of the boiled saliva into tube D. Place it in the rack next to tube B and let it cool down. (See Figure 2.8.)

4. Add 2 cm³ of 1% starch solution to each of the four test-tubes A, B, C, D. Use starch solution which has been kept in the fridge for tube A because it has to stay cold. Remember to put tube A back into the fridge.

5. Wait 2 minutes.

6. Using the glass rod, take a drop of the mixture from tube A and place it on the white tile. Add a drop of iodine to it (iodine turns blue/black if starch is present). Wipe the glass rod and repeat for tubes B, C and then D.

7. Repeat this every 2 minutes until at least one of the tubes shows no more starch present.

8. Now add about 1 cm³ of Benedict's solution to each tube and heat the contents gently until they boil. An orange/yellow colour will show lots of glucose present. A green colour will show only a little glucose. Any other colour means there is no glucose.

9. Record your results in a chart like the one below.

First tube to show no starch	
	Results of the Benedict's test
Tube A	
Tube B	
Tube C	
Tube D	

10. In which tube did the starch disappear first?

11.   What effect did boiling the saliva have?

12.   At what temperature did you find the amylase worked best?

13.   Did the amylase work well in the fridge?

Experiment 2.2

To investigate the effect of pH on an enzyme

The enzyme for this experiment is *pepsin*, found in the stomach. It controls the digestion of *protein* into *amino acids*.

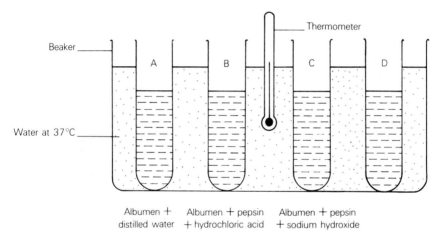

Figure 2.9   Investigating the activity of pepsin at varying pH

1.   Take four clean test-tubes and label them A, B, C, D.

2.   Treat the tubes in the following way:
     Tube A. Add about 2 cm^3 of albumen suspension (albumen suspension is made by boiling an egg white with lots of water) and 1 cm^3 of distilled water.
     Tube B. Add about 2 cm^3 of albumen suspension and 1 cm^3 of pepsin solution and four drops of dilute hydrochloric acid.
     Tube C. Add about 2 cm^3 of albumen suspension and 1 cm^3 of pepsin solution and four drops of dilute sodium hydroxide.
     Tube D. Add about 2 cm^3 of albumen suspension and 1 cm^3 of distilled water and four drops of dilute hydrochloric acid. (See Figure 2.9.)

3.   Place all the tubes in a beaker of water at 37°C and leave for 15 minutes.

4. You will be able to see that all the albumen has been digested when the liquid goes from being cloudy to being clean.

5. In which tube was the albumen digested?

6. What conditions does pepsin need in order to work?

7. How do you know it was not the acid which digested the albumen?

8. Tubes A and D were controls. What do you think tube A showed?

Digestion in humans

Our digestive system, or gut, can be thought of as a very long tube which goes from the mouth to the anus (Figure 2.10).

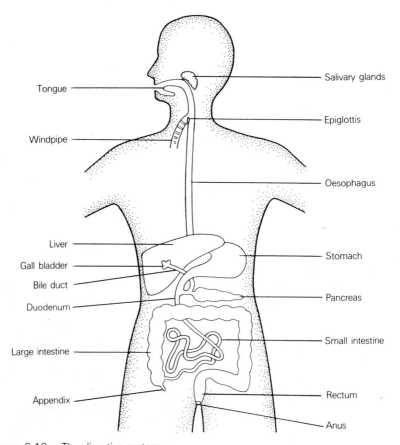

Figure 2.10   The digestive system

In some places the tube is quite narrow and in others it has become a large bag. The wall of the tube contains muscles which squeeze food along and in some parts help to mix food with enzymes.

Inside the tube, food is first digested by enzymes and then *absorbed* into the blood. 'Absorbed' means that the tiny molecules of food substances, like glucose and amino acids, pass from the gut into the blood. Some substances can be absorbed in the stomach — for example, alcohol, aspirin and glucose. Most substances, however, are absorbed in the small intestine.

We can see how the gut works by looking at what the different parts do.

The mouth. Food is chewed in the mouth. Saliva produced by the salivary glands contains the enzyme amylase. This digests starch into the sugars maltose and glucose. This can be written as

$$\text{Starch} \xrightarrow{\text{Amylase}} \text{Maltose} + \underline{\text{Glucose}}$$

(All substances which are underlined in the next few pages are ones which cannot be digested any further and can be absorbed into the blood.)

Since food does not spend very much time in the mouth, not a lot of starch is digested. However, in the mouth, food is mixed with a watery, slippery liquid called mucus. This makes it easier for the food to pass through the gut.

The oesophagus (gullet). This is just a long tube which connects the mouth to the stomach. The oesophagus is not an open tube — nothing falls down it. All food is carried through it by a system of muscle movement called *peristalsis* (Figure 2.11). This is rather like squeezing the last bit of toothpaste from the end of the tube.

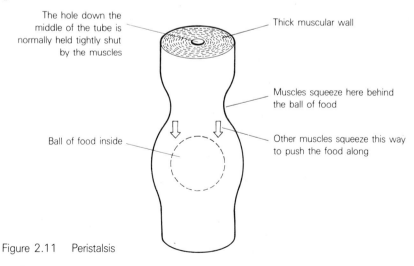

The hole down the middle of the tube is normally held tightly shut by the muscles

Thick muscular wall

Muscles squeeze here behind the ball of food

Ball of food inside

Other muscles squeeze this way to push the food along

Figure 2.11   Peristalsis

Muscles squeeze behind a piece of food and so push it along the tube. Peristalsis normally works in the direction mouth to anus. It can go backwards, however — as you were probably aware the last time you were sick!

The stomach. This is a large bag just under your left ribs. It has strong muscles in its walls which mix the food with hydrochloric acid, mucus and the enzymes *pepsin* and *rennin.* The acid kills bacteria and provides the right pH for the enzymes to work. Pepsin digests proteins into smaller substances called *peptides.* Rennin is only really useful when we are babies because it clots milk, separating the solid foods from the liquid. In this way the solids can be kept in the stomach for digestion and the liquid can be moved on. Here are the word equations:

$$\text{Proteins} \xrightarrow{\text{Pepsin}} \text{Peptides}$$

$$\text{Milk} \xrightarrow{\text{Rennin}} \text{Separates solid and liquid parts}$$

Food stays in the stomach for about 6 hours. At the end of this time it has become a watery mash.

The duodenum. This is a very important short length of tube. Both the *liver* and the *pancreas* pass substances into the duodenum to digest the food.

The liver produces a powerful, useful liquid called *bile* which is stored in the gall bladder. It is released down the bile duct to the duodenum. Bile is a strong alkali. It neutralises the acid from the stomach and makes the food alkaline. It also breaks large fat droplets into very tiny ones which are easier to digest. Some of these fat droplets are so small they can be absorbed without being digested any further.

The pancreas produces three enzymes: *trypsin,* which digests proteins into peptides; *lipase,* which digests fats into fatty acids and glycerol; *amylase,* which digests starch into glucose and maltose. In equations:

$$\text{Proteins} \xrightarrow{\text{Trypsin}} \text{Peptides}$$

$$\text{Fats} \xrightarrow{\text{Lipase}} \underline{\text{Fatty acids}} + \underline{\text{Glycerol}}$$

$$\text{Starch} \xrightarrow{\text{Amylase}} \text{Maltose} + \underline{\text{Glucose}}$$

The small intestine. This is a very long, narrow tube. It is between 6 and 10 metres long and is coiled and twisted. It is found in the place we normally point to if we mean our stomach. When we talk about having 'stomach ache' we usually mean 'intestine ache'. Part of the job of the small intestine is to complete digestion. *Peptidase* digests peptides into amino acids. *Maltase* digests maltose into glucose. There are also other enzymes but their names are not so important. In equations:

$$\text{Peptides} \xrightarrow{\text{Peptidase}} \text{Amino acids}$$

$$\text{Maltose} \xrightarrow{\text{Maltase}} \text{Glucose}$$

The other job of the small intestine is to absorb the digested food. If you look back through the parts of the gut, you will see that the substances which will be absorbed are glucose, amino acids, fatty acids and glycerol, and the tiny fat droplets produced by bile. Absorbing these is a slow job which is why the small intestine is so long. It also has a very special inside surface which is folded and folded again to produce a huge surface area for the food to pass through. The result of all this folding is to produce tiny projections which look like fingers (Figure 2.12). Each one is called a *villus* (plural: *villi*). Inside every villus are a lot of tiny blood tubes which take the digested food away. Another tube called a *lacteal* takes away the tiny fat droplets.

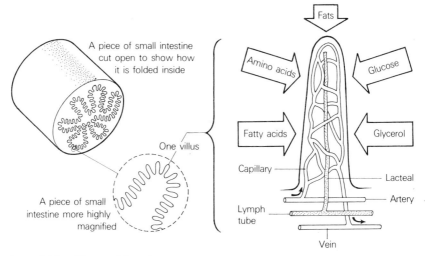

Figure 2.12   The small intestine

The large intestine. This tube is wider but much shorter than the small intestine. It contains all the substances which the gut could not digest, like plant fibres, mixed with lots of water. We cannot afford to waste this water, so the large intestine takes it back into the blood. What is then left is stored for a while in the *rectum,* then passed out through a small muscular hole called the *anus.*

Experiment 2.3

To show that food does not fall through the oesophagus

Figure 2.13   A demonstration

1. All you need is a piece of bread.

2. Prop yourself upside down against a wall and eat the bread (Figure 2.13).

3. Could you swallow the bread while you were upside down?

Experiment 2.4

Making a model of the digestive system to show digestion and absorption

1. You will need two boiling tubes, a piece of visking tube, a paperclip, a dropper, a piece of cotton, a test-tube and a white tile. (Visking tubing behaves in much the same way as the walls of the small intestine.)

2. Collect about 3 cm^3 of saliva in a boiling tube.

3. Add to this about 6–8 cm^3 of starch solution. This mixture will represent the food digesting in the model gut.

4. Carefully, half fill the visking tube with the starch/saliva mixture and tie the top of the visking tube with the thread. Now rinse the outside of the tube under a tap to make sure there is no starch or saliva on the outside.

5. Half fill the second boiling tube with distilled water and drop the visking tube in, as in Figure 2.14.

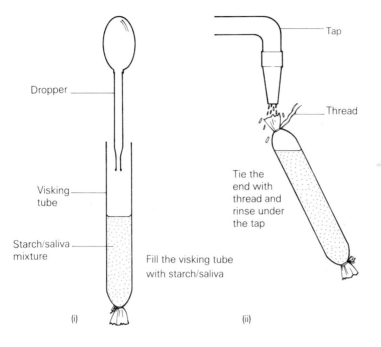

Dropper

Visking tube

Starch/saliva mixture

Fill the visking tube with starch/saliva

(i)

Tap

Thread

Tie the end with thread and rinse under the tap

(ii)

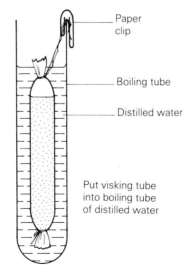

Paper clip

Boiling tube

Distilled water

Put visking tube into boiling tube of distilled water

(iii)

Figure 2.14(i)−(iii)   A model of the digestive system

6. Test the water in the boiling tube straight away for starch (take a drop out
    and mix on a tile with iodine) and glucose (add a few drops of water to
    1 cm^3 of Benedict's solution in the test-tube and heat gently until it boils).
    Record your results in a table.

7. Wait 15 minutes, now test the water in the boiling tube again for starch and
    glucose.

	Starch	Glucose
Test on the water immediately after visking tube was added		
Test on the water 15 minutes later		

8. Did the starch pass through the visking tube?

9. Did glucose pass through it?

10. Where did the glucose come from?

Summary

1. Food is needed for energy and to provide the materials for growth.

2. Animals eat other living things for food.

3. Food is digested in the gut. It is broken down by chewing, and then by
    enzymes into very tiny molecules.

4. Digested food is absorbed into the blood so that it can be carried to the
    cells that need it.

2.2 The breathing system

Breathing in animals

Oxygen in the air must be transferred into the blood. Carbon dioxide in
the blood must be transferred into the air. This is a slow process because it
relies on *diffusion*. Diffusion is the movement of gases and liquids from
places where there is a high concentration to places where there is a low
concentration (Figure 2.15).

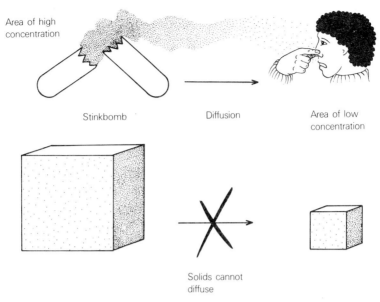

Figure 2.15   Diffusion

To cope with the slowness of diffusion, breathing surfaces in all living organisms have a large surface area. They also have a layer of water for oxygen to dissolve in before it diffuses into the blood.

Worms breathe through their skin, which is why they are always covered in a thin layer of slime. Insects have a system of tubes called *tracheae* (pronounced 'track-ee-yee') which carry air to all the parts (Figure 2.17). Fish have gills to obtain oxygen that has dissolved in the water. Each gill is made of millions of tiny layers to give as large a surface area as possible. Mammals, birds, reptiles and amphibians all breathe with lungs.

Figure 2.17 (overleaf) shows some different ways of breathing.

Figure 2.16   The whale is a mammal. It breathes with lungs just like we do

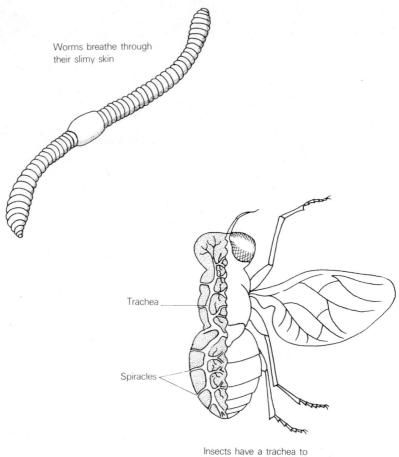

Worms breathe through
their slimy skin

Trachea

Spiracles

Insects have a trachea to
carry air to the tissues

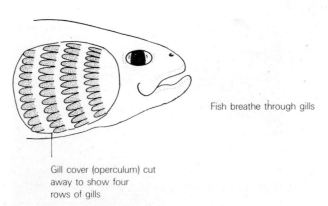

Fish breathe through gills

Gill cover (operculum) cut
away to show four
rows of gills

Figure 2.17   Ways of breathing

Breathing in humans

We breathe using our lungs. As you can see in Figure 2.18, the two lungs are contained in a completely airtight chamber formed by the *ribs* and the *diaphragm.* The lungs connect to the mouth by a tube called the *trachea.* It has rings of *cartilage* around it which stop it from collapsing when air is sucked in (rather like the rings on a vacuum cleaner hose). Each lung is surrounded by two thin membranes called the *pleural membranes.* These are covered with liquid and are very slippery. They stop the lungs from rubbing against the ribs during breathing.

You can see, too, that the heart is between the lungs. The heart pumps blood through the lungs to pick up oxygen and get rid of carbon dioxide.

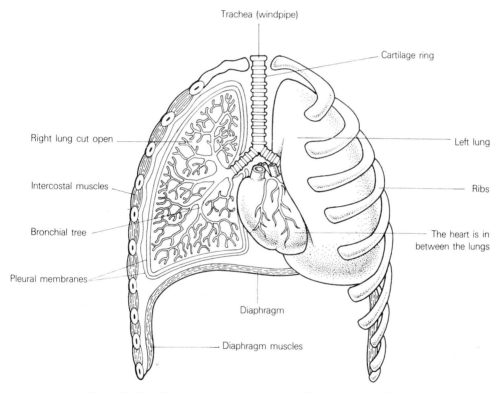

Figure 2.18   Diagram of the human lungs (with the right side of the rib cage cut away)

What are the lungs like?

The lungs are rather like a sponge. Inside each lung there is a system of tubes called the *bronchial tree* (Figure 2.19). All these tubes connect to the *bronchii* and then to the trachea. Air can pass through these tubes to all parts of the lung.

Figure 2.19   A bronchial tree

These tubes become smaller and smaller until they are too small to be seen, except with a microscope (Figure 2.20). Each one ends in a group of tiny air bags which look a little like a bunch of grapes. Each tiny air bag is called an *alveolus* (plural: *alveoli*).

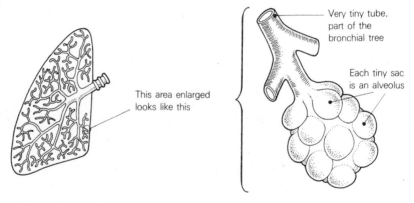

Figure 2.20   Enlargement of the smallest part of the bronchial tree

Each alveolus has a wall only one cell thick. Next to this are many blood *capillaries* which also have walls one cell thick. Inside the capillaries are the blood cells. Oxygen diffuses from the air in the alveolus through the cells and into the blood. Carbon dioxide diffuses from the blood into the air in the alveolus. (See Figure 2.21 (opposite).)

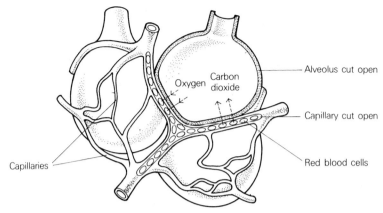

Figure 2.21   How oxygen gets into the blood and carbon dioxide gets out

How air gets into the lungs

We *breathe* by using our *ribs* and *diaphragm.* Together these create a suction which pulls air into the lungs. You can see how this works in the following simple model.

Experiment 2.5

Using a model to show how breathing works

1.   The rubber sheet under the jar represents the diaphragm (Figure 2.22). Pull the rubber down.

2.   Now let the rubber sheet go.

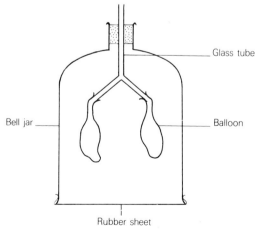

Figure 2.22   How the lungs are filled with air

3. What happens to the balloons when the sheet is pulled?

4. What happens when the rubber sheet is released?

5. Explain how this works.

An explanation of breathing is as follows. The ribs move up and out and the diaphragm moves down. This makes the volume inside the chest cavity larger. Something has to fill this larger space. The lungs stretch to fill this space and this stretches the alveoli inside the lungs. Air rushes down the trachea and through the bronchial tree to fill the alveoli. This is breathing in. Breathing out is simply a case of the ribs going in and the diaphragm moving up. The alveoli are elastic like tiny balloons. When there is no suction they go back to their original size. (See Figure 2.23.)

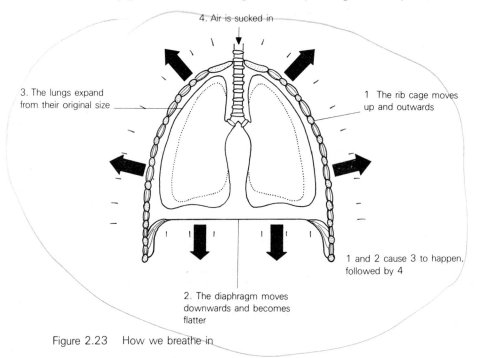

4. Air is sucked in

3. The lungs expand from their original size

1 The rib cage moves up and outwards

1 and 2 cause 3 to happen, followed by 4

2. The diaphragm moves downwards and becomes flatter

Figure 2.23   How we breathe in

How is the suction caused?

The ribs are moved in and out by two sets of muscles called *intercostal muscles*. These connect all the ribs together. They are the meat of cows, pigs and lambs that you eat if you have 'spare ribs' for dinner. The two sets are arranged so that they connect the ribs at different angles (Figure 2.24). When the set on the outside contracts they pull the ribs up and out. When the set on the inside contracts they pull the ribs down and in.

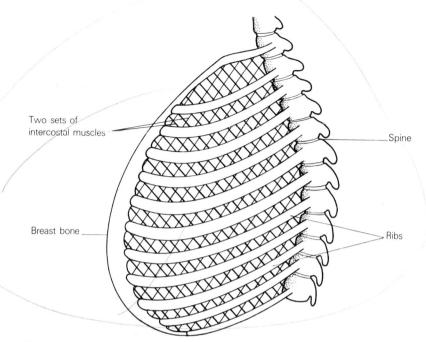

Figure 2.24   The intercostal muscles

The diaphragm is a tough sheet of fibre which has muscles all around the edge (Figure 2.25). These muscles connect to the lower part of the rib cage. The diaphragm is normally shaped like a dome. When the muscles contract, they pull the diaphragm down and make it flatter.

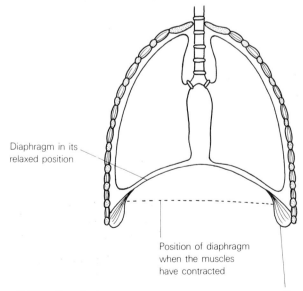

Figure 2.25   The diaphragm

Experiment 2.6

Using a model to show how the intercostal muscles work

1. Obtain or assemble a model like the one in Figure 2.26. It can be made of wood or stiff cardboard. Work in pairs.

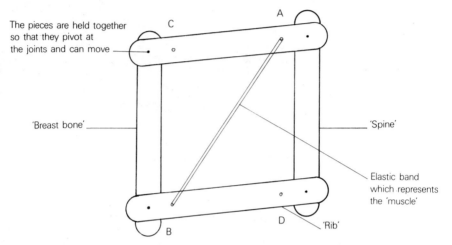

The pieces are held together so that they pivot at the joints and can move

'Breast bone'

'Spine'

Elastic band which represents the 'muscle'

'Rib'

Figure 2.26　　How the intercostal muscles work

2. One person holds the 'spine' and 'breastbone' firmly while the other connects an elastic band between pins A and B.

3. Keep a firm hold on the 'spine' and let the 'breastbone' go.

4. Now repeat 2 and 3 but this time connect the elastic band to pins C and D.

5. Which 'muscle' raised the 'ribs'? Which one lowered them?

How much air do we breathe?

How much air we breathe depends on how much oxygen our cells need. If you are resting, you breathe slowly and not very deeply. As you do more exercise, you begin to breathe more deeply and quickly.

The largest amount of air you can take in one breath will be between 3 and 3½ litres. Breathing normally you will probably take in between ½ and 1 litre of air per breath.

Experiment 2.7

Experiment to find the maximum lung volumes for the class

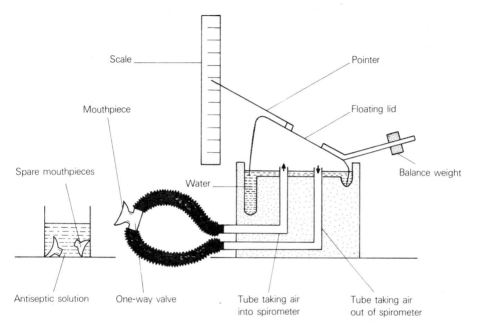

Figure 2.27   Apparatus used to measure the volume of air breathed (a spirometer)

1. A spirometer (Figure 2.27) is a machine which measures the volume of air you breathe. There are a number of different sorts of spirometer. Make sure you know how yours works.

2. Take a clean, disinfected mouthpiece and connect it to the spirometer.

3. Take a few practice deep breaths. Then take as deep a breath as you can. Gently breathe out into the spirometer until you have squeezed all the air out of your lungs. Get one member of the class to read the volume.

4. Remove your mouthpiece and rinse it under a tap. Then replace it in the antiseptic solution. The spirometer must be emptied and set to zero again.

5. Write your lung volume on the blackboard.

6. When the volumes for the whole class have been written down, organise the results into a chart like the one below.

Lung volume (litres)	Number of people with that volume
½–1	
1–1½	
1½–2	
2–2½	
2½–3	
3–3½	
3½–4	
4–4½	
4½–5	

7. Now draw a bar chart of these results like the one below.

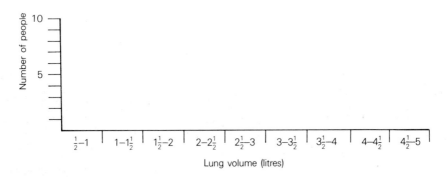

8. Finally, work out the *average* lung volume by adding all the class results together and dividing this by the number of pupils who took part in the experiment.

9. What is the most common lung volume?

10. What is the average lung volume?

11. Do boys generally have a larger lung volume than girls?

What do we breathe?

We breathe *air* into our lungs and we breathe air out of them again. Whilst the air is in our lungs we take a little oxygen out of it and add a little carbon dioxide to it. We do *not* breathe in 'nothing but oxygen' and breathe out 'nothing but carbon dioxide'.

In fact, nearly 80% of air is a gas called nitrogen. It is a gas which has almost no use to any living organism except some bacteria. It is very important, however, because it keeps the amount of oxygen down. We would die if we breathed pure oxygen for long. The other 20% of air is made up mainly of oxygen and carbon dioxide. The proportions of each are shown in Figure 2.28.

You should remember, too, that gases like hydrogen and helium etc. are so rare in air that they can be detected only by using special apparatus.

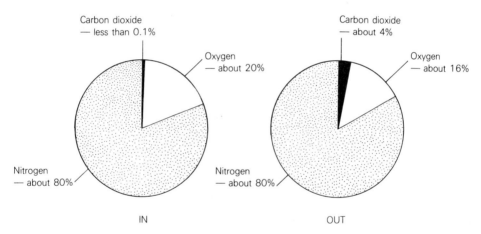

Figure 2.28   Proportions of the main gases that we breathe in and out

Summary

1. Oxygen is needed for energy.

2. Oxygen gets into the blood by diffusion. Carbon dioxide diffuses out.

3. Humans have lungs to give a large surface area for oxygen to get into the blood.

2.3 The blood system

The blood system has to get food and oxygen to the cells and take carbon dioxide and other waste products away. To make sure this is done efficiently blood is pumped by the heart through a system of tubes or vessels. This tube system appears quite complicated but is really quite simple.

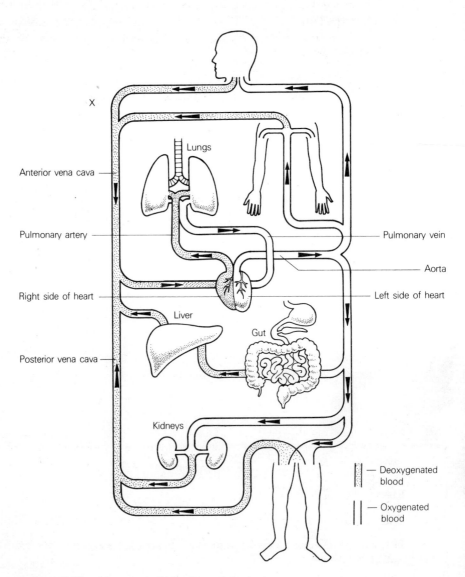

Figure 2.29   Movement of blood round the body

To understand it you must remember that before the blood can go to any cell it has to go to the lungs to collect more oxygen. Also, pumping the blood through any group of cells is hard work. The heart cannot produce enough force to push blood through two areas of cells one after another. This means that once the blood has gone through a group of cells it has to go back to the heart again. Try following this in Figure 2.29.

Imagine blood which has just passed through your brain. It has very little oxygen. It is at point X on the diagram. It flows down to the heart through a tube called the *anterior vena cava* (anterior means front). It passes through the right side of the heart and then is pumped to the lungs through the *pulmonary artery*. At the lungs it picks up oxygen, and gets rid of carbon dioxide. It also loses most of its force as it squeezes through the millions of tiny blood tubes in the lung. It has to go back to the heart to be pumped again. It passes through the *pulmonary vein* and into the left side of the heart. Here it is pumped again and leaves the heart through a large and important tube called the *aorta*. The aorta quickly divides into a number of branches and the blood can pass out through any of them. It may go to the feet and deliver its oxygen to the foot cells. Wherever the blood goes it must squeeze through more tiny blood tubes and so lose all its force again. It must then return to either the anterior or *posterior vena cava* (posterior means back). The blood goes back to the heart to begin the cycle again.

What is blood like?

Blood is a liquid which contains a lot of cells. It is made up of four parts:

Red blood cells (erythrocytes) are shown in Figure 2.30. These are unusual cells because they do not have a nucleus. This means that they can only live for about 120 days. They also have an unusual shape. They are thinner in the

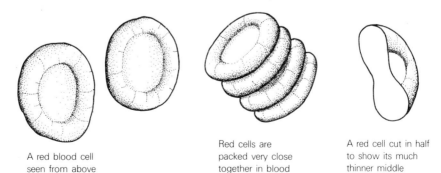

A red blood cell
seen from above

Red cells are
packed very close
together in blood

A red cell cut in half
to show its much
thinner middle

Figure 2.30   A red blood cell

middle than they are at the edges. They contain a red substance called *haemoglobin* which can carry a lot of oxygen. Haemoglobin gives blood its red colour. There are about 5½ million red blood cells in every mm³ of blood.

White blood cells (leucocytes). These are shown in Figure 2.31. They are larger than red blood cells but there are not so many of them. They are not white but transparent. They do have a nucleus and this can easily be stained to make the cells show up. There are different sorts of white blood cells but they are all involved in keeping the body free from infection. Some white blood cells produce *antibodies* to destroy infection. Others destroy bacteria and viruses by engulfing and digesting them.

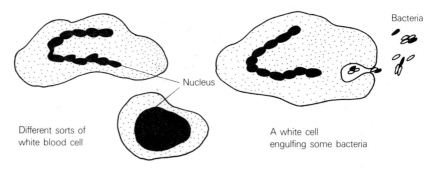

Figure 2.31   White blood cells

Platelets. These are tiny fragments of cells which help form clots to seal wounds (Figure 2.32).

Plasma. This is a watery liquid which is a very pale yellow colour. It contains foods and many other substances dissolved in it.

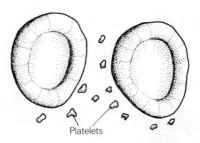

Figure 2.32   Red blood cells and platelets

Experiment 2.8

Looking at blood

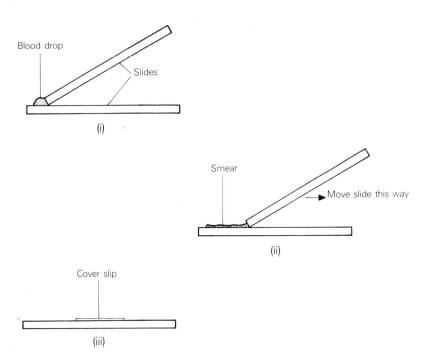

Figure 2.33   Preparing a slide

1. Obtain three clean microscope slides, two cover slips, and some Leishman's stain.

2. Place a drop of blood on one slide and bring the edge of another slide up to it as shown in Figure 2.33(i).

3. Draw a smear of blood across the slide by moving the second slide as shown in (ii).

4. Quickly drop a cover slip on to the blood smear.

5. Observe the red blood cells first using the low-power lens of the microscope and then the high-power lens.

6. Draw a few red blood cells.

7. Repeat 1, 2 and 3 but then wave the slide gently from side to side to allow the smear to dry.

8. Add a drop of Leishman's stain and leave it for a minute.

9. Run any excess stain off the slide then wash very gently to get rid of the stain (Figure 2.34). Add a cover slip and dry the underside of the slide.

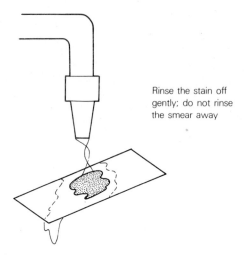

Rinse the stain off gently; do not rinse the smear away

Figure 2.34   Swilling the stain from the slide

10. Observe the dark blue nuclei of white blood cells under low power and then high power. Having found a cell nucleus, try to see the rest of the cell using high power.

11. Draw a few white blood cells.

What are blood vessels (tubes) like?

There are three sorts of blood vessel, *arteries, capillaries* and *veins* (see Figure 2.35 opposite). Blood is pumped out of the heart through arteries. These divide into smaller and smaller tubes until they become tiny tubes called capillaries. There are thousands of miles of capillaries in our bodies and they make sure blood is delivered to all our cells. Eventually capillaries join up to become larger and larger tubes and end up as veins. Veins carry blood back to the heart again.

Arteries. These are strong thick tubes. They are stretchy and can withstand the pressure of the heart pumping. If you squeeze an artery, you can feel the blood being pumped through it. You can feel a *pulse* like this in your wrist (see Figure 2.36 opposite).

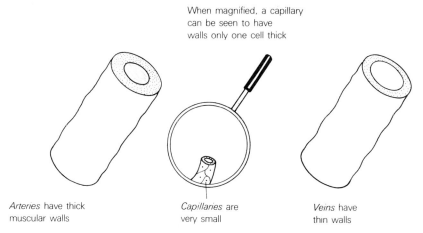

When magnified, a capillary
can be seen to have
walls only one cell thick

Arteries have thick
muscular walls

Capillaries are
very small

Veins have
thin walls

Figure 2.35   The three sorts of blood vessel

Capillaries. These are very tiny tubes which often have walls only one cell
thick. This allows food and oxygen to pass easily out of them and into the
cells. Similarly, waste products and carbon dioxide can pass easily into
them from the cells around.

Veins. These are large tubes but they have thin walls. They are not stretchy
and do not have to stand much pressure. In fact, the blood in the veins is
often under such low pressure that it has to be helped back to the heart. To
do this veins have valves which are tiny flaps which work like canal lock

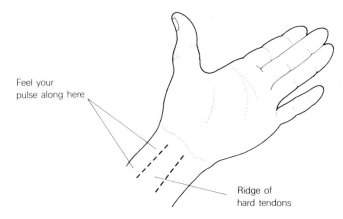

Feel your
pulse along here

Ridge of
hard tendons

Figure 2.36   Finding a pulse

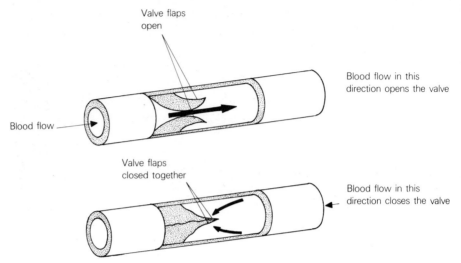

Figure 2.37   One-way valve in a vein

gates. The blood can pass one way through the valve, but if it tries to go the other way it gets behind the flaps and closes the valve. (See Figure 2.37.)

You can see how these valves work by doing an experiment first done by a man called William Harvey around the year 1600.

Experiment 2.9

William Harvey's experiment to see the effects of valves in veins

1. Obtain a volunteer with large visible veins in his/her arm.

2. Gently tie a band around the upper arm to prevent blood from flowing away from the arm through the veins.

3. Find a suitable stretch of unbranched vein like stretch A–B in Figure 2.38.

4. Press a finger on the vein at point A. This will close the vein.

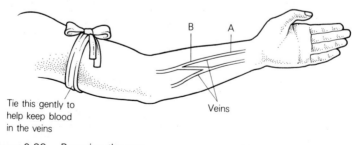

Figure 2.38   Preparing the arm

5. Use a finger of your other hand to press the vein next to point A. Still pressing on the vein move this finger towards point B. This will push the blood towards B.

6. What happens to the blood in the vein?

7. Can you see the position of the valve?

8. What happens when you release the finger pressing point A?

What is the heart like?

The first thing to remember is that the heart is simply a pump made out of muscle. It pumps blood. It is not the part of the body which 'feels' love — that all goes on in the brain. The reason why people used to think that the heart was the centre of emotions is that when we get excited or nervous our heart beats faster. It does this to make sure that the whole of the body is getting enough oxygen in case we need to react quickly.

The heart is not one pump but two. It is divided into two sides, right and left. The right side collects blood from the body and pumps it to the lungs. The left side collects blood from the lungs and pumps it around the body. (See Figure 2.39.)

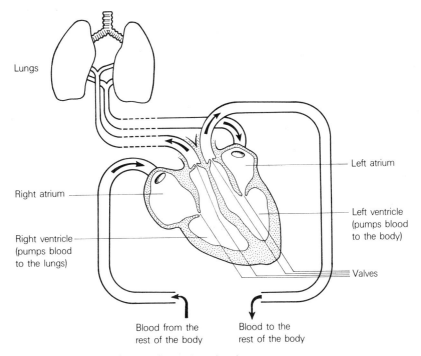

Figure 2.39   The heart's pair of pumping chambers

Each side of the heart has a collecting chamber called the *atrium* and a pumping chamber called the *ventricle*. There is a valve between the atrium and the ventricle to stop the blood going back into the atrium when the ventricle pumps. This valve is very much like the valves in the veins. It is made of flaps of thin membrane which catch blood underneath them and slam together when the ventricle pumps. (See Figure 2.40.)

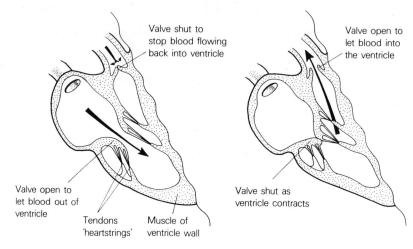

Figure 2.40   How the heart valves work

There are also tiny tendons ('heartstrings') which hold the valve flaps down so that they do not blow through into the atrium. There is another valve in the artery which leads from the ventricle. This stops blood from going back into the ventricle when it is filling up with blood from the atrium.

All these valves have different names as you can see in Figure 2.41. If you cannot remember the names just remember that all the valves work in the same way. They all stop blood from flowing backwards in the heart.

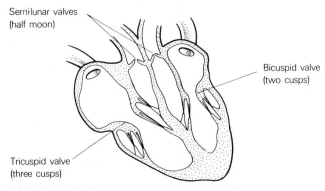

Figure 2.41   The heart valves

Figures 2.39, 2.40, and 2.41 are simplified to help you understand how the heart works. Figure 2.42 is a little more like the real thing. As you can see, the blood vessels wrap around each other. Drawings like this are very useful but not always easy to follow.

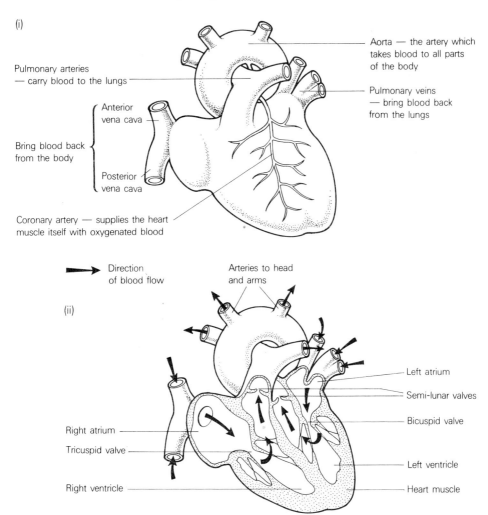

(i)

Aorta — the artery which takes blood to all parts of the body

Pulmonary arteries — carry blood to the lungs

Pulmonary veins — bring blood back from the lungs

Anterior vena cava

Bring blood back from the body

Posterior vena cava

Coronary artery — supplies the heart muscle itself with oxygenated blood

Direction of blood flow

Arteries to head and arms

(ii)

Left atrium

Semi-lunar valves

Bicuspid valve

Right atrium

Tricuspid valve

Left ventricle

Heart muscle

Right ventricle

Figure 2.42   The heart seen from the front (i); The heart cut open (ii)

How does the heart work?

The heart works by squeezing the blood out. The ventricle and atrium walls are made of muscle and almost nothing else. As the muscle contracts it gets smaller and makes the space inside smaller. The blood is squeezed through whatever opening it can find.

When the heart works the two atria squeeze together followed by the two ventricles. This gives a regular heartbeat which is the sound of the valve flaps slamming shut. The heartbeat has a loud sound followed by a softer one — a sort of 'lub-dub' sound. The loud sound is made when the valves between the atria and the ventricles shut. The softer sound is made when the semi-lunar valves in the two arteries shut as the ventricles are filling.

Experiment 2.10

Experiment to hear your heartbeat

1. Obtain a stethescope or make one using a funnel and rubber tubing.

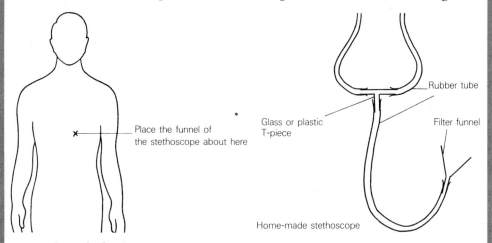

Place the funnel of the stethoscope about here

Glass or plastic T-piece

Rubber tube

Filter funnel

Home-made stethoscope

Figure 2.43   Listening to the heart

2. Place the funnel of the stethescope as close as you can to your skin so that it presses near where the ribs and the breastbone join, just below the breast on the left.

3. Do not move the funnel because every sound will be magnified and you will not be able to hear your heartbeat (Figure 2.43).

4. It may help you to hold your breath for a while.

5. Listen carefully until you can hear the lub-dub sound.

How quickly does the heart beat?

Your heart beats as fast as is necessary to supply your cells with oxygen. The number of beats per minute will be different for different people because of their size, the size of their heart, and what they are doing. An average heart rate is said to be about 70 beats per minute. You can check your heart rate by counting the number of pulses per minute you can feel in your wrist.

Experiment 2.11

Experiment to find your heart rate

1. Work in pairs. You will need a clock or watch which shows seconds. Find your partner's pulse in his/her wrist (Figure 2.36).

2. With your partner sitting perfectly still and relaxed count the number of pulses in one minute.

3. Record these results on the blackboard for the whole class and in a chart like the one below.

Name	Resting heart rate	Exercising heart rate

4. Now let your partner find your resting heart rate.

5. Send your partner off to do some exercise like running once around the playground. Immediately your partner returns count the number of pulses in a minute again. Record this result on your chart.

6. Now you do 5 and let your partner take your exercising heart rate.

7. Use the class results for resting heart rate to work out an average value. Add all the results together and divide by the number of people in the class.

8. Collect the results in a chart like the one below. Once you have collected them use them to draw a bar chart of resting heart rates.

Heart rate (beats/min)	Number of pupils
51–55	
56–60	
61–65	
66–70	
71–75	
76–80	
81–85	

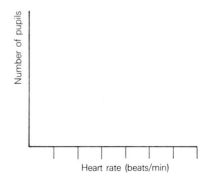

Resting heart rate for the class

Number of pupils

Heart rate (beats/min)

9. Was *your* resting heart rate average?

10. Was the class average the same as the average in this book?

11. Why did your heart rate change when you did some exercise?

What else does blood do?

Apart from carrying oxygen and food to the cells and removing wastes from them, the blood has other jobs:

It fights infection using the white blood cells.

It carries hormones around the body. These help control how the body grows and works.

It carries heat around the body. This is important in animals like ourselves which have to keep their temperature constant.

It is also able to heal wounds in the body, by first making a clot and then repairing and replacing cells.

Summary

1. Blood transports substances around the body.

2. Because oxygen is one of the most important of these substances, blood has to keep going back to the lungs to get more.

3. The heart pumps blood through a well organised system of tubes.

4. Valves in the heart stop the blood from flowing backwards.

5. The heart pumps by squeezing the blood.

Questions on Chapter 2

1. An animal which eats only plants is called a _____ .
   An animal which eats only animals is called a _____ .
   An animal which eats both plants and animals is called an _____ .

2. Describe simply how the teeth of (a) a dog and (b) a sheep are suited to the food that they eat.

3. (a) In our gut food is digested by special chemicals called _____ .
   (b) Describe some of the important facts about these chemicals.

4. Below is a list of parts of a human gut. The parts are not in any order. List them in the correct order that food passes through them:
    mouth, small intestine, rectum, stomach,
    duodenum, large intestine, oesophagus, anus

5. Write a paragraph which explains simply and in your own words what a villus is and what it does.

6. Fill in the blanks in the following digestion reactions:

    Starch $\xrightarrow{\text{Amylase}}$ _____ + Glucose   In the mouth

    _____ $\xrightarrow{\text{Pepsin}}$ _____   In the stomach

    Proteins $\Longrightarrow$ Peptides   In the _____

    _____ $\Longrightarrow$ Fatty acids + glycerol   In the duodenum

    Peptides $\Longrightarrow$ _____ _____   In the small intestine

    _____ $\xrightarrow{\text{Maltase}}$ _____   In the small intestine

7. Explain what diffusion is.

8. Fill in the blanks in the following explanation of breathing:
    We breathe in when the _____ move out and the _____ moves down. This causes the _____ inside the chest to get _____ . The lungs expand to fill this space and air is _____ into the _____ .

9. A pupil wrote a passage describing the lungs. Unfortunately this pupil got some of his words mixed up. Write out the following paragraph, correcting the mistakes.
    The two lungs are in an air tight box formed by the *trachea* and the *bronchial tube*. A tube called the *diaphragm* connects the lungs to the mouth. It has rings of *ribs* around it to stop it from collapsing. Each lung is wrapped up in two *alveoli* which stop the lungs from rubbing during breathing. Inside the lungs is a system of tubes called the *pleural membranes* which connect the *diaphragm* to the tiny air spaces called *cartilage*.

10. It has been said that there is about 50 m^2 of surface area inside the lungs. A friend of yours asks how all that surface gets into such a small space. Explain to your friend how the lungs are constructed.

11. Blood flows around the body in an organised way. Copy the passage below
     and fill in the missing parts of the blood system.
     After blood has passed through the legs it travels through the _____
     _____ _____ to the _____ side of the heart. It is then
     pumped along the _____ _____ to the lungs. It goes back to
     the _____ side of the heart through the _____ _____ and
     leaves the heart through the _____ . From here it can go to any part of
     the body.

12. (a) Draw a diagram of red blood cells.
     (b) Why are red blood cells unusual?
     (c) What is their job?

13. (a) How would you tell a white blood cell from a red one, apart from
         colour?
     (b) What do white blood cells do?

14. Fill in the blanks in the following passage on blood vessels. (Copy the
     passage first.)
     _____ are thick-walled tubes. They are stretchy and can withstand a
     lot of _____ such as when the heart pumps. _____ are thin-
     walled tubes. They carry blood which has so little pressure that they have to
     have _____ to help blood get back to the _____ . The smallest
     blood tubes are called _____ . They have walls which are only
     _____ _____ thick.

15. The heart is not one pump but two. Explain as simply as possible and in
     your own words exactly what this means.

16. (a) How many valves are there in the heart?
     (b) What do these valves do?
     (c) Explain simply (with a diagram if you need one) how they work.

17. Make a list of all the jobs that your *blood* has to do.

18. The class results for an experiment to measure the pulse rate were as
     follows:

     A   67 beats per minute   F   74 beats per minute
     B   71 beats per minute   G   77 beats per minute
     C   68 beats per minute   H   67 beats per minute
     D   58 beats per minute   I   71 beats per minute
     E   82 beats per minute   J   65 beats per minute

     What is the average rate for the class?

19. Blood enters the heart at the right atrium and leaves the heart from the left
     ventricle. Make a list, in the correct order, of all the parts of the heart that
     the blood passes through between the right atrium and left ventricle.

Crossword on Chapter 2

(Teacher, please see special note in front of book.)

Copy this grid, then fill in the answers. Do not write on this page.

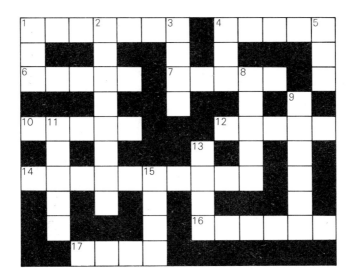

Down

1 One of the bones that helps us breathe (3)
2 When digested they produce amino acids (8)
3 These animals are 14 across (4)
4 A healthy body gets _____ the substances it needs (3)
5 8 down fill up with _____ (3)
8 We need them to breathe (5)
9 It is near the end of the large intestine (6)
11 It pumps 6 across (5)
13 The bronchial _____ is a system of tubes (4)
15, 17 across   6 across from the brain passes to the 11 down through the anterior _____ _____ (4, 4)

Across

1 If our muscles need extra oxygen, our 11 down must _____ by pumping harder (7)
4 A very important artery (5)
6 Liquid pumped through the body (5)
7 Fish have _____ not 8 down (5)
10 A herbivore (5)
12 Food can _____ the body through the mouth (5)
14 Animals that eat other animals are called _____ (10)
16 A special chemical controlling a chemical reaction in the body (6)
17 See 15 down

3. How plant cells obtain energy

Plant cells need energy to grow and to stay alive. They get this energy by respiration in exactly the same way as animal cells. Thus all plant cells need a supply of food, usually glucose, and oxygen. However, because plants do not move or need to keep warm, they use much less energy than animals like us. You can see some plant cells in Figures 3.1 and 3.2.

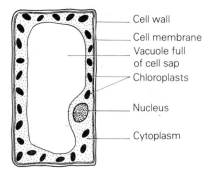

Cell wall
Cell membrane
Vacuole full
of cell sap
Chloroplasts

Nucleus

Cytoplasm

Figure 3.1   A drawing of a plant cell

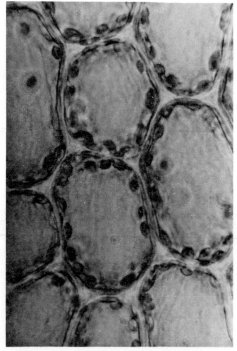

Figure 3.2   Plant cells seen under the microscope

Plants get their oxygen from the air (or water in the case of water plants), but they do not get their glucose by feeding. Instead they use the energy in sunlight to *build* carbon dioxide gas and water into glucose. This process is called *photosynthesis*.

Photosynthesis only occurs in *green* plant cells. These contain the green substance called *chlorophyll* which is able to trap the sunlight and use its energy. Living plant cells which are not green or which are underground do not photosynthesise. They must be supplied with glucose for respiration. (See Figure 3.3.)

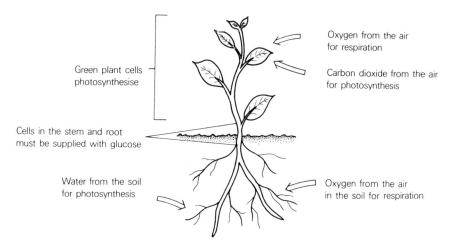

Green plant cells photosynthesise

Oxygen from the air for respiration

Carbon dioxide from the air for photosynthesis

Cells in the stem and root must be supplied with glucose

Water from the soil for photosynthesis

Oxygen from the air in the soil for respiration

Figure 3.3   The activities in a plant

3.1 Photosynthesis — the food supply

Photosynthesis can be summarised as

$$\text{Carbon dioxide} + \text{Water} \xrightarrow{\text{Light}} \text{Glucose} + \text{Oxygen}$$

this can be written as

$$6\,CO_2 + 6\,H_2O \xrightarrow{\text{Light}} C_6H_{12}O_6 + 6\,O_2$$

In the cell, the glucose is quickly turned into other substances. A common one is *starch*, which is stored in the cell until it can be taken away to other parts of the plant. The glucose can also be made into *amino acids* and then *proteins* which can be used to make new living plant material. To make amino acids, the plant also needs small amounts of minerals like nitrates and sulphates. The plant gets these from the soil.

Although photosynthesis takes place in all green plant cells, most plants have leaves which are specially adapted to photosynthesise efficiently.

They are wide and flat to obtain lots of light. They are thin so that the carbon dioxide gas can easily get to all the cells. They are often held on the plant so that they face the sun and shade each other as little as possible.

Leaf structure

A *cross-section* of a leaf shows that the leaf itself is carefully arranged into layers (Figures 3.5 and 3.6). Figure 3.4 shows how a leaf section is cut.)

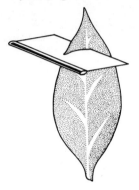

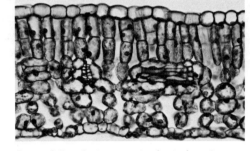

Figure 3.5   A photograph of a leaf section

How to cut a
cross-section of a leaf

Figure 3.4   Cutting a leaf section

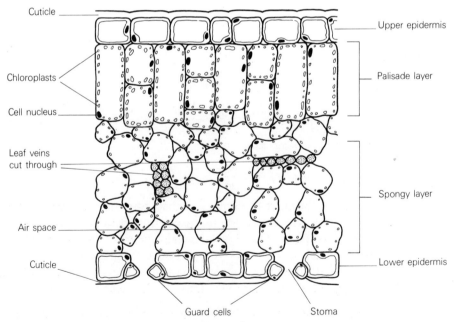

Figure 3.6   Leaf and leaf section (diagram)

The *cuticle* is waterproof and stops leaves losing too much water. The *upper epidermis* is the transparent outer layer of cells. The *palisade layer* is made of tightly packed tall thin cells. These have lots of *chloroplasts* which contain the chlorophyll. This layer does most of the photosynthesis because it is nearest the light. The *spongy layer* helps to supply the palisade layer with all the carbon dioxide gas it needs for photosynthesis. The *lower epidermis* is also transparent with a cuticle. It has lots of holes in it which are known as *stomata*. The stomata let gases in and out of the leaf and also let water out. To prevent too much water being lost each stoma has two *guard cells* which close it at night when photosynthesis does not take place — leaf veins bring water to the photosynthesising cells and take substances made by photosynthesis to other parts of the plant.

Experiment 3.1

How to do a starch test on a leaf

Many experiments on photosynthesis rely on the fact that a lot of the glucose produced is turned into starch. This can be easily tested for in a small piece of leaf. The starch test uses iodine solution which turns blue/black with starch. Before the iodine can be used, the piece of leaf has to be treated so that the iodine can reach the starch.

1. Cut a small piece from a leaf. A geranium leaf works well.

2. Put the piece of leaf into boiling water for about a minute to soften it and break down the cuticle. (See Figure 3.7.)

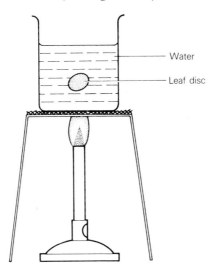

Water

Leaf disc

Figure 3.7   Softening a leaf

3. Put about 10 cm³ of ethanol in a boiling tube along with the leaf. *Remove the bunsen* from under the beaker, because ethanol, liquid or vapour, catches fire very easily and must *never* be put near a naked flame. Stand the boiling tube in the beaker and the ethanol will begin to boil (Figure 3.8).

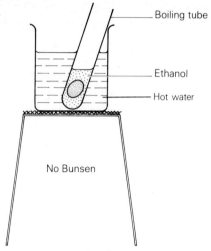

Figure 3.8   Do not heat ethanol with a flame

4. Allow the ethanol to boil until the leaf has turned white. If the ethanol stops boiling then heat the water again but take the boiling tube out of the beaker first.

5. Remove the white piece of leaf from the ethanol and put it back into the hot water for a few seconds.

6. Put the leaf on to a white tile and add one or two drops of iodine (Figure 3.9). Wait a few minutes for a blue/black colour to appear showing starch is present.

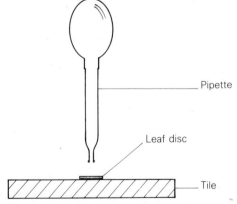

Figure 3.9   The test for starch

Experiment 3.2

Investigating photosynthesis
Part I: To see whether carbon dioxide is necessary

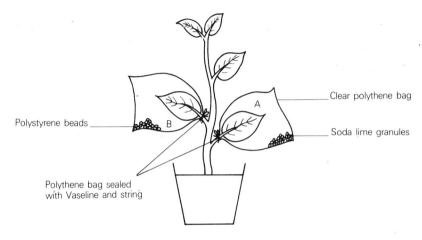

Figure 3.10   Comparing photosynthesis in leaves with and without carbon dioxide

1. Take a large plant and treat it as shown in Figure 3.10. Soda lime absorbs carbon dioxide gas. Leaf A will therefore have no carbon dioxide gas providing the polythene bag is well sealed on to the leaf stalk. Polystyrene beads have no effect on the air.

2. Leave the plant set up in the light for a few days.

3. Do a starch test on leaves A and B.

4. Did both leaves show starch?

5. What does the experiment show?

6. Leaf B is called a control. Why do you think it was included in the experiment?

Part II: To see whether light is necessary

Part III: To see whether chlorophyll is necessary

Design your own experiments to investigate light and chlorophyll. Do not forget that each experiment must have a control.

Summary

1.   Green plant cells photosynthesise.

2.   Photosynthesis supplies all the plant cells with food.

3.   Photosynthesis needs light, chlorophyll, carbon dioxide and water.

4.   The equation for photosynthesis is

$$\text{Carbon dioxide} + \text{Water} \xrightarrow{\text{Light}} \text{Glucose} + \text{Oxygen}$$

3.2 The plant and air

There are two processes going on in plants which need gases from the air:

Photosynthesis, which needs carbon dioxide and produces oxygen.
Respiration, which needs oxygen and produces carbon dioxide.

Leaves during the day

During the day both photosynthesis and respiration are taking place in leaf cells. Respiration will be happening very slowly but photosynthesis will be quite fast. The leaf cells will need much more carbon dioxide for photosynthesis than they produce by respiration. They will also give off much more oxygen by photosynthesis than they need for respiration. (See Figure 3.11.)

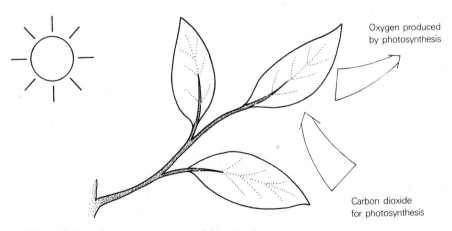

Oxygen produced
by photosynthesis

Carbon dioxide
for photosynthesis

Figure 3.11   Gas exchange in a leaf (day time)

Leaves at night

No photosynthesis will take place during the night. The leaf cells will need oxygen for respiration and produce carbon dioxide. (See Figure 3.12.)

Figure 3.12   Gas exchange in a leaf (night-time)

Experiment 3.3

Investigating gas exchange in a plant in the light and the dark

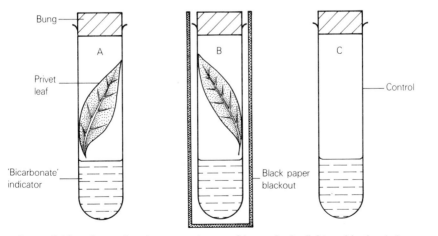

Figure 3.13   Comparing the gas exchange of leaves in the light and in the dark

This experiment uses 'bicarbonate' indicator which is red but changes to yellow with carbon dioxide. It also turns dark red/purple if the small amount of carbon dioxide, normally dissolved in it, is removed.

1. Take three test-tubes marked A, B and C.

2. To each tube add about 2 cm depth of 'bicarbonate' indicator. Do not breathe on the tubes.

3. Wedge a single large privet leaf into tubes A and B and put bungs into all the tubes. Tube C is a control.

4. Wrap black paper around tube B so that no light can get in.

5. Leave in a well-lit place, e.g. by a window, for 4–6 hours.

6. Draw a results chart like the one below. Write in the colour of the indicator at the start of the experiment. In the next column predict what colours the indicator will be in a few hours time. To do this you need to work out what you think will happen. This will be your hypothesis. After 4–6 hours, fill in the actual colours of the indicator.

Tube	Colour of indicator at start	Predicted colour of indicator at end	Actual colour of indicator at end
A			
B			
C			

7. Were your predictions accurate?

8. What does the experiment tell you about gas exchange in the leaf during the day?

9. What does the experiment tell you about gas exchange in the leaf during the night (in the dark)?

10. What was the control (tube C) for?

Plant roots and air

Root cells only respire — they do not photosynthesise. Thus root cells need oxygen and give off carbon dioxide. They get the oxygen from the tiny air spaces in soil (Figure 3.14 (opposite)). Oxygen diffuses into the root and carbon dioxide diffuses out. When a root becomes waterlogged many of the tiny air spaces fill up with water. There is no air for the plant roots to use. If the soil stays waterlogged for some time, the root cells begin to die because of a lack of oxygen. This, of course, may lead to the plant dying. This is why over-watering will often kill your plants at home.

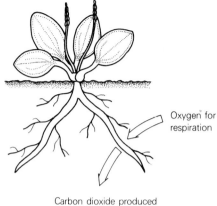

Oxygen for
respiration

Carbon dioxide produced
by respiration

Figure 3.14   Gas exchange in plant roots

Experiment 3.4

Experiment to demonstrate gas exchange in plant roots

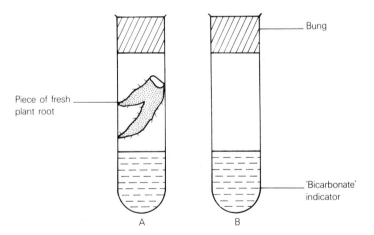

Bung

Piece of fresh
plant root

'Bicarbonate'
indicator

A   B

Figure 3.15   Investigating gas exchange in a root

1. Take two test-tubes marked A and B.

2. To each tube add 2 cm depth of 'bicarbonate' indicator.

3. Wedge a piece of fresh plant root into tube A and put bungs into both tubes. Tube B is a control. (See Figure 3.15 (p. 65).)

4. Leave for 3–4 hours.

5. Check the colour of the indicator in each tube. Record your results in a table:

Tube	Colour at start	Colour at end
A		
B		

6. Which gas did the root give off?

7. Which gas do you think the root was using?

8. What was tube B for?

Stomata

Stomata are tiny holes, usually found on the underside of leaves (Figure 3.16). They remain open to allow carbon dioxide in and oxygen out of the leaf during photosynthesis. The cells inside the leaf are covered with a water layer as are the alveoli in our lungs. This water layer allows the gases to dissolve and diffuse in and out of the cells. The water evaporates all the time and diffuses out of the stomata into the air. To prevent too much

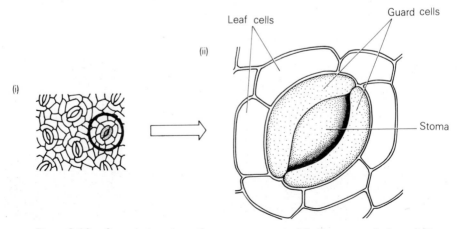

Figure 3.16   Several stomata as they appear on a leaf (i); One stoma (enlarged) (ii)

water being lost this way the stomata are closed at night when photo-synthesis does not happen. Stomata are opened and closed by the two guard cells (Figure 3.17). A stoma is simply the hole between two guard cells — Figure 3.18 shows one magnified about 500 times under the microscope.

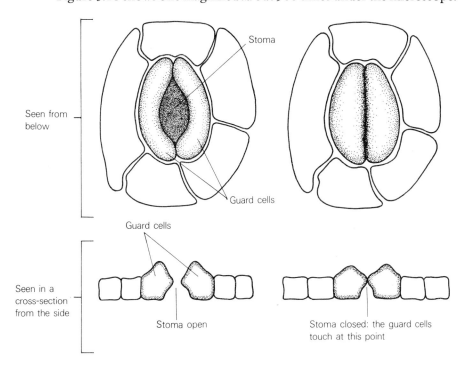

Figure 3.17   A stoma open (left) and closed

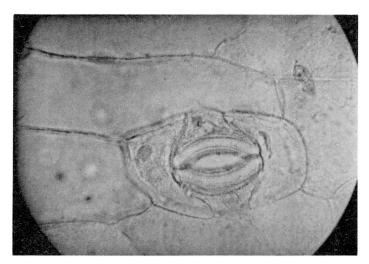

Figure 3.18   A single stoma highly magnified

Experiment 3.5

Looking at open and closed stomata

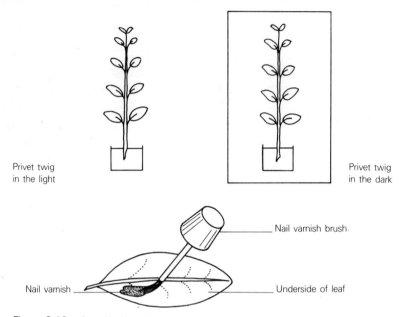

Figure 3.19   Investigating stomata

1. You need two privet leaves. One must be in the dark and have been kept in the dark for an hour. You also need two microscope slides, a pair of forceps and some nail varnish.

2. Paint a thin layer of nail varnish on the underside of both leaves (Figure 3.19). The one in the dark must be kept in the dark until the nail varnish has dried.

3. Using forceps peel off the dry nail varnish from the leaf in the light and place it on a microscope slide.

4. Using a microscope, examine the nail varnish for impressions of stomata. They are very small. Can you think of a way of measuring or estimating how wide and long a stomata is? If so, measure two or three stomata.

5. Make a clear labelled sketch of two or three open stomata.

6. Now repeat this for the leaf in the dark. Observe and sketch two or three closed stomata.

7. Approximately how wide and long are stomata?

Summary

1. All plant cells respire using oxygen and giving off carbon dioxide.

2. Green plant cells photosynthesise in the light. They use carbon dioxide and give off oxygen.

3. Stomata are tiny holes in leaves which allow gases in and out of the leaf.

3.3 Photosynthesis — air and agriculture

Farmers grow plants to supply our needs. We either eat the plants or feed them to animals. The more plants a farmer can grow, then the more he can sell. Perhaps more importantly, the more plants a farmer grows, then the more people can be fed. The world's population is getting larger all the time. Farmers must increase the amount of food they produce to keep up with the population.

To grow more food may not simply be a case of sowing more plants. There may not be enough room to do this. What is needed is to get each plant to grow bigger or to produce more seed. One way of doing this is to try and make the plant photosynthesise more.

Figure 3.20   Farmers need to increase food production

Photosynthesis is a chemical reaction which speeds up as the temperature rises. The enzymes which control photosynthesis work more quickly as the temperature goes up. The rate of photosynthesis is fastest at about 25 °C. Much above this, the enzymes start being destroyed by the heat. Photosynthesis can also be speeded up by increasing the amount of carbon dioxide in the air. Normal air has about 0.03% carbon dioxide. By raising this to 0.1% the rate of photosynthesis can be increased quite a lot. (See Figure 3.21.)

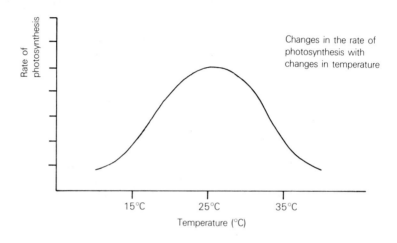

Changes in the rate of photosynthesis with changes in temperature

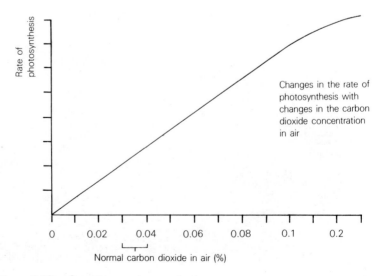

Changes in the rate of photosynthesis with changes in the carbon dioxide concentration in air

Figure 3.21   Speeding up photosynthesis

What a farmer has to do is to examine how much it costs to increase photosynthesis and how much extra money it will make for him. At the moment, most crops are grown in fields where it is impossible to raise either the temperature or the carbon dioxide level. The only way this can be done is if the crop is grown inside some sort of building. Crops like tomatoes and cucumbers are grown inside large glasshouses. Farmers find it economic to increase the rate of photosynthesis because of the extra crop produced. The glasshouse by itself increases the temperature during the day. (See Figure 3.22.)

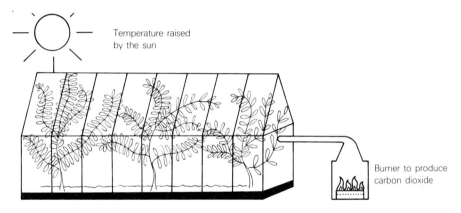

Figure 3.22   Improving the yield of crops in a glasshouse

The amount of carbon dioxide can be increased by burning propane gas heaters in the glasshouse. Farmers used to burn paraffin, but they found that impurities in the paraffin were released into the air and damaged the plants. Heaters also warm up the glasshouse, but this may be a disadvantage in the summer. To get around this, some farmers put the heaters outside the glasshouse and pipe the gas through coolers and into the glasshouse. Other farmers use cylinders of carbon dioxide gas instead.

As farmers try new methods of improving their crop yield, so they become more skilled at it. The advances made in increasing the yield of a crop in one part of the world, can often be applied to another crop somewhere else. The technology and research can be passed from one country to another. This means that we are learning how to get more from our plants. Therefore as the world population continues to rise we will be in a better position to feed all the people.

3.4 Plant transport systems

Figure 3.23 shows the transport system inside a plant. It has two jobs:

1. To take water and minerals from the roots to the cells of the leaves for photosynthesis.

2. To take foods made in the leaves by photosynthesis to all the other cells of the plant.

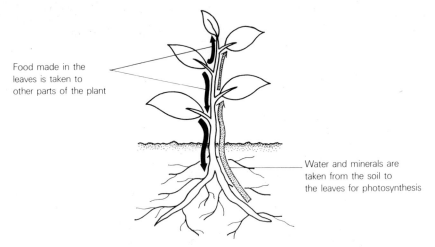

Food made in the leaves is taken to other parts of the plant

Water and minerals are taken from the soil to the leaves for photosynthesis

Figure 3.23   A plant's transport system

Plants have two separate systems of tubes. *Xylem* tubes carry out job 1, and *phloem* tubes carry out job 2. Xylem and phloem tubes are often found together in the plant as groups of tubes called *vascular bundles*.

Vascular bundles

Figure 3.24 shows the arrangements of vascular bundles in two different plants.

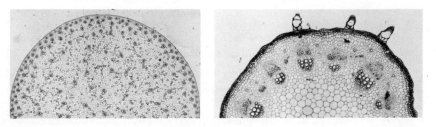

Figure 3.24   Vascular bundles in different plants

In the stem, the vascular bundles are found near the surface. In roots, they run down the centre. In leaves the vascular bundles are often called *veins*. They branch off the *midrib* of the leaf to form smaller and smaller veins which reach all the cells of the leaf.

Whilst there are a great many differences between different plants, vascular bundles are generally arranged as shown in Figure 3.25.

The xylem and phloem are made of tube cells packed on top of each other. They run continuously all the way up the plant with branches off to supply twigs and leaves.

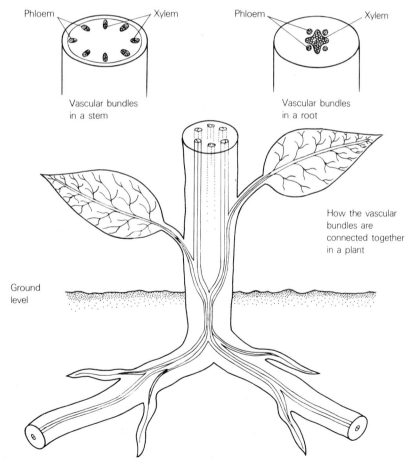

Figure 3.25   The general arrangement of vascular bundles in roots and stems

Experiment 3.6

Experiment to look at vascular bundles

1. You will need a microscope, a razor blade, some microscope slides and some plant stems and roots.

2. Use the razor blade to cut very thin slices, or sections, of a stem or root (Figure 3.26). These must be so thin that you can hardly see them. It takes practice to do this.

3. Put a couple of thin sections on a slide. Cover the sections with a few drops of a stain called FABIL. Leave for a minute.

4. Gently run off any stain left. Be careful not to lose the sections. Cover them with a cover slip.

5. Look at the sections through the microscope to see vascular bundles.

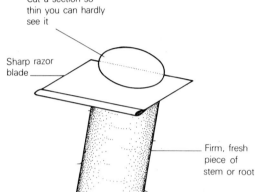

Figure 3.26   Cutting a root or stem section

6. Your teacher may supply you with prepared microscope slides instead or as well.

7. Make clear, labelled sketches of one or two vascular bundles. Do not forget to include the name of your plant on your sketch.

Experiment 3.7

Experiment to see the veins in leaves

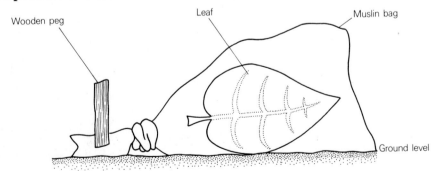

Figure 3.27   Allowing a leaf to decay

1. Take a single leaf from a plant. Wrap it loosely in a layer of muslin. This will stop larger animals getting the leaf. (See Figure 3.27 (opposite).)

2. Peg the muslin to the ground in a place where it will not be disturbed for a couple of weeks. Micro-organisms in the soil will rot the leaf. The veins will be the last parts to decay.

3. Examine your leaf every couple of days until most of it has rotted away.

4. Draw a sketch of the decayed leaf to show the arrangement of veins.

5. How does the arrangement of veins in the leaf compare with the arrangement of capillaries in part of your body?

Xylem

Xylem carries water and any substances dissolved in it from the roots to the leaves. Xylem tubes are also known as *vessels*. They are made of dead cells which are hollow and joined end to end. To stop them collapsing, the xylem vessels have thicker cell walls often made stronger by rings of a woody substance called *lignin*. (See Figure 3.28.)

Water travels up the xylem by a force called *transpiration*. Water passes into the roots by *osmosis* from the solution in the soil. It enters the xylem tubes

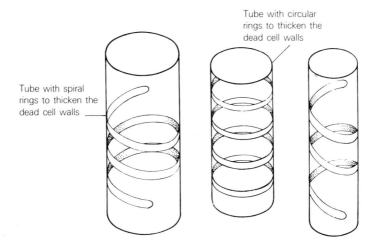

Figure 3.28   Xylem tubes seen from the side (highly magnified)

and is pulled up the tube by the force of the water evaporating from the leaves. This is transpiration. The way the xylem vessels are made also helps the water to move up them. (See Figures 3.29 and 3.30.)

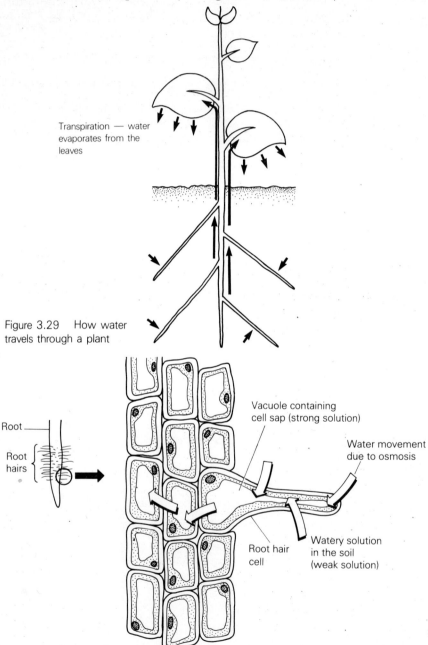

Transpiration — water evaporates from the leaves

Figure 3.29   How water travels through a plant

Root

Root hairs

Vacuole containing cell sap (strong solution)

Water movement due to osmosis

Root hair cell

Watery solution in the soil (weak solution)

Figure 3.30   A root hair cell showing how water is absorbed from the soil

The rate of transpiration depends upon how quickly water evaporates from the leaves. This can easily be investigated using a potometer. There are a number of different sorts of potometer. The following experiments use two of them.

Experiment 3.8

Using a weight potometer to measure transpiration

Water passes out of leaves through the stomata. Transpiration should therefore be less in the dark than in the light.

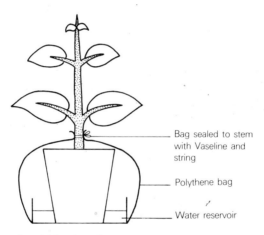

Bag sealed to stem
with Vaseline and
string

Polythene bag

Water reservoir

Figure 3.31   A weight potometer

1. Set up a plant as in Figure 3.31. This is called a *weight potometer*. Make sure there is a good supply of water inside the polythene bag and that the seal around the stem is watertight.

2. Weigh the potometer and record the weight in a chart like the one overleaf. Note the time.

3. Leave the plant for 6–8 hours in the light in the lab. Then reweigh it and note the time and weight.

4. Place the plant in a cupboard and leave it overnight. Next day note the time and weigh the plant.

5. Calculate the average loss of water in grams per hour from the plant in daylight and in darkness.

6. You may wish to repeat the experiment to get more accurate average weights.

	Weight at start	Time	Weight at end	Time	Weight loss	Time for experiment	Average loss of weight/ hour
In the light							
In the dark							

7. Why was the polythene bag placed around the plant pot and sealed tightly?
8. Why did you calculate average weight loss per hour?
9. Why would repeating the experiment have given more accurate averages?
10. Is transpiration faster in the light or dark?

Experiment 3.9

Using a bubble potometer to measure transpiration

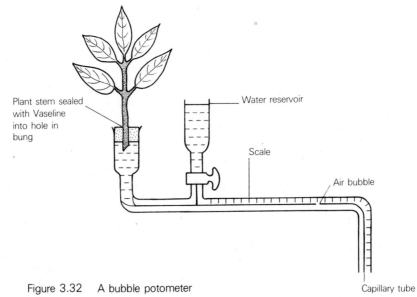

Plant stem sealed with Vaseline into hole in bung

Water reservoir

Scale

Air bubble

Figure 3.32   A bubble potometer

Capillary tube

Assemble a bubble potometer as follows:

1. Put a ring of Vaseline about 1 cm from the cut end of the twig. Put the twig through the hole in the bung until it comes out of the other side. The Vaseline should make an airtight seal.

2. Using a sharp razor cut the twig near the end to expose a fresh surface. Then put the cut end and bung in a bowl of water so that they are both below the water level (Figure 3.32 (opposite)).

3. Making sure that the entire potometer and the bung are under water, quickly insert the bung into the potometer.

4. Now remove the assembled potometer from the water and clamp it in position (Figure 3.33).

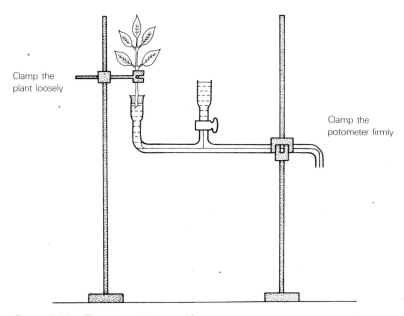

Figure 3.33 The potometer in position

5. As water evaporates from the leaves of the twig, a bubble of air will be drawn through the potometer. For each experiment measure how far the bubble moves in 10 minutes. By opening the reservoir tap you can move the bubble back to the end again.

6. The rest of this experiment is up to you. Water evaporates more quickly in warm, dry, windy conditions. You can compare the rate of transpiration in the following conditions:

   (a) A warm place and a cool place.
   (b) A windy place and a still place.
   (c) A damp place and a dry place.

   Or you can compare the rate of transpiration with all the leaves on the twig and with only half of them.

   Whichever experiment you choose, first write down your hypothesis, i.e. what you think will happen. Then measure the rate of transpiration for each condition. If there is time, repeat the experiment.

7. What was your hypothesis?

8. Was your hypothesis proved correct?

9. Were you accurate enough with your experiment?

10. Did you repeat your experiment? Should you have done?

Limiting transpiration

Some plants would lose so much water by transpiration that they would wilt and die. Plants that live in warm, windy and dry places have adaptations to stop them losing so much water (Figure 3.34).

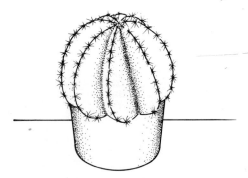

Figure 3.34   A plant which retains water

The leaves of a cactus have reduced in size to become spines. Such small leaves have very few stomata, and so they cannot lose much water.

Some plants have hairy leaves. The hairs trap moist air and stop it from being blown away from the leaf so quickly. Other plants have stomata sunk into tiny pits. This has the same effect as hairy leaves. (See Figure 3.35 (opposite).)

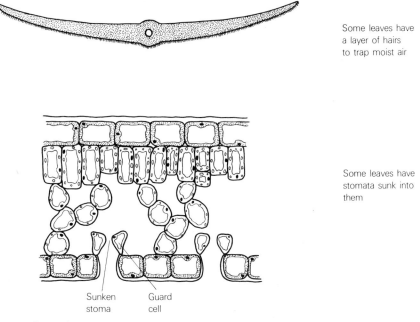

Some leaves have
a layer of hairs
to trap moist air

Some leaves have
stomata sunk into
them

Sunken   Guard
stoma   cell

Figure 3.35   Ways of reducing water loss from leaves

Marram grass grows on sand dunes by the sea. It has hairy leaves, but when conditions are dry the leaves roll up. This keeps moist air inside the rolled-up leaf and reduces transpiration. (See Figure 3.36.)

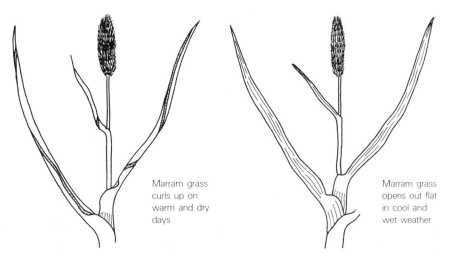

Marram grass
curls up on
warm and dry
days

Marram grass
opens out flat
in cool and
wet weather

Figure 3.36   Marram grass: reaction to weather conditions

Phloem   Phloem carries the substances made in the leaf to all the other cells of the plant (Figure 3.37). Sugars and amino acids are taken to the growing parts of the plant to provide energy and to make new cells. Sugars may be taken to the roots to be stored as starch, as in carrots and turnips. They may be taken to the seeds to be stored. This provides the seed with a food store for when it starts to grow. Very often we eat seeds like this and use the stored food for ourselves. Crops like wheat and rice and broad beans and peas are grown for food.

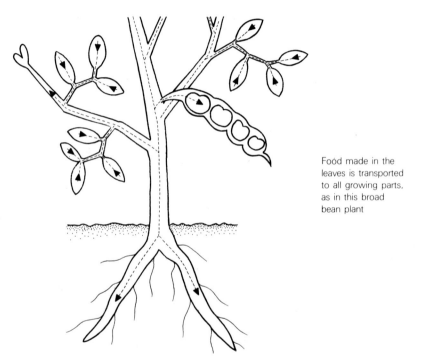

Food made in the leaves is transported to all growing parts, as in this broad bean plant

Figure 3.37   Food is transported by phloem

Phloem is made of tube-cells called *sieve tubes* (Figure 3.38 (opposite)). These are living cells joined end to end by a special cell wall which looks a little like a sieve. It is called a *sieve plate*. We are not really sure how phloem works. It seems that the sieve cells pass substances from one cell to another. To do this they must have energy and they must be alive.

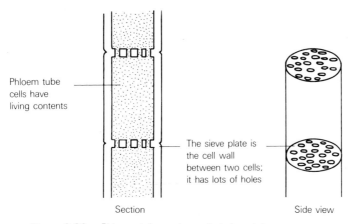

Phloem tube cells have living contents

The sieve plate is the cell wall between two cells; it has lots of holes

Section   Side view

Figure 3.38   Phloem tubes, also called sieve tubes

There are not many experiments which you can do to see phloem in action. The following one was first done by Stephen Hales around the year 1727.

Experiment 3.10

Experiment to show that phloem carries substances from the leaves to the roots of a plant

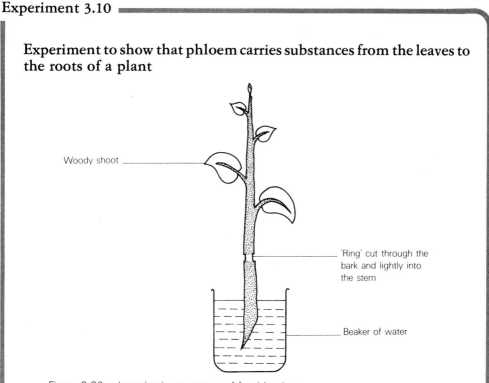

Woody shoot

'Ring' cut through the bark and lightly into the stem

Beaker of water

Figure 3.39   Investigating transport of food in plants

1. Take a shoot of a woody plant such as elder.

2. Cut a ring of bark away and cut a ring into the woody part to a depth of about ½–1 mm (Figure 3.39 (p. 83)). This will remove the phloem tubes but leave at least some xylem.

3. Make an accurate sketch of the area of the stem which includes the ring.

4. Leave the 'ringed' shoot in a beaker of water for a week or so.

5. Now look at the ring. Can you see any changes in the tissue above and below the ring? When Hales did this experiment he found that after a while his shoot looked like the one in Figure 3.40.

6. Make a sketch of your plant stem.

7. What changes did you see above the ring?

8. What changes did you see below the ring?

9. Can you explain how the changes may have come about?

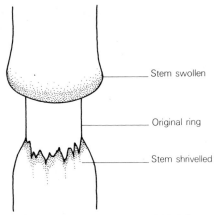

Figure 3.40   The results of Hales's original experiment

Stem swollen

Original ring

Stem shrivelled

Summary

1. Plants have two transport systems.

2. Xylem tubes carry water and dissolved substances from the soil to the leaves for photosynthesis.

3. Xylem is made of dead cells.

4. Phloem carries the foods made by photosynthesis to all the cells of the plant that need them.

5. Phloem is made of living cells.

Questions on Chapter 3

1. How are plant cells and animal cells similar in the way they get energy?

2. (a) What is photosynthesis?
   (b) Write out the equation for photosynthesis.

3. (a) Name a to l in the drawing of a cross-section of a leaf in Figure 3.41.
   (b) Describe in your own words how the leaf is organised to be an efficient photosynthesis 'factory'.

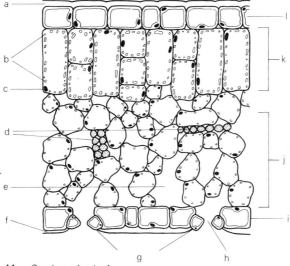

Figure 3.41   Section of a leaf

4. What are the two jobs of a plant transport system?
   Which job does xylem do and which does phloem do?

5. Copy from Figure 3.42 these two cross-sections of a stem with a leaf attached and a root. Draw on your copy where you would expect to find vascular bundles.

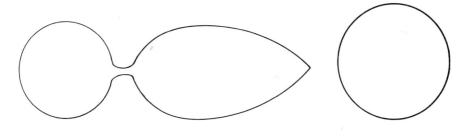

Stem with leaf (cross-section)   Root (cross-section)

Figure 3.42   Locating vascular bundles

6. Explain why each of the following steps in the starch test on a leaf is necessary:
   (a) Dip the piece of leaf in boiling water.
   (b) Boil the piece of leaf in ethanol.
   (c) Boil the ethanol in a hot water bath and never over a flame.
   (d) Add iodine to the piece of leaf.

7. (a) In Figure 3.43 which gas would you expect plant A to be using most of?
   (b) Which gas would it be producing?
   (c) Which gases would plant B be using and producing?

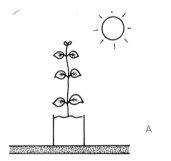
A
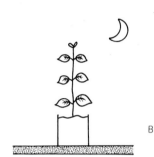
B

Figure 3.43   A plant by day and night

8. Describe some of the differences between xylem and phloem.

9. Describe some of the ways a plant which lives in a hot climate could be adapted to reduce transpiration.

10. The following results were obtained using a bubble potometer to measure transpiration.

	Distance bubble moved in 10 min (cm)					Average
	1	*2*	*3*	*4*	*5*	
Plant in still air	4	5.2	3.6	4.1	4.6	
Plant in air moved by an electric fan	6.2	7.2	8.3	7.5	6.8	

Calculate the average values for each experiment. Why is it important to do the experiment several times and calculate an average? What would you conclude from this experiment?

11.   Copy out the following and fill in the blanks.
Gases pass in and out of a leaf by _____ . During the day gases pass in and out of the open _____ . At night these are _____ to prevent too much _____ loss from the leaf.

Acrostic on Chapter 3

(Teacher, please see special note in front of book.)

Copy or photocopy the acrostic. Do not write on this page. Solve the clues and write the answers in the spaces. This will give you a 13-letter word going down from 15. Write your own clue for 15.

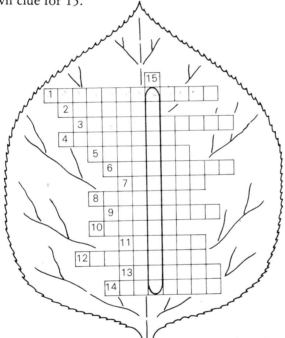

1   What makes plants green (11)
2   Plants can turn glucose into this (6)
3   Plants can use glucose to make _____ , which are then made into proteins (5, 5)
4   They let gases in and out of leaves (7)
5   _____ tubes transport foods away from the leaves (6)
6   5 and 7 together form _____ bundles (8)
7   _____ carries water from roots to leaves (5)

8   A woody substance (6)
9   A waterproof layer on the leaf (7)
10   15 cannot occur at _____ (5)
11   The 6 in leaves are often called _____ (5)
12   The _____ layer of a leaf has tightly packed thin cells (8)
13   The central 11 in a leaf is called the _____ (6)
14   7 tubes are sometimes called _____ (7)

4. Keeping body conditions stable

4.1 Why conditions must be stable

A body like ours contains millions of cells doing many different jobs. Inside each cell there are hundreds of chemical reactions, all controlled by enzymes.

For the whole body to work efficiently each cell must work properly (Figure 4.1).

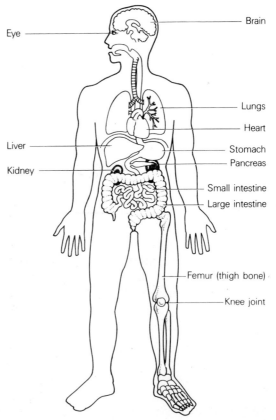

Figure 4.1 Body parts must work together efficiently

All the different parts of the body depend upon each other. It is no good if some parts work well and others do not. For each cell to work properly the chemical reaction inside it must work as quickly as possible. That means the enzymes must be able to work as quickly as possible. For all this to happen the conditions for each cell must be kept stable. A cell cannot work efficiently if the temperature suddenly changes or if it begins to gain or lose water. It will not work if it is not supplied with food or oxygen. Nor will it function if its waste products are not taken away regularly.

Homeostasis

Keeping conditions inside the body as stable as possible is called *homeostasis*. In a complex body like ours, there are some parts whose job it is to make sure conditions remain stable. These parts are often called *homeostatic organs*. Some examples of these include the skin, the kidneys and the liver (Figure 4.2).

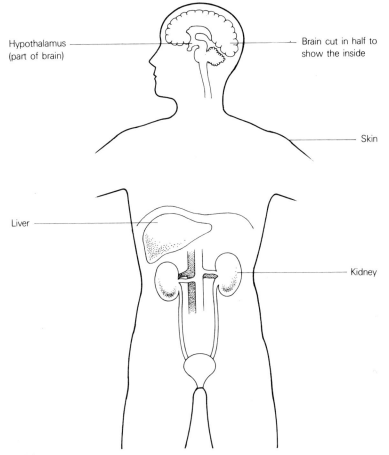

Hypothalamus
(part of brain)

Brain cut in half to
show the inside

Skin

Liver

Kidney

Figure 4.2   Important homeostatic organs

Conditions inside the body are constantly checked by a part of the brain known as the *hypothalamus*. This sends instructions to the homeostatic organs when any changes are necessary.

Negative feedback control

Homeostasis works through a system called *negative feedback control* (Figure 4.3). Take, for example, temperature control. The hypothalamus is connected to temperature sensors in the skin and in some blood vessels in the neck. If the temperature of the blood falls below what it should be, the hypothalamus sends messages to the skin to reduce the amount of heat lost. The body makes heat all the time with the muscles, the gut and the liver. When only a little of this heat is being lost, the body temperature will rise. It may easily go higher than it should be. The hypothalamus will detect this rise and send a message to the skin to lose more heat. This of course will lead to the temperature falling again, and so the process is repeated.

All homeostatic control works like this. The hypothalamus detects changes in conditions. Different parts of the body then make adjustments. This keeps conditions as near as possible to what they should be.

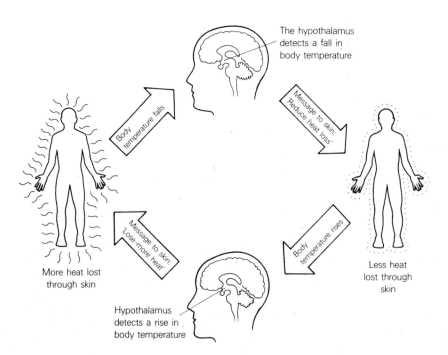

The hypothalamus detects a fall in body temperature

Body temperature falls

Message to skin: 'Reduce heat loss'

Less heat lost through skin

Body temperature rises

More heat lost through skin

Message to skin: 'Lose more heat'

Hypothalamus detects a rise in body temperature

Figure 4.3   Negative feedback control of body temperature

4.2 Keeping temperature stable

We keep our temperature as stable as possible so that the enzymes in the cells work as quickly as they can. The temperature must not fall because the enzymes would slow up. It must not rise because the heat would begin to destroy the enzymes.

Each person is an individual. Each body is slightly different to all other bodies. Thus, each person's temperature is adjusted to suit their own body.

Experiment 4.1

Experiment to find body temperatures

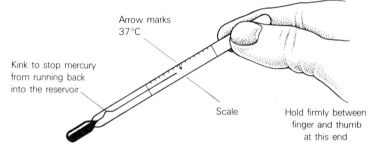

Figure 4.4   Clinical thermometer

1. Take a clinical thermometer (Figure 4.4). This has a small kink in the tube near the mercury reservoir. This kink stops the mercury running back into the reservoir when the thermometer is taken out of your mouth.

2. Check that you can see the mercury inside the thermometer. The triangular thermometer tube magnifies the mercury, but you have to look in the correct position to see it. Figure 4.5 shows you how to do this.

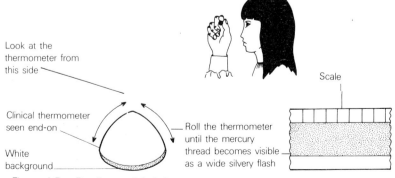

Figure 4.5   Reading a clinical thermometer

3. Shake the mercury down by grasping the thermometer with your finger and thumb firmly at the top end. Shake by flicking your wrist. *Do not* stand near a bench when you do this in case you smash the thermometer.

4. Now dip the reservoir end of the thermometer into dilute antiseptic. Rinse off under a tap.

5. Put the reservoir end of the thermometer under your tongue and leave it for at least a minute.

6. Take it out and check your temperature.

7. Write your temperature in a chart of the class results on the blackboard. Copy down this chart for your write up.

8. Work out the average class temperature.

9. How much variation was there in the temperature of the class?

10. What was the average temperature? Was this the figure you expected to get?

11. Why did you dip the thermometer into antiseptic?

The skin   The structure of skin is shown in Figure 4.6. The skin is the largest organ in the body. It has a number of jobs:

(a) It holds the body together.

(b) It protects the body from attack by microbes.

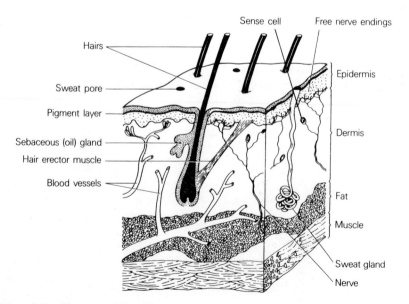

Figure 4.6   Structure of the skin

(c) It is waterproof and therefore stops the body gaining or losing water.

(d) It has sense cells which can detect touch, pain and temperature.

(e) It protects the body against harmful ultra-violet light from the sun. This light is absorbed by a pigment layer in the epidermis. The more we are exposed to sunlight, the darker the pigment becomes. This is called a *sun-tan*.

(f) It helps to control the body temperature.

The epidermis

Figure 4.7 shows a cross-section through the epidermis, which is the outer layer of the skin. It consists of layers of cells, but only the bottom layers are living. The lowest layer consists of cells which are growing and dividing all the time. This layer gradually pushes the other cells away, towards the surface. As the cells get pushed up, they die and become flatter. They are filled with a hard protein called *keratin*. These dead, flat cells make the skin tough and waterproof.

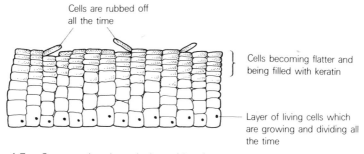

Cells are rubbed off all the time

Cells becoming flatter and being filled with keratin

Layer of living cells which are growing and dividing all the time

Figure 4.7   Cross-section through the epidermis

Since the outer cells are dead they are easily worn away. It is said that the outer layer of skin cells over our entire body gets worn away every three weeks. You can see that the epidermis cells must grow constantly to keep up with this.

The dermis

The dermis contains most of the living skin cells. It contains the hair-producing cells, the sebaceous glands, the sweat glands, blood capillaries and most of the sensory cells. At the base of the dermis is a fat layer. This varies in thickness between different people, from a few millimetres to several centimetres. Fat is an insulator, and its job is to prevent heat loss.

How does the skin help control body temperature?

There are two basic body conditions to which the skin reacts:

(a) When the body is too cold and less heat must be lost.

(b) When the body is too hot and more heat must be lost.

The skin is able to make very small adjustments and may not always do all of the following reactions. What is described below are the possible reactions the skin can make.

When the body is too cold

On a cold day, the following skin reactions help us to stay warm (Figure 4.8).

(a) Many of the tiny arteries in the dermis close up a little. This is called *vasoconstriction*. It reduces the amount of warm blood passing near the skin's surface where it could lose heat to the air. In fair-skinned people, the skin grows paler.

(b) Goose pimples are produced when the hairs in our skin stand up on end. They are pulled up by the hair erector muscles. In animals with lots of fur, it makes a thicker layer around the body. The hair traps a layer of air which is an insulator. This means less heat is lost. Since we do not have much hair, this reaction is not very useful to us. We manage to achieve the same effect by putting on extra clothes.

(c) Shivering is not really a skin reaction although skin muscles can do it. The muscles make heat by working and this helps to warm the body up. We usually shiver only when we are very cold.

(d) Our skin, of course, stops sweating.

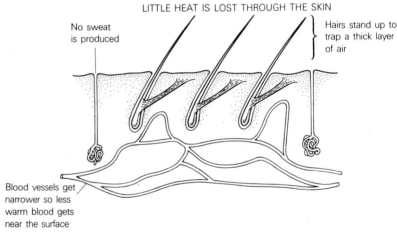

LITTLE HEAT IS LOST THROUGH THE SKIN

No sweat is produced

Hairs stand up to trap a thick layer of air

Blood vessels get narrower so less warm blood gets near the surface

Figure 4.8   How the skin reacts when we are cold

When the body is too hot

On a hot day the following skin reactions help us keep cool (Figure 4.9 (opposite)).

(a) The tiny arteries in the dermis open wide. This is called *vasodilation*. It brings lots of warm blood close to the skin's surface. More heat can be lost to the air. In fair-skinned people, the skin becomes redder.

(b) Sweating cools us down. Sweat is a watery liquid which is poured on to the skin by the sweat glands. This itself does not cool the skin, but when the sweat *evaporates* it does. To evaporate the sweat needs heat. It takes this from the skin and so cools it.

(c) The hairs on the skin lie as flat as possible to keep the insulating air layer thin. This is useful only to furry animals, not to humans.

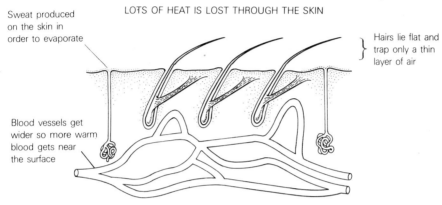

Sweat produced on the skin in order to evaporate

LOTS OF HEAT IS LOST THROUGH THE SKIN

Hairs lie flat and trap only a thin layer of air

Blood vessels get wider so more warm blood gets near the surface

Figure 4.9   How the skin reacts when we are hot

Experiment 4.2

Experiment to see the effects of sweating

1. Place a drop of alcohol on the back of your hand. The alcohol should be at room temperature and not particularly cold. (Figure 4.10.)

2. Blow gently across the alcohol to make it evaporate.

3. How did your skin feel as the alcohol evaporated?

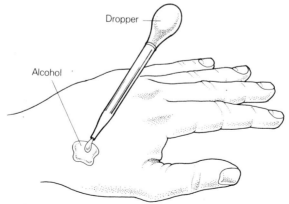

Dropper

Alcohol

Figure 4.10   To see how evaporation cools the skin

Experiment 4.3

Experiment to investigate the effects of thick and thin fur on the amount of heat lost by a body

This is a simple experiment which you should be able to design for yourself. If you use hot water in your 'body' you can check the temperature easily. Remember too that both your 'bodies' must start as close as possible to the same temperature. Things you will have to decide are:

What will you use for a 'body'?
What will you use for its fur?
How often will you take its temperature?

After the experiment you should display your results on a graph with axes like the ones in Figure 4.11.

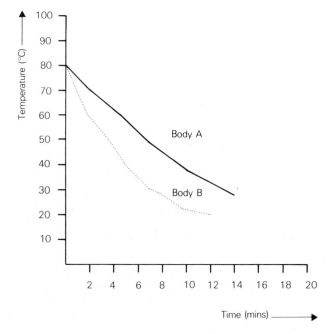

Figure 4.11   Graph of the heat lost by different bodies

1.   For the same amount of time, which body lost most heat?

2.   Why did this happen?

4.3 Warm-blooded and cold-blooded animals

The terms 'warm-blooded' and 'cold-blooded' are not very accurate. A warm-blooded animal is one which can control its body temperature. It keeps the temperature fairly stable. Only mammals and birds can do this. They are called *homeothermic*.

A cold-blooded animal is one which cannot control its body temperature. Its temperature depends upon how much heat it can make and the temperature of its surroundings. Most animals except mammals and birds are like this. They are called *poikilothermic*.

The problem with being poikilothermic is that when the surroundings are cold then the animal's body is cold. All the enzymes in the cells work more slowly, and the whole body will slow down. For this reason, poikilothermic animals often disappear during the winter. They may hibernate like grass snakes and tortoises or they may spend the winter as eggs or some other resting stage. You may have noticed how few flies are about in the winter. It is generally too cold for them to survive.

Poikilothermic animals which live in hot climates may really have warm blood. Tropical fish do. So, too, do crocodiles and alligators, at least during the day. However, if the night is cold, then the blood of these animals cools down.

Summary

1. Conditions inside the body must be as stable as possible so that all the cells can work efficiently.

2. Keeping conditions stable is called homeostasis.

3. Homeostasis works through negative feedback control.

4. The skin helps keep our temperature constant.

5. Animals which can keep their temperature constant are called homeothermic.

6. Animals whose body temperature depends on their surroundings are called poikilothermic.

4.4 The kidney — an important homeostatic organ

We have two kidneys, as shown in Figure 4.12. They are found either side of the backbone, just below the ribs. Each kidney is connected by a tube called the *ureter* to the *bladder*. The bladder stores the liquid *urine* until it can be passed out of the body. Each kidney has a *renal artery* bringing blood to it and a *renal vein* taking blood away.

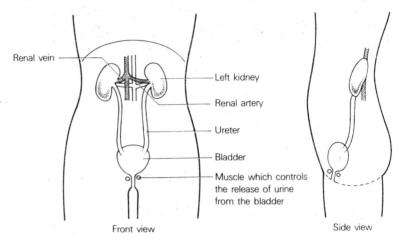

Figure 4.12   Position of the kidneys

What the kidneys do

The kidneys have two jobs:

(a) To get rid of poisonous waste substances made by the body. Most of these come from dead cells. In the liver the proteins from the cells are broken down. This makes ammonium compounds which are very poisonous. The liver turns these into a less poisonous substance called *urea*. It is the job of the kidneys to get rid of urea. Removing poisonous waste substances is called *excretion.*

(b) To make sure the water content of the body stays more or less constant. We take water in all the time in food and drink. The kidneys control how much is got rid of.

What are the kidneys like?

If you cut a kidney in half you will see that it is made up of three parts (Figure 4.13 (opposite)). These are:

(a) an outer 'grainy' region called the *cortex.*
(b) an inner striped region called the *medulla.*

(c) a whitish central region called the *pelvis* which leads to the ureter.

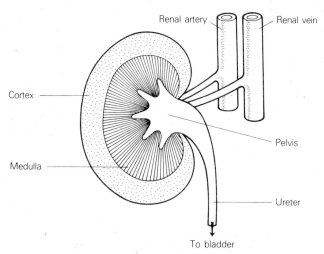

Figure 4.13   Cross-section through the kidney

It is very difficult to imagine what the kidney is like. Each kidney is made up of about a million tube systems called *nephrons*. These are all packed into the cortex region. The blood vessels and urine tubes which supply the nephrons all run through the medulla. The medulla is striped because it contains thousands of these tiny tubes. Figure 4.14 gives you some idea of what this is like.

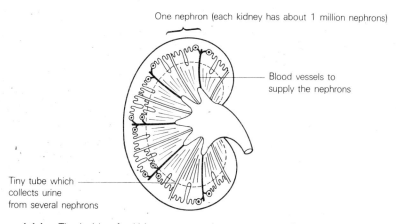

Figure 4.14   The inside of a kidney

Each nephron is able to remove urea from blood and help control its water content. Each nephron can do both of the jobs that the kidney does. Thus if you understand how one nephron works then you will understand how the whole kidney works.

What is the nephron like?

Figure 4.15 shows a nephron unravelled from the kidney. It has been drawn a little more simply so that you can follow it.

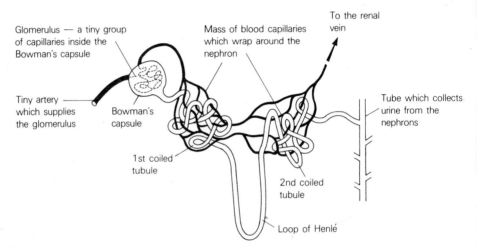

Figure 4.15   A single nephron dissected out of a kidney

The nephron itself has one end swollen called the *Bowman's capsule*. The tube then wiggles about a little before becoming a hairpin loop. This is called the *loop of Henlé*. After this the tube wiggles about a little more and joins on to a main *urine-collecting tube*. The twisted parts of the nephron are sometimes known as the *first* and *second coiled tubules*.

A tiny artery which has branched from the renal artery enters the Bowman's capsule. Inside, it divides into a tightly bunched group of capillaries called the *glomerulus*. The capillaries join up and leave the glomerulus as another tiny artery. This then quickly divides into more capillaries which spread out and wrap around the first and second coiled tubules. There are many more capillaries than are shown in the diagram.

Finally, these capillaries join up to become a tiny vein. This joins with other veins and eventually becomes the *renal vein* leaving the kidney.

How does the nephron work?

Look at Figure 4.16. Blood from the artery is squeezed through the glomerulus. The tiny artery which leaves the glomerulus is smaller than the one going into it. This squeezes the blood even more. The capillary walls have microscopic holes. These allow much of the liquid in the blood to be filtered into the Bowman's capsule. This is called *ultrafiltration*.

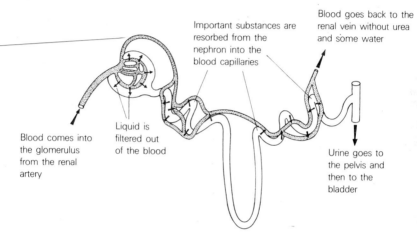

Important substances are resorbed from the nephron into the blood capillaries

Blood goes back to the renal vein without urea and some water

Blood comes into the glomerulus from the renal artery

Liquid is filtered out of the blood

Urine goes to the pelvis and then to the bladder

Figure 4.16   What happens in the nephron

All the urea gets filtered into the Bowman's capsule. So too do water, glucose, amino acids, salt and many other substances in the blood. These substances are very important to the body. They cannot be wasted and must be taken back into the blood.

The filtered liquid trickles out of the Bowman's capsule and into the first coiled tubule. The blood capillaries which wrap around the nephron take back useful substances as the filtered liquid trickles through. This process is called *resorption* and no one is really sure how it works. However, the blood capillaries resorb most of the useful substances like glucose, amino acids and water. Urea is not resorbed.

What is left of the filtered liquid trickles through the loop of Henlé. This helps to control how much water is finally removed. It then passes through the second coiled tubule where more water and salt are resorbed into the blood.

Finally, what is left in the nephron is called *urine*. It contains water, urea, some salt and a few other poisonous compounds. Urine passes into the collecting tube and down to the bladder.

The blood has now been cleaned. It passes into the renal vein to go back to the heart again.

The homeostatic control of body water content

Look at Figure 4.17. The hypothalamus of the brain checks the water level of blood constantly. If the water level falls then the hypothalamus tells the *pituitary gland* to produce the chemical ADH (anti-diuretic hormone). ADH is one of the body's *hormones*. These are chemical messengers passed around the body in the blood.

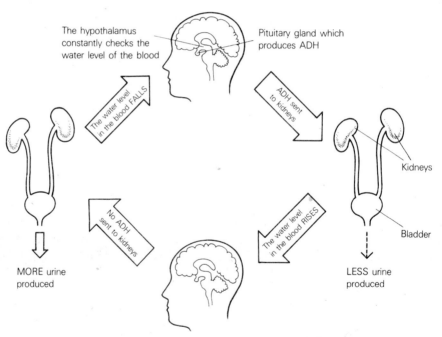

Figure 4.17   How the water content of the body is controlled

ADH makes the kidneys resorb more water into the blood, less is released into the urine. This keeps the water level of blood up.

If the water level rises, say after a drink, then no ADH is produced. The kidneys then remove more water in the urine and the blood water level falls.

This is another example of **negative feedback control**.

Summary

1. The kidney has two jobs — to remove poisonous wastes and to control the water content of the body.

2. Removing poisonous wastes is called excretion.

3. A single kidney is made of about a million tiny tubes called nephrons.

4. Each nephron is able to do both of the kidney's jobs.

5. The water content of the body is controlled by the hypothalamus using the hormone ADH.

Excretion and water control in other animals

Most vertebrates have kidneys which work like ours. Freshwater fish gain water from their surroundings by osmosis. (For a reminder of *osmosis,* see *A First Biology Course,* Chapter 9.) Their kidneys get rid of lots of water. Saltwater fish lose water to the sea by osmosis; their kidneys have to get rid of as little water as possible. (See Figure 4.18.)

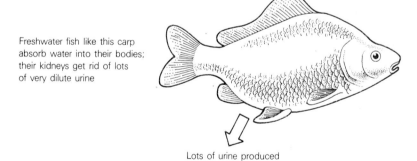

Freshwater fish like this carp absorb water into their bodies; their kidneys get rid of lots of very dilute urine

Lots of urine produced

Sea water fish like this mackerel lose water by osmosis from their bodies; their kidneys get rid of only a little very concentrated urine

Little urine produced

Figure 4.18   Water control in fish

Insects have tiny tubes attached to their gut which remove poisonous wastes (Figure 4.19). They cannot afford to waste any water, so they produce solid *uric acid* instead of urea. This is passed out with their faeces.

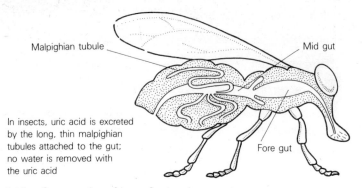

Malpighian tubule

Mid gut

In insects, uric acid is excreted
by the long, thin malpighian
tubules attached to the gut;
no water is removed with
the uric acid

Fore gut

Figure 4.19   Cross-section of housefly showing excretory organs

Birds produce the same solid uric acid. They could not fly if they had a bladder which constantly changed weight as urine was added and removed. They would not be able to keep proper balance.

One-celled water animals like the *Amoeba* do not have a problem with poisonous wastes. These simply diffuse out of the body into the water. They do have a problem with osmosis because the cell constantly fills up with water. To stop itself from bursting an Amoeba has a *contractile vacuole*. This is a part of the cell which fills up with water and bursts through the cell membrane, dumping the water outside. (See Figure 4.20.)

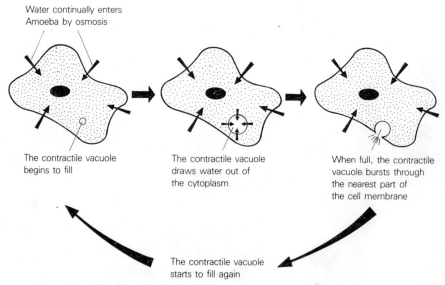

Water continually enters
Amoeba by osmosis

The contractile vacuole
begins to fill

The contractile vacuole
draws water out of
the cytoplasm

When full, the contractile
vacuole bursts through
the nearest part of
the cell membrane

The contractile vacuole
starts to fill again

Figure 4.20   Water control in *Amoeba*

Questions on Chapter 4

1. (a) What is homeostasis?
   (b) Name three homeostatic organs in the human body.

2. (a) What is negative feedback control?
   (b) Give an example of negative feedback control in the body.

3. The following results were obtained when a class took their body temperatures:

36.5 °C	36.6 °C	37.4 °C	36.8 °C	37.3 °C
37.2 °C	37.1 °C	36.8 °C	37.0 °C	36.8 °C

   What is the average body temperature for the class? Why is it important that humans keep their temperature around this level?

4. When you come out of the swimming pool you feel cold, especially if there is a slight breeze. You do not feel so cold when you have dried yourself. Why is this?

5. Copy out the following and fill in the blanks.
   When we are cold our skin looks _____ . This is because all the tiny arteries have _____ . This is called _____ . The hairs on our skin stand up on end and we may also _____ . When we are hot, our skin looks _____ . This helps to cool us because it allows _____ blood close to the surface of the skin. To do this the tiny arteries _____ . This is called _____ . We also _____ which cools us down by _____ and taking heat from the skin.

6. (a) What do homeothermic and poikilothermic mean?
   (b) Give three examples of a homeothermic animal and three of a poikilotherm.

7. Copy out the following and fill in the blanks.
   We have _____ kidneys. Each one has a _____ artery and _____ vein. There is also a tube which connects them to the bladder called the _____ . Each kidney contains about a million _____ . Each of these has a swollen end called a _____ _____ which contains a group of capillaries inside called the _____ . The rest of the tube is divided into two _____ parts and a loop of _____ . Tiny blood _____ wrap around the tube.

8. Describe in your own words what ultrafiltration and resorption are.

9. Mammals excrete urea but some other animals excrete uric acid instead.
   (a) What types of animals excrete urea or uric acid?
   (b) Why do they do so?

Crossword on Chapter 4

Across

3   This animal cannot live out of water (4)

5   A mixture of gases, mostly nitrogen (3)

7   Striped region of the 16 down (7)

11   See 26 across

13   Tree home for a bird (4)

14   _____ dilation is happening when the arteries in the 28 across open wider (4)

15   Cold-blooded (14)

17   Oxygen is a _____ (3)

19   The hypothalamus can control the amount of heat that is _____ from the body (4)

20   A kidney tube (7)

24   The outer layer of the 28 across (9)

26, 11   The swollen end of a 20 across (7, 7)

27   It is produced by the pituitary gland (1, 1, 1)

28   The body's largest organ (4)

29   Produced to cool us down (5)

30   A hard protein found in the 28 across (7)

Down

1   Central area of a 16 down (6)

2   Tiny blood vessels (11)

4   If homeostasis doesn't work, you may become _____ (3)

6   These little animals are 15 across (7)

8   Part of the 20 across (4, 2, 5)

9   One of these is not a plant (6)

10   A cell will not work without food or _____ (6)

12   Liquid in the blood undergoes _____ filtration into the 26, 11 across (5)

16   A homeostatic organ (6)

18   It contains hair-producing cells (6)

21   We need to do this to replace lost liquid (5)

22   Another homeostatic organ (5)

23   We 29 across to keep _____ (4)

25   2 down are very _____ (4)

27   A common type of 6 down (3)

(Teacher, please see special note in front of book.)

Copy this grid, then fill in the answers. Do not write on this page.

5. Changes in the environment

5.1 What is the environment?

Environment means everything around a living organism. We can think of this in two parts:

(a) The physical environment.
(b) The biological environment.

The physical environment

Think of your environment. Your physical environment includes everything which is non-living — for example, the temperature and the amount of water (Figure 5.1).

Figure 5.1   The physical environment

Temperature can affect whether you live or die. It can affect whether the water is snow, rain or ice and whether it evaporates quickly or not.

Rocks, too, are part of the physical environment. What they are made of is important, and whether the land is hilly or flat. This affects the behaviour of water, which may form fast-flowing streams, lakes or seas.

Wind affects how quickly the rocks are eroded. As rocks dissolve away they may alter the chemical composition of the environment.

The amount of light is important to plants.

The biological environment

Your biological environment includes everything that is living — all plants and animals (Figure 5.2). You may eat plants for food or use them for shelter. You may eat other animals or they may eat you! Micro-organisms may live off you or your food. They will decompose dead plants and animals and help recycle important chemicals.

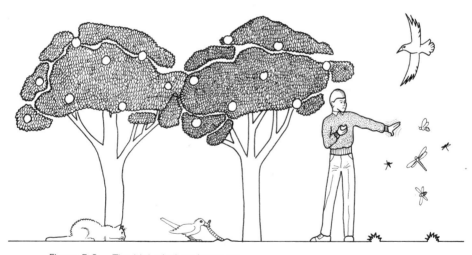

Figure 5.2   The biological environment

Every living organism is part of the environment of the other living organisms around it. If something happens to one organism, it may affect many others in some way.

The environment in balance

The environment is extremely complex. In any one place it will have evolved over many, many years. This does not mean that it is fixed. It might, for example, change at different times of the year. In general, however, the environment is *balanced*. The numbers of animals and plants are such that neither animals nor plants die out. Changes are often gradual and this gives the animals and plants time to adapt to them.

Humans sometimes bring changes much more quickly to the environment. In order to grow food or provide housing, or for many other good reasons, we may very suddenly change large areas of land. Because of the complex balance which exists such changes can affect all sorts of animals and plants. Some of these may live far away, as happened when farmers used the insecticide DDT on crops in Europe and North America. It was found that DDT was killing peregrine falcons in Scotland and affecting penguins in the Antarctic. The poison had been passed from plants to animals and through food chains until it ended up in these unlikely victims.

Before we make any changes to the environment, we should investigate carefully what effects they may have. It is easy to upset the balance and create areas where, in the end, few organisms can live. Some changes must take place, but the environment is *our* responsibility. We must not ruin it.

Summary

1. The environment is everything around an animal or plant.

2. The environment can be divided into the physical and the biological environment.

3. The environment is in balance. Large changes can seriously upset the balance.

5.2 Detecting the environment

Animals have *senses* which they use to detect any changes in the environment. They use these to move to environments which suit them best. In general, animals have the following senses:

    (a) Touch
    (b) Temperature detection
    (c) Pain
    (d) Taste/smell
    (e) Sight
    (f) Hearing
    (g) Balance

Some animals have one sense which is more highly developed than the others. Dogs, for example, have a very good sense of smell. Bats have highly developed hearing which they use like radar to guide them when flying. Birds of prey have good vision for seeing the animals they feed on. The senses in humans are all quite well developed, but none is as specialised as the three examples given below (Figure 5.3).

Dogs have a good
sense of smell

Bats have highly
developed hearing

Birds of prey have
good vision

Figure 5.3   Highly developed senses in animals

5.3 How we detect the environment

Touch   The sense of touch is very important, especially for the blind (Figure 5.4). We all have *touch receptor cells* in our skin. Our hairs are attached to nerves, and hairs, too, can detect when something is touching them. Some areas of

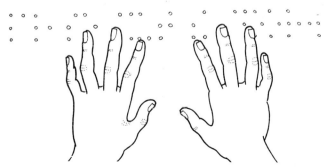

Figure 5.4   The sense of touch: the hands of a blind person 'reading' braille

our skin have more touch cells than others. Our fingers and lips and tongue are particularly sensitive. As babies we learn a lot about things around us either by picking them up or by putting them in our mouths.

Experiment 5.1

An investigation into the sense of touch in different parts of the body

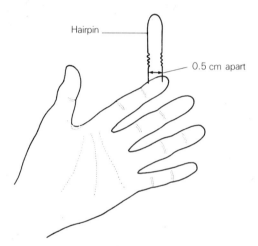

Hairpin

0.5 cm apart

Figure 5.5   Investigating sensitivity of touch

1. Work in pairs. You will need a hairpin with the ends 0.5 cm apart.

2. One partner should be blindfolded or must look away.

3. The other partner uses the hairpin to touch the skin of the fingertips lightly (Figure 5.5). The skin is touched ten times with either one or both points of the hairpin. Try to vary the order of touching so that the person touched cannot guess whether it is with one or both points.

4. After each touch, the subject (the person who is being touched) should say whether he/she felt one or both points.

5. Record the total number of correct answers out of ten.

6. Repeat this investigation using skin on the back of the hand, the arm, the cheek and the neck.

7. Swap over so that the person who did the touching now becomes the subject.

8. Which areas of skin gave the most correct scores?

9. Is there any reason why this part of the skin should detect touch more accurately?

10. Which area gave the least correct scores?

11. Is there any reason why this part of the skin should not detect touch so accurately?

Temperature detection

We have temperature detecting cells in the skin. They do not measure temperature, like thermometers, but detect temperature changes. You can see this in the following simple experiment.

Experiment 5.2

Investigating temperature detection

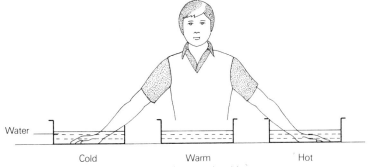

Water

Cold   Warm   Hot

Figure 5.6   Investigating reaction to heat and cold

1. You need three bowls of water. The first holds very cold water; the middle bowl holds lukewarm water; the last holds hot water.

2. Put one hand in the cold water and the other in the hot (Figure 5.6). Leave for a minute.

3. Put both hands at the same time into the middle bowl. Think carefully what each hand feels.

4. In the middle bowl, which hand felt cold? Can you explain why?

5. In the middle bowl, which hand felt warm? Again, explain why.

6. What does this demonstrate about your ability to tell the temperature of your surroundings?

Pain

We feel pain whenever a nerve cell is damaged. Pain tells us something is wrong and we must do something about it. There are no special pain receptors in the body. Not everybody has the same sensitivity to pain. Some people find the prick of a doctor's needle very painful. Others, particularly the mystics of Far Eastern countries, can lie all day on a bed of nails and apparently not feel uncomfortable. (See Figure 5.7.)

Pain has a lot to do with your state of mind. Athletes in a marathon can develop painful blisters, but because they think only about running they do not notice the pain until the race is over. This is true of many minor sports injuries.

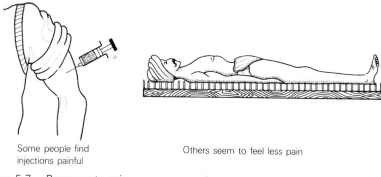

Some people find
injections painful

Others seem to feel less pain

Figure 5.7   Response to pain

Taste and smell

These two have been put together because they both involve detecting chemicals in the environment. In fact, although we say that we can taste the food we eat, much of this 'tasting' is done in the nose.

Experiment 5.3

Investigating taste

1. You need a subject to work with who must be blindfolded. You also need a small amount of crushed onion and crushed apple in separate containers. Use a fresh onion and a crisp apple. (See Figure 5.8 (opposite).)

2. Feed your subject with very small amounts of *either* the apple or the onion. Do not mix them. The subject is given only up to 5 seconds to taste the food and then must tell you whether it is apple or onion.

3. Repeat this until you have given five lots of apple and five lots of onion. Vary the order in which you give them so that the subject cannot guess what they are being given.

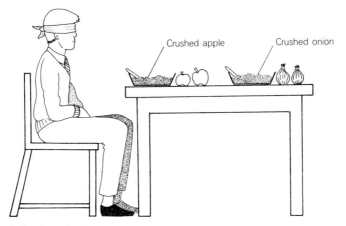

Figure 5.8   Investigating taste

4.   Score the number of correct answers out of ten.

5.   Repeat the experiment, asking your subject to pinch his/her nose for the whole time during tasting.

6.   Score the number of correct answers out of ten.

7.   Did pinching the subject's nose make any difference to his/her ability to taste?

Our tongue has taste buds. These are groups of cells which lie in tiny holes in the tongue. Food dissolves in water and fills the holes. The taste cells can't then detect the food. Our tongues can only detect four basic tastes: sweet, salt, sour and bitter. Even these cannot be detected in the same parts of the tongue. Figure 5.9 is a 'map' of the tongue showing which areas can taste what.

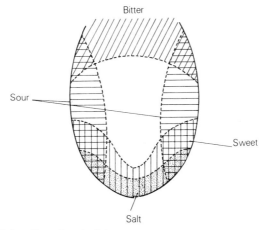

Figure 5.9   Taste 'map' of the tongue

Summary

1. Most animals can detect touch, temperature change, pain, tastes/smells, light, and sounds.

2. Touch receptors and temperature receptors are both found in our skin.

3. Damage to any nerve cell produces the sensation of pain.

4. Taste and smell are very similar.

5. Our tongue can only taste four tastes: sweet, salt, sour and bitter. All other 'tastes' are detected in our nose.

Sight

Being able to see is one of our most useful senses. You can understand this if you close your eyes for a minute. Imagine how you would move around. Which parts of your environment would you no longer be able to detect? How would that affect your life? Most blind people cope well with their handicap but life is much easier for those who can see.

To understand how the eyes work you must try to answer a few simple questions.

Why do we have two eyes?

Close one eye. You will find that using one eye you can still see about two-thirds of what you could see using two eyes. The picture is still as clear and in focus. Therefore, you do not need two eyes to see the world clearly. Try this experiment.

Experiment 5.4

Investigating why we need two eyes

Part I

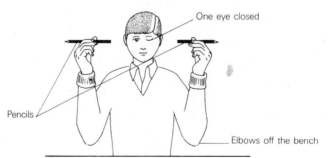

Pencils

One eye closed

Elbows off the bench

Figure 5.10   How to do Part I

1. Pick up two pencils or pens, one in each hand. Hold them out in front of you as shown in Figure 5.10. Bend your arms a little.

2. Now close one eye and bring the pencils together so that they touch end to end. Do this quite quickly.

3. Repeat this several times, and then do it with the other eye shut.

4. Try the experiment again but with both eyes open.

5. Was it easier to bring the pencils together with one eye open or with both eyes open?

6. What difference did using two eyes make?

Part II

1. Now work with a partner. Get your partner to read a book held quite close to the face.

2. Measure the distance between the middles of the two pupils, as shown in Figure 5.11.

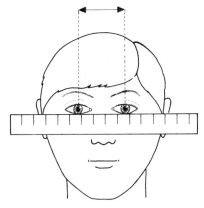

Figure 5.11   Measure the distance between the pupils as accurately as possible

3. Your partner should now look at an object a long way away. If possible look out of the window. Measure the distance between the pupil middles again.

4. Record your results in a chart like the one below.

	Distance between pupils
When looking at a close object	
When looking at a far object	

5. Is there a change in the distance between the pupils?

6. What have the eyes done to produce such a change?

7. Why do you think the eyes produced this change?

Having two eyes means that each eye can look at the same object from a different position. This ability allows us to see in three dimensions and to judge distance accurately. Our brain can measure the angle at which each eye is pointing. It uses this to work out how far away an object is. Also it can work out which objects are near and which are further away from the eye. (See Figure 5.12.)

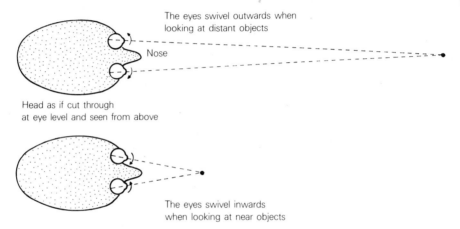

Figure 5.12   How two eyes are used to judge distance

To understand this more fully you must remember that each eye sees objects accurately only when it is pointing straight at them. The eyes can be swivelled in their sockets to keep them pointing at the objects you want to look at.

Field of vision

Your field of vision is what you can see with both eyes. This depends on where the eyes are on the head. The more the view from one eye overlaps with the view from the other, the smaller the field of vision.

To judge distance accurately the view from one eye must overlap with the view from the other. In this way, both eyes can look at the same object at once and the distance to the object can then be worked out accurately. Hunting animals, like hawks, need to judge the distance to their prey very accurately. They have eyes set in the front of their heads. This gives them a small total field of vision (Figure 5.13 (opposite)).

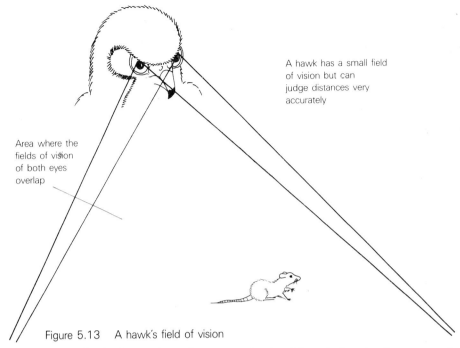

A hawk has a small field of vision but can judge distances very accurately

Area where the fields of vision of both eyes overlap

Figure 5.13   A hawk's field of vision

Animals which eat plants do not need to be able to judge the distance to the plant so well. They are often hunted, however, and they need to see as much as possible. They often have eyes at the side of their head. This gives them a very wide field of vision to see predators (Figure 5.14).

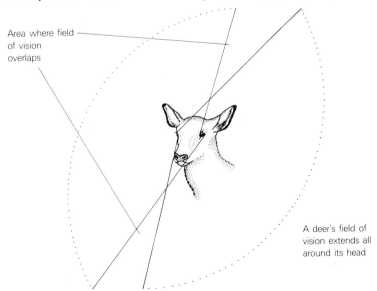

Area where field of vision overlaps

A deer's field of vision extends all around its head

Figure 5.14   A deer's field of vision

Experiment 5.5

Investigation to find your field of vision

1. Work in pairs. Bend down until your eye is level with the top of the bench.

2. Your partner holds a pencil in front of your head. The pencil is moved in a circle to the right side of your head — as shown in Figure 5.15.

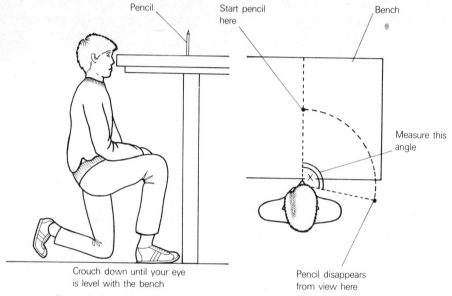

Figure 5.15   How to do the experiment

3. Without moving your head, tell your partner when you can no longer see the pencil.

4. Using a protractor measure the angle X in the diagram. This is the angle between where the pencil started and where it disappeared from view.

5. Repeat this for the left side.

6. Add the two angles together to find your total field of vision.

7. What is your field of vision?

8. Is it similar to your partner's?

9. Can you work out the average field of vision for the class?

10. Do you think you have a wide field of vision or a narrow one — or is yours in between wide and narrow?

11. How does your field of vision fit in with the way we live?

How does the eye work?

Figures 5.16 and 5.17 give you two different views of the eye. Figure 5.16 is a three-dimensional picture and Figure 5.17 shows a cross-section of an eye. This second picture shows a thin slice taken horizontally through the eye across its middle.

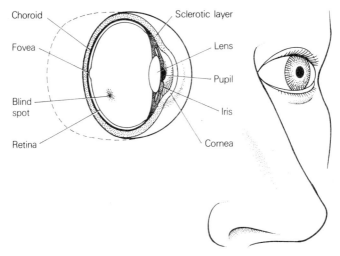

Figure 5.16   A three-dimensional view of the eye

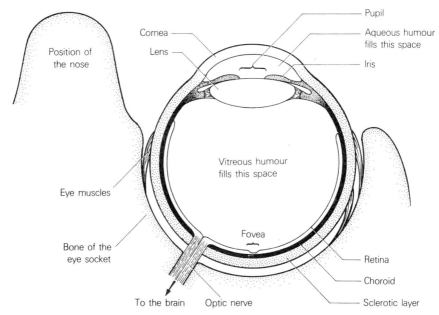

Figure 5.17   A cross-section of the eye seen from above

The following sequence describes how the eye works:

(a) The *brain* produces the 'pictures' you see. It does this using information from the eyes. This information travels from the eye along the *optic nerve*.

(b) The *retina* detects the objects you are looking at. Light from these objects passes into the eye and hits the millions of light-sensitive cells which make up the retina. Each cell sends a message to the brain. There are more of these light-sensitive cells in a tiny area called the *fovea* than in any other area of the retina. Your eyes are pointed at objects so that the light from them hits the fovea.

(c) Once the light has passed through the retina it is absorbed by a totally black layer called the *choroid*. This stops light reflecting inside the eye. The choroid also contains blood vessels which supply the retina cells.

(d) Light is focused by the *lens* and the *cornea* so that the retina cells receive a sharp picture. The lens shape can be changed to focus objects at different distances.

(e) The amount of light which passes into the eye is controlled by the *iris*. This changes the size of a hole called the *pupil* to let more or less light into the eye. The light-sensitive cells of the retina do not work well if they receive too much or too little light.

(f) The eye is kept in shape by the tough outer coat called the *sclerotic layer*, and the two liquids which fill the eye called the *aqueous* and *vitreous humours*. Muscles join the sclerotic and the skull. These are used to swivel the eye.

Experiment 5.6

Investigating how the amount of light affects the size of the pupil

1. Work in pairs. Stand in a darkened corner of the room. Measure the size of your partner's pupil (Figure 5.18).

2. Move to a brightly lit part of the room and measure the pupil size again.

3. When is the pupil biggest?

4. When is the pupil smallest?

5. Why does the pupil change size?

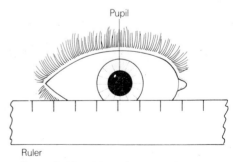

Figure 5.18   Measuring a pupil

The change in pupil size is produced by two sets of muscles which form the iris (Figure 5.19). To make the pupil smaller the circular muscles contract. To make it larger, the radial muscles contract.

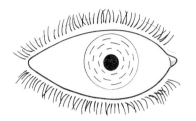
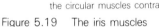
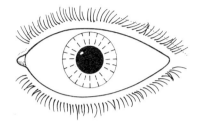

To make the pupil smaller,
the circular muscles contract

To make the pupil larger,
the radial muscles contract

Figure 5.19   The iris muscles

Experiment 5.7

Dissecting a bull's eye to see its structure

1. Take a bull's eye, a pair of scissors and a sharp scalpel. Be careful not to cut yourself.

2. Cut away all the fat and tissue from around the eye until you can find the optic nerve. Carefully remove everything from the surface of the eye except the optic nerve.

3. There is only one cut you can make through an eye. This is shown in Figure 5.20. Make this cut gently using the scalpel. Do not press too hard on the eye. Remember — it is full of liquid.

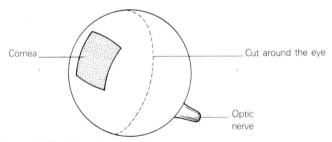

Cornea

Cut around the eye

Optic
nerve

Figure 5.20   Dissecting a bull's eye

4. Once you have made your first cut it is easier to finish off the eye with scissors.

5. Disturb the eye contents as little as possible. Examine the eye to answer the following questions (6 – 10).

6. What colour is the optic nerve?

7. What colour is the liquid in the eye? Why should it be this colour?

8. What colour is the retina?

9. What colour is the choroid?

10. Was the sclerotic as tough as you expected?

11. Now make two labelled sketches of the eye. One should be of the inside of the back of the eye, labelling where the optic nerve entered the eye. This point is called the *blind spot* because it has no retina cells. Did you find the fovea? It is a tiny yellowish dip in the middle of the back of the eye.

   The second sketch should be of the inside of the front of the eye. Label the iris and the muscles which held the lens.

12. Before you pack away, compare your dissected eye with Figures 5.16 and 5.17. Can you see how the drawings were made?

Seeing in colour

There are two sorts of light-sensitive cells in the retina — *rod cells* and *cone cells*. They get their names from the fact that rods are rod-shaped and cones are cone-shaped.

Rods can only produce a black and white picture in the brain. They can detect very small amounts of light and work only at night or when it is dark. During the day, there is so much light that the rod cells are permanently stimulated. If you sit in a lit room at night and then switch the lights off it takes about a minute for you to be able to see. This is the time it takes for your rod cells to begin working again.

Cones produce a coloured picture in the brain. Cone cells only work in bright light. This means we can only see in black and white in very dim light. Cone cells do not work so well in the dull lighting in some clothes shops. This is one reason why a garment may seem one colour in the shop but a very different colour outside in daylight.

There are three sorts of cone cells. Some detect red light, some detect green light, and the others detect blue light. Depending on how many of each sort of cone cell are stimulated our brains can create all the colours that we see.

Colour blindness is often caused when one sort of cone cell is missing. Many people suffer from red/green colour blindness. This means that either the red-sensitive cones or the green-sensitive cones are absent. The person cannot, therefore, easily tell the difference between red and green.

All the cone cells are found in the fovea part of the retina. This is why we must look straight at objects when we want to see them accurately and in colour.

Eye problems

The commonest eye problem occurs when a person cannot focus properly. There can be a number of reasons for this. The lens may be the wrong shape or the eye may not be completely round. The lens may get hard, as it does in older people. The problem usually shows itself in one of two ways. Either the person can see things which are close by and cannot accurately see objects which are far away — this is called being *short-sighted*. Or the person can see things far away but cannot accurately see them when they are close — this is called being *long-sighted*. The cure is to put a lens in front of the eye to do part of the focusing. This lens can be either in a pair of spectacles or be a contact lens. Short sight is cured with a *diverging* lens and long sight with a *converging* lens. This is explained in Figure 5.21.

Occasionally the lens may become cloudy so that very little light can pass through it. This is called a *cataract*. Modern surgery can remove such a lens

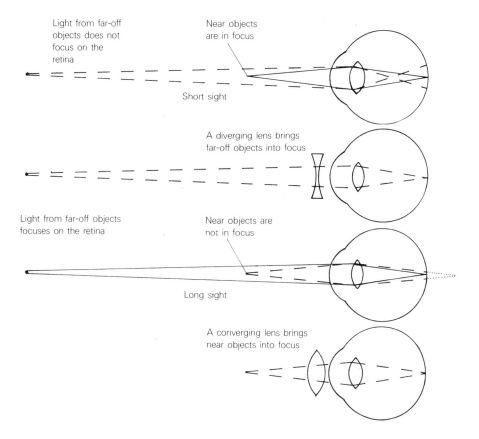

Figure 5.21   Short and long sight

and even replace it with a plastic one. A plastic lens can only focus objects over a small range of distances. To help the person see properly they may have to have glasses as well.

The cornea of the eye may become damaged or diseased. This can make a person blind even though the rest of the eye can still work properly. It is possible to remove a healthy cornea from the eye of a dead person and use it to replace a diseased one. This operation is quite common. This is why eyes are now included on organ donor cards.

Fooling the eye

Optical illusions are pictures which are not quite what they seem. We are fooled because our brain expects to see things arranged in certain ways. What happens is that our brain makes sense of the picture. Only by looking carefully do we realise that the brain has made a mistake. The drawings in Figure 5.22 show some optical illusions.

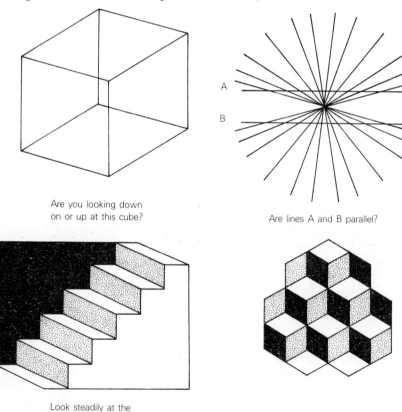

Are you looking down on or up at this cube?

Are lines A and B parallel?

Look steadily at the staircase. Turn the page slowly to the left and back, then look again.

Count the cubes and then carefully recount them

Figure 5.22   Optical illusions

Summary

1. We have two eyes to help us judge distance and depth accurately.

2. Each eye 'sees' because it has light-sensitive cells in the retina.

3. These cells send impulses to the brain. It is the brain which produces the pictures of what we are looking at.

4. Focusing is done by the lens and the cornea.

5. The pupil is a hole. Its size is changed by the iris. This allows enough light into the eye for the light sensitive cells to work.

6. To see an object accurately we must look straight at it.

Hearing The ear is not just a hearing organ, it also contains organs which tell us whether our bodies are upright and whether we are moving around or not. These are part of the *sense of balance.*

Why do we have two ears?

Experiment 5.8

Investigating why we have two ears

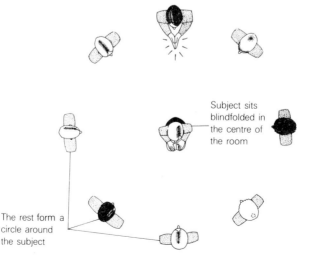

Subject sits blindfolded in the centre of the room

The rest form a circle around the subject

Figure 5.23   The arrangement for Experiment 5.8

1. You need between eight and twelve people for this experiment.

2. One person is blindfolded and sits in the centre of the room. The others stand or sit in a circle around, as shown in Figure 5.23 (on the previous page). There must be no noise at all.

3. One person organises the experiment (this could be the teacher). This person points at random to the people in the circle. Each time a person is pointed at he or she must make a single hand-clap. The subject in the centre must then point to where the sound came from.

4. It is important that everybody tries to make his or her hand-clap the same loudness as everybody else's. It is also important that one person must be exactly in front of the subject and another exactly behind.

5. After about a dozen hand-claps change the person in the centre.

6. Can the subject always accurately tell where the sound came from?

7. Sounds from which direction gave the most problems?

8. Why do you think this is?

Two ears are necessary to tell the direction of a sound. Sound waves travel through the air at about 330 metres per second. This is quite slow and therefore sounds reach each ear at slightly different times. The brain can measure this time difference and work out where the sound came from.

How the ear works

To understand this you need to know that the ear contains large numbers of *hair cells* (Figure 5.24). These are cells which are stimulated when their tiny hair is pulled or pushed. All the jobs of the ear depend upon hair cells.

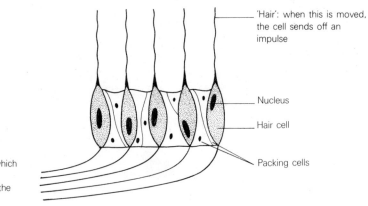

'Hair': when this is moved, the cell sends off an impulse

Nucleus

Hair cell

Packing cells

Nerve fibres which carry a nerve impulse from the hair cells

Figure 5.24   Hair cells of the ear

Figure 5.25 is a drawing of a slice or section through the ear. Since most of the ear is well inside the skull, it is very difficult to see. This sometimes makes the diagram more difficult to follow. The diagram has been drawn as if the ear has been cut vertically, straight through the middle from the side of the head.

Sound waves are vibrations in the air. When they arrive at the ear the following happens:

(a) The sound waves are directed into the *ear canal* by the outside part of the ear called the *pinna* (plural: *pinnae*). We could hear just as well without pinnae, but in some animals they are very important. Dogs, for example, can 'prick up' their ears if they want to listen. Birds, however, do not have pinnae and yet they still manage to hear well.

(b) The *eardrum* is a thin membrane stretched across the end of the ear canal. Vibrations in the air make the eardrum vibrate. So that the eardrum can vibrate freely and easily it has an air chamber on either side of it. The ear canal is on the outside, and on the inside the chamber connects to the throat by the *eustachian tube.* This allows the *air pressure* to be the same on both sides of the eardrum. If you travel uphill or downhill quite quickly the air pressure outside will change. This may make your ears feel odd. Yawning or swallowing opens up the entrance to the eustachian tube and the air pressure can adjust itself. Sometimes you may feel your ears pop as this happens.

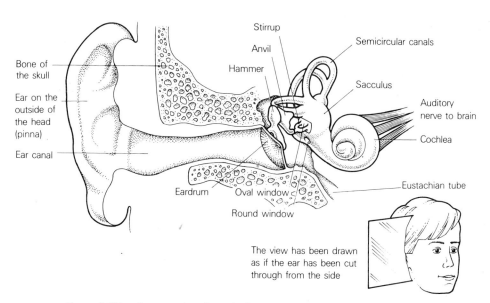

Figure 5.25   Cross-section through the ear

(c) The eardrum is connected to three tiny bones called the *hammer,* the *anvil* and the *stirrup.* As the eardrum vibrates then these three bones vibrate. They *amplify* the vibrations which allows the ear to work better.

The three bones are attached to the skull by muscles and ligaments. When a very loud sound is heard the muscles tighten up to prevent the bones from vibrating. This prevents damage to the ear.

(d) The stirrup connects to another tiny membrane called the *oval window.* Vibrations pass from the stirrup to the oval window and into a long, coiled structure called the *cochlea.* Inside the cochlea are the hair cells. These are stimulated when the liquid inside the cochlea vibrates. Each hair cell sends an impulse to the brain along the *auditory nerve* and the brain then 'hears' the sound.

Hearing and listening

You do not listen to all the sounds you hear. For instance, suppose you are having lunch in a crowded dining hall. If you stop and listen, you will realise that there are many sounds around you. Even so, you do not usually notice them, and you can quite easily hold a conversation with a friend. Your brain only listens to what it wants. Your ears hear all the sounds but your brain sorts them into useful and not useful ones. In this way you do not have to cope with too much information at once.

The ear and balance

The ear helps us to keep our balance in two ways. It detects whether the body is upright or not and it detects movements of the head.

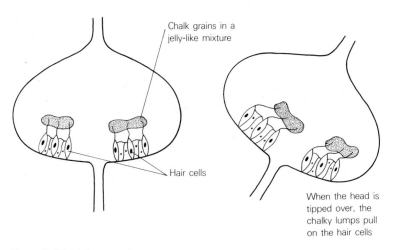

Figure 5.26   The sacculus

(a) Keeping upright. There is a swelling just above the cochlea which is filled with liquid. It is called the *sacculus* and is shown in Figure 5.26 (opposite). It contains a few small pieces of a chalky material attached to the hairs of some hair cells. When the head is upright the chalky lumps press on some hair cells. As the head tilts, gravity makes them move and they pull on some hair cells and press on others. The brain uses this information to tell if the body is upright or not.

(b) Head movements. Just above the sacculus is an arrangement called the *semicircular canals* (Figure 5.27). These are three tiny tubes which are filled with liquid. The three tubes are arranged at right angles to each other. At one end of each tube is a swelling which has hair cells in it. Attached to these is a small plate. As the liquid in the tubes moves so the plates are pushed about.

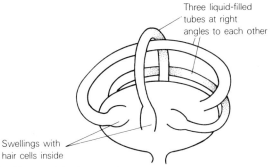

Three liquid-filled tubes at right angles to each other

Swellings with hair cells inside

Figure 5.27   The semicircular canals

Figure 5.28 should help you understand how the semicircular canals work. When the head moves, the liquid tends to stay in the same place. It pushes against the plates and stimulates the hair cells. Having three tubes at right angles means that any movement of the head will move the liquid in at least one tube. The brain works out how much movement there is in each tube and uses this to detect head movements.

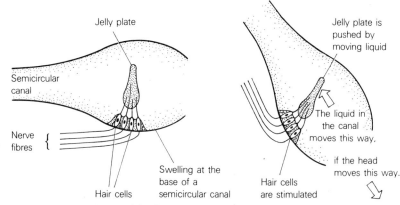

Jelly plate

Semicircular canal

Nerve fibres {

Hair cells

Swelling at the base of a semicircular canal

Jelly plate is pushed by moving liquid

The liquid in the canal moves this way,

if the head moves this way.

Hair cells are stimulated

Figure 5.28   How the semicircular canals detect head movements

Other organs of balance

Our eyes are very important in balance. We see the world around us and use this information to keep our bodies in the correct position. We also have *stretch receptors* in all of our muscles. These tell the brain when the muscle is stretched. By knowing which muscles are stretched and which are not, the brain can work out exactly the position of each part of the body.

Experiment 5.9

Balancing without our eyes

1. Stand upright without touching any object around you.
2. Now close your eyes. Remain standing for about a minute.
3. Did you feel your body sway?
4. Why do you think it is necessary to sway a little to remain upright?
5. Repeat the experiment but stand on one leg only.
6. Could you feel the muscles contracting and relaxing?

Ear problems

Deafness is the most obvious ear problem. It can be caused by a burst eardrum, the three ear bones not working, or the cochlea being diseased. If deafness is caused by damage to the eardrum or the ear bones, then it can be helped a little. A deaf person like this can wear a hearing aid which picks up sounds and transmits them through the bones of the skull to the cochlea.

Ear infections often occur with throat and nose infections. This is because the ear is connected to the throat by the eustachian tube. Microbes can pass from the throat into the chamber of the middle ear. The infection, and your body's attempt to control it, may stop ear bones vibrating freely. This may make you feel a little deaf for a while. Sometimes infection can pass into the balancing organs of the ear; this can make you feel dizzy.

If you go on a roundabout in a park or at a fair you usually become dizzy. Going round in circles several times starts the liquid in the semicircular canals spinning. When you get off the roundabout, you stop spinning but the liquid does not. Messages go from the hair cells to the brain telling it that the head is moving. Messages go from the eyes to the brain telling it that the body is not moving. This confuses the brain and produces dizziness.

In some cases the brain cannot cope with this confusion. Instead it makes the body fall over until everything gets back to normal. You can lessen the effects of dizziness by closing your eyes.

Summary

1. We have two ears to tell accurately the direction from which sound comes.

2. As well as detecting sounds, the ear helps to keep the body balanced.

3. All the work of the ear depends on hair cells.

4. Sound is vibration in the air.

5. Sound waves are picked up by the eardrum, amplified by the ear bones and turned into nerve messages in the cochlea.

6. The ear detects all the sounds but the brain only 'listens' to some of them.

7. The three semicircular canals detect head movements in any direction.

8. Balance relies a great deal on eyes as well as ears.

Questions on Chapter 5

1. Describe, in your own words, what the environment is.

2. The country was affected by a sudden change in temperature. The temperature fell so that it became like winter all the time. Write about how you think this would affect the animals and plants.

3. The following animals have one sense more highly developed than the others. Write down which sense you think it is and why.

   (a) bat   (b) owl   (c) mole   (d) whale
   (e) shark   (f) rattlesnake   (g) eagle   (h) rabbit

4. Jimmy asked Kate out for a meal. Kate said she would love to go but she had such a bad cold she would not be able to enjoy her food. What do you think she meant by this?

5. Copy out the following and fill in the blanks.
   In the eye the _____ has rod cells and _____ cells. These detect light and send impulses along the _____ _____ to the brain. Light is focused by the _____ and the _____ , whose shape can be changed to adjust the focus. The coloured part of your eye is called the _____ . It controls how much light enters the eye by making the _____ larger or smaller. The job of the choroid is to _____ all light so that none reflects inside the eye.

6. Which animal has the larger field of vision — a fox or a rabbit? Why do you think this is?

7. In an accident you damaged your left eye and had to have it bandaged to let it heal. Describe some of the problems this might give you. (Try walking around your house for 15 minutes with your left eye covered.)

8. To treat short sight, you need a _____ lens and to treat long sight you need a _____ lens.

9. Copy out the following and fill in the blanks.
    In the ear, sound waves first strike the _____ . This is connected to the three _____ of the ear called the _____ , _____ and _____ . These _____ sounds and pass them to the _____ which is able to detect them. The _____ _____ connects the ear to the throat. It is there to keep _____ _____ the same on both sides of the eardrum. This allows the eardrum to _____ freely.

10. You took your young brother to the park and gave him a ride on a roundabout. When it stopped he got off, wobbled about a bit and fell down. Explain why this happened.

Crossword on Chapter 5

Across

1   The eye is kept in shape by the _____ layer (9)
7   One of the bones in the ear (7)
9   It transmits 14 down to the brain (5)
10 An optical illusion is a sort of _____ our eyes play on us (5)
11 An insecticide (1, 1, 1)
12 Part of the eye which focuses light (4)
13 It can make your eyes water (5)
18 This eye problem is caused when the 12 across becomes cloudy (8)
21 A change in its pressure can affect your ears (3)
22 Bird with good 5 down (3)
24 Our 14 down are _____ to changes in the environment (9)
25 Our 7 down has 20 down _____ cells (8)
26 A basic 15 down (4)

Down

1   One of our 14 down (5)
2   Organisms are _____ things (6)
3   The _____ 9 across goes from the eye to the brain (5)
4   Part of the eye controlling the amount of light entering (4)
5   Another word for sight (6)
6   Each eye has a blind one (4)
7   Hairs grow in it (4)
8   Some cones in the eye are _____ -sensitive (3)
13, 16 A membrane in the ear (4, 6)
14   They help us detect changes in the environment — don't take leave of yours (6)
15   It is closely related to smell (5)
16   See 13 down
17   The ear _____ is *not* a waterway! (5)
19   Another bone in the ear (5)
20   One of our 14 down (5)
23   They are particularly 24 across to 20 down (4)

(Teacher, please see special note in front of book.)

Copy this grid, then fill in the answers. Do not write on this page.

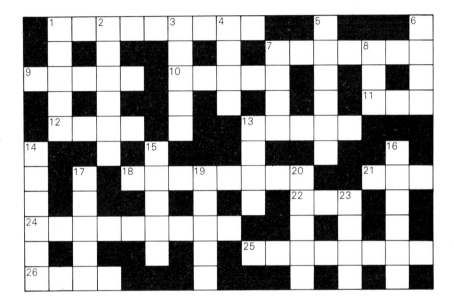

6. Getting information around the body

Having senses is no use unless the changes they detect can be used to help you (or any other animal) decide what you should do. This means that information from sense cells must pass to your brain which controls your body. The brain then sends information to your muscles to produce movement. This information is carried through the nervous system.

6.1 What is the nervous system?

The nervous system is made up of the brain and the spinal cord. These are called the *central nervous system* (CNS) — see Figure 6.1. They are connected to all other parts of the body by nerves.

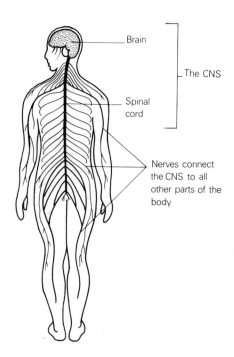

Brain

The CNS

Spinal cord

Nerves connect the CNS to all other parts of the body

Figure 6.1   The central nervous system

The whole nervous system is made of special cells called *nerve cells* or *neurons*. There are several different sorts:

(a) *Sensory* nerve cells which carry messages from sense cells to the CNS.

(b) *Motor* nerve cells which carry messages from the CNS to muscles.

(c) *Brain* nerve cells which do the work of the brain. There are many different sorts of nerve cell in the brain and nobody is very sure exactly how they work.

6.2 What is a nerve cell?

A nerve cell is very much like other cells in the body (Figure 6.2). It has cytoplasm, a nucleus and a cell membrane. Also, parts of the membrane become extended away from the cell to make connections with other cells. In sensory and motor nerve cells one piece of membrane grows

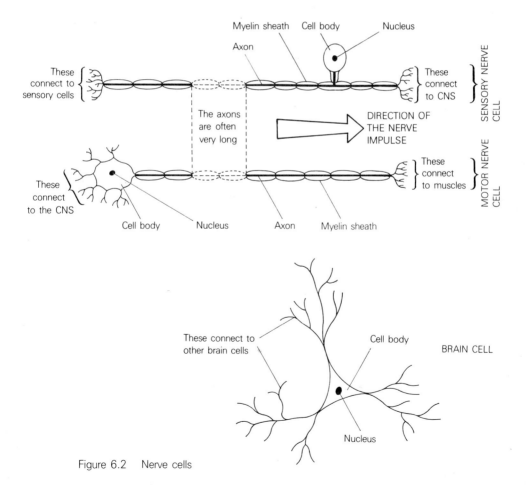

Figure 6.2   Nerve cells

much larger than the others. It is called the *axon*. Axons can be very long. For instance, each sense cell in your toes is connected to the spinal cord by a single sensory nerve cell. Its axon will be nearly one metre long. Axons grow whilst your body is growing. Once you stop growing at around 20 years old your axons also stop growing. If after that you should break an axon, the two halves will not join back together again. If a person breaks nerve cells in the spinal cord, he or she will become paralysed for ever. This is because no information can get across the break. Although the body will continue to work properly, the brain cannot control it and gets no information from it.

What does a nerve cell do?

A nerve cell carries a tiny electrical impulse from one part of the body to another. The impulse travels along the axon of the nerve cell. It uses energy supplied by the nerve cell body and other cells around the axon.

This process is quite slow. To speed it up the longer axons have a wrapping of a fatty substance called *myelin*. This is the *myelin sheath*. Although nobody is sure how this works, the myelin sheath makes the impulse travel much more quickly. It travels at up to 100 metres per second in some axons.

What is a nerve?

A nerve is a collection of nerve cell axons. A cross-section of one is shown in Figure 6.3. Any one nerve may contain thousands of axons, some sensory and some motor. A nerve will look white because the fatty substance, myelin, is white. As well as speeding up the impulses the myelin also insulates one axon from others around it.

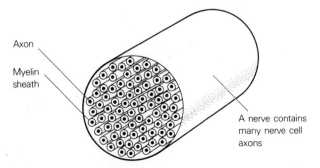

Axon

Myelin sheath

A nerve contains many nerve cell axons

Figure 6.3   Cross-section through a nerve

6.3 The synapse

When nerve cells join other cells they do not touch but are separated by small gaps called *synapses*. Every time a nerve cell connects to another cell there will be many synapses as shown in Figure 6.4.

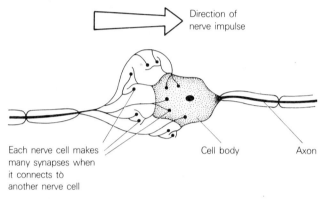

Figure 6.4   The tiny gaps are called synapses

To get the impulse across the gap the nerve cell releases a tiny amount of a chemical, usually *acetylcholine*. This crosses the gap and is received by a special surface on the next nerve cell. The special surface then starts a new electrical impulse. (See Figure 6.5.)

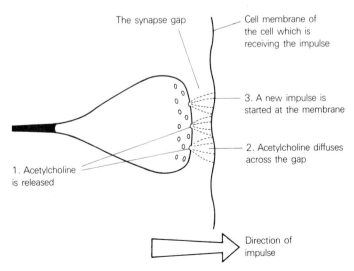

Figure 6.5   How a synapse works

Why have synapses?

Synapses are important because impulses can only cross them one way. This means that impulses go to the brain along one group of nerve cells and leave the brain along a different group. In this way impulses do not get mixed up.

Synapses also mean that one nerve cell can connect to several others at once. Connections like this are important in the brain.

The chemical acetylcholine is generally broken down after it has triggered an impulse. This prevents it from starting more than one impulse. Alcohol prevents acetylcholine from being broken down so quickly. It produces all the symptoms of drunkenness. Slurred speech, slow reactions etc. are all caused because the synapses are not working as well as they should.

6.4 The spinal cord

The spinal cord carries many millions of nerve cells (Figure 6.6). Some have a myelin sheath around them and others do not.

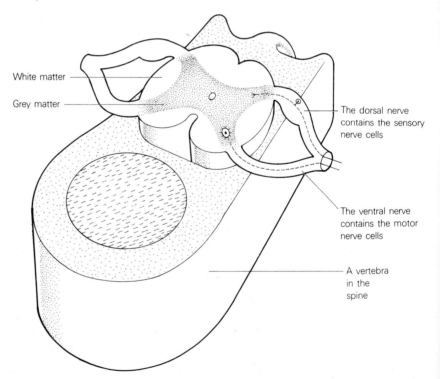

White matter

Grey matter

The dorsal nerve contains the sensory nerve cells

The ventral nerve contains the motor nerve cells

A vertebra in the spine

Figure 6.6   A cross-section of the spinal column showing the spinal cord inside

Cells with a sheath appear white and ones without look grey. This is why the spinal cord has both *white* and *grey matter* in it. Nerves enter and leave the spinal cord in gaps between the bones of the spine. The spinal cord itself runs through the centre of the bones of the spine.

All sensory nerve cells enter the spinal cord through the upper or dorsal nerve. The swelling in this nerve is the place where all the cell bodies of the sensory neurons are found. All motor nerve cells leave the spinal cord through the lower or ventral nerve. A short distance from the spinal cord the upper and lower nerves join to become one nerve.

6.5 Reflexes

A reflex is a fast reaction. It is usually automatic — we do not have to think about it. Reflex actions often help to protect the body from harm. They include blinking the eye when something comes quickly towards it and pulling your hand quickly away from a hot surface (Figure 6.7). Perhaps the best-known reflex action is the knee jerk, although it is difficult to think of what use this could be to the body.

Doctors will sometimes test your reflexes by testing the knee jerk reaction. By doing this they can check that your nervous system is working correctly.

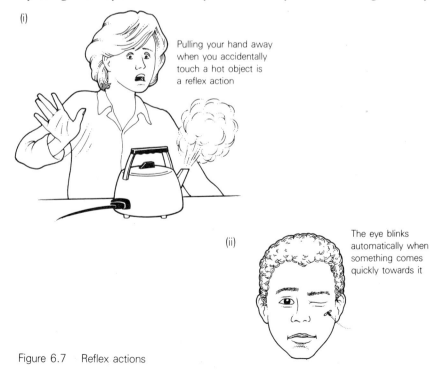

(i)

Pulling your hand away when you accidentally touch a hot object is a reflex action

(ii)

The eye blinks automatically when something comes quickly towards it

Figure 6.7   Reflex actions

Experiment 6.1

Investigating the knee jerk reaction

1. Work in pairs. One person sits completely relaxed on a chair with his or her legs crossed.

2. The other person taps gently just below the subject's knee-cap (Figure 6.8), using either the edge of the hand or the edge of a ruler.

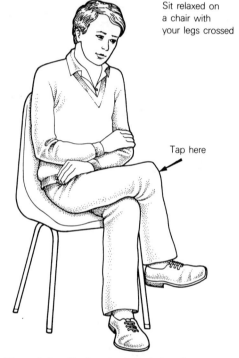

Sit relaxed on a chair with your legs crossed

3. Watch for the knee jerk reaction. The foot will be lifted up a little as the leg muscles contract.

4. Once you have found where to tap, test the reflex several times. After this the subject must try to prevent the reflex action from happening by conciously controlling the leg.

Tap here

5. Then swap places with your partner.

6. Did you find the reflex action?

7. Was it a fast reaction?

8. Is it possible to prevent it from happening?

Figure 6.8   Finding the knee jerk reflex

9. If so, how did you prevent the reflex from happening?

How a reflex action works

In any reflex action there will be nerve cells connecting the sense cells to the muscles. There will usually be only three nerve cells involved and they link together to form a system called the *reflex arc*.

Figure 6.9 shows the reflex arc for the reaction which pulls the hand away from a hot surface. The sense cell in the finger detects the hot surface. This sends an impulse along the sensory nerve cell to the spinal cord. In the spinal cord, as well as connecting to a nerve cell going to the brain, the sensory nerve cell also connects to a second very small nerve cell. This *relay nerve cell* connects to a motor nerve cell, which then connects to the arm muscle. When the muscle receives the impulse it contracts, pulling the hand away.

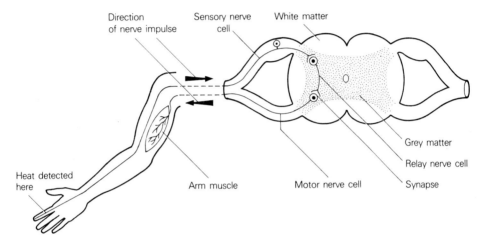

Figure 6.9   The nerves of a reflex arc

As well as going around the reflex arc, an impulse also goes to the brain. The brain receives it and produces the sensation of heat and possible pain. However, the impulse takes longer to get to the brain than to get to the arm muscle. You pull your hand away before your brain tells you that the surface is hot. The 'short-circuit' of the reflex arc prevents your hand from being badly burned.

Learned reflex actions

Riding a bicycle or driving a car involves a large number of automatic reactions that must be learned. Learning them is not always easy, but once they are learned you can do them without thinking. They are *learned* reflex actions. They are more complex than the simple reflex arc because they involve nerve pathways in the brain. Even walking can be thought of as a series of learned reflex actions. As a baby you had to learn to walk. Now you never give it a moment's thought. You can walk in straight lines or around corners completely automatically.

Conditioned reflex action

Look at Figure 6.10. A Russian scientist called Pavlov trained some dogs to perform an unusual reflex action. Dogs, like us, produce saliva in their mouths when they are hungry and smell food. We call it 'mouth watering'. You may have experienced it when walking past a bread shop, for example. The smell of freshly baked bread makes your mouth water.

Pavlov fed his dogs each day at much the same time. Just before he produced the food, he rang a bell. After a while the dogs learned that the bell meant food was coming. They began to produce saliva as soon as the bell was rung, but before they had seen or smelled any food. It became possible to get the dogs to produce saliva just by ringing the bell. It was not necessary to bring food at all. Thus the dogs had been trained to perform a reflex action to completely the wrong stimulus. This became known as a *conditioned reflex* action or *conditioning*.

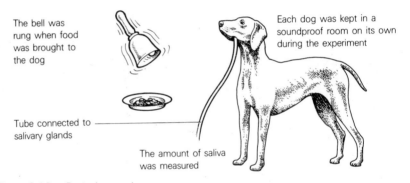

The bell was rung when food was brought to the dog

Each dog was kept in a soundproof room on its own during the experiment

Tube connected to salivary glands

The amount of saliva was measured

Figure 6.10   Pavlov's experiment

Conditioning is important because it is a form of learning. A lot of animal training involves conditioning, and it is probably also involved in human actions like learning to drive a car.

Human learning is much more complex than Pavlov's dogs. However, by studying simple learned reactions we may be able to begin to understand how we learn.

6.6 The brain

Our brain is one of the most complex parts of our body. It is made of millions and millions of tiny nerve cells. It works by impulses passing between these cells but we know very little of exactly how this happens.

We do know which parts of the brain do which jobs. You can see these in Figure 6.11.

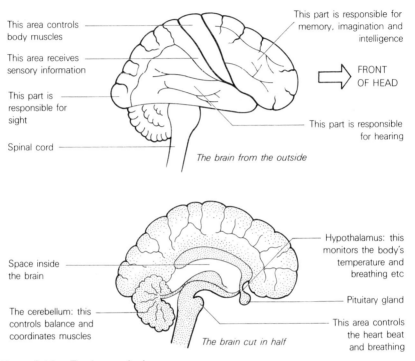

This area controls body muscles

This area receives sensory information

This part is responsible for sight

Spinal cord

This part is responsible for memory, imagination and intelligence

FRONT OF HEAD

This part is responsible for hearing

The brain from the outside

Space inside the brain

The cerebellum: this controls balance and coordinates muscles

Hypothalamus: this monitors the body's temperature and breathing etc

Pituitary gland

This area controls the heart beat and breathing

The brain cut in half

Figure 6.11   The human brain

The job of the whole brain is to control the body. To do this:

(a) It receives information from all the nerve cells in the body.
(b) It processes and compares all this information.
(c) It remembers information. Some it remembers for only a short while and some for a longer time.
(d) It uses new information and that which is stored in the memory to decide what the body shall do.
(e) It then sends impulses to the muscles to make the body move.

Sometimes the brain does all this *subconsciously,* without our thinking about it. For instance, our body temperature and heart rate and breathing rate are all controlled like this. At other times we *consciously* think about what we want to do.

The brain does more than just this. It also provides us with emotions like love and hate, fear and pleasure. It allows us to dream and imagine. The brain lets us remember what happened before and also predict what will happen later.

Although scientists have studied the brain for many years, we have very little idea of how it works. We know that the brain needs a constant supply of oxygen for energy. It can only survive for about four minutes without oxygen. After that it quickly begins to die. We know, too, that the best computer in the world cannot do all the things that the brain can do.

Our brain consists of about 1.4 kg of nerve cells, blood cells and other sorts of cell. For the moment we can only wonder at all the remarkable things it can do.

Anaesthetics and drugs

Anaesthetics stop the nervous system from working correctly. They may block synapses or they may stop the nerve cell from carrying an impulse. Used carefully they allow doctors to perform operations without the patient feeling too much pain. Before anaesthetics were discovered, operations were done with the patient fully aware of what was happening. The patient often had to be held or strapped down and sometimes they were given alcoholic drinks to make them drunk. Operations like this were usually done quickly and, as a result, not always carefully. Nowadays, during an operation, one doctor is in charge of the anaesthetics. He or she makes sure that the patient is given just enough anaesthetic to keep them unconscious for the operation.

Too much of an anaesthetic can kill because it disrupts the nervous system. Some poisons do the same thing. Some insecticide poisons kill insects by attacking their nervous systems. They will attack us, too. People who handle insecticides should use great care (Figure 6.12). They should avoid getting the insecticide on their skin or breathing in the dust or spray.

Figure 6.12   Protective clothing while using insecticides

Drugs like heroin and cocaine also disrupt our nervous systems. They prevent certain parts of the brain working correctly. This can give pleasant sensations, but these only last for a short time. The problem with these drugs is that people become addicted to them. Their bodies start to need the sensations they provide. To an addict, reality exists only when he or she has the drug. Normal life seems unreal and frightening. Many addicts die, not because of the drug, but because of the life it forces them to lead. An addict is helpless without the drug and will steal and starve to buy it.

Other drugs are useful if taken under doctors' instructions. Tranquillisers and barbiturates have an important job to do. Tranquillisers help calm people down and make them less anxious. They are useful because they have a calming effect without making the patient sleepy. Barbiturates calm people and make them sleep. They can be used as anaesthetics.

The nervous system is finely balanced and easily damaged by uncontrolled drug-taking. Being 'high' means that the brain is not working properly and at risk of serious and permanent harm. Once damaged, the brain never recovers.

Summary

1. The nervous system is made of nerve cells or neurons.

2. There are three sorts of nerve cells: sensory nerve cells, motor nerve cells, brain nerve cells.

3. Nerve cells conduct electrical impulses.

4. Nerve cells connect to other cells at gaps called synapses.

5. An impulse crosses the synapse by a chemical, usually acetylcholine.

6. Synapses allow one cell to connect to many others. They are also 'one-way' only. This means that impulses travel either towards the CNS or away from it, but never in both directions along the same nerve cell.

7. A reflex arc is a simple nerve pathway which allows quick, automatic reactions to happen.

6.7 Chemical control of the body

As well as being controlled by the nervous system, our body is controlled by chemicals. They are called *hormones* and they are produced by special glands called *endocrine glands*. The main endocrine glands can be seen in Figure 6.13.

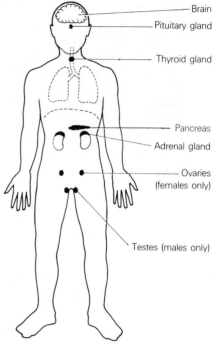

Figure 6.13   The endocrine glands

Brain
Pituitary gland
Thyroid gland
Pancreas
Adrenal gland
Ovaries (females only)
Testes (males only)

How do hormones work?

Hormones are passed out of the glands which make them and into the nearest blood vein. They are carried all around the body in the blood. Hormones cause changes in some cells but not others. Not all cells can pick up the hormone and respond to it. Cells which can respond to a particular hormone are called the *target cells* for the hormone. (See Figure 6.14.)

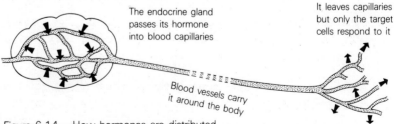

The endocrine gland passes its hormone into blood capillaries

It leaves capillaries but only the target cells respond to it

Blood vessels carry it around the body

Figure 6.14   How hormones are distributed

Why have a hormone system?

Nerve impulses last for only a short time and go to particular parts of the body only. Hormones, however, go to all parts of the body and they can remain in the blood for a long time. Hormones are more able to control slow, long-term reactions than nerves are. For example, as you grow so cells all over your body grow. This makes sure that your body grows evenly. A steady supply of a hormone in the blood will make sure that all cells grow at the same rate. It would not be possible for nerves to do this.

The endocrine glands and their hormones

The pituitary gland

This is actually part of the brain. It produces a large number of hormones, some of which control what other glands do. Because of this, the pituitary gland is sometimes called the *master gland.*

The pituitary gland produces *ADH* (anti-diuretic hormone) which acts on the kidneys to control how much water is removed from the body.

FSH (follicle-stimulating hormone) and *LH* (*luteinising hormone*) act on the ovaries to control the menstrual cycle.

Growth hormone controls the rate of growth of bone and muscle. A child who does not make enough of this may not grow enough and will become a midget. A child who makes too much growth hormone will grow too large and become a giant.

TSH (thyroid-stimulating hormone) controls how quickly the thyroid gland works.

The pituitary gland produces many other hormones as well as these.

The thyroid gland

This produces *thyroxin* which controls the speed of the chemical reactions in the body. The amount of thyroxin is very important especially in growing children. Too little of it slows up the growth rate and will make a child mentally retarded. Children who suffered from this used to be known as *cretins.* Too much will make a person overactive.

In tadpoles thyroxin controls the change from tadpole to frog.

The pancreas

This produces *insulin,* which controls how much glucose our body stores. After a meal we have lots of glucose in our blood. If some of this were not stored, our kidneys would remove it. Later on there would be none left for energy. Insulin makes the liver store glucose and then slowly releases it as the glucose in the blood is used up.

People whose pancreas stops making insulin are known as *diabetics*. They must take insulin either by mouth or by injection. If they did not they could easily run out of glucose. This would affect their brain first and they would black out. Without help, they would die. Diabetics also need a carefully balanced diet of regular meals to help their bodies keep a constant glucose level.

The adrenals

These are attached to the kidneys. They produce *adrenalin* which prepares the body for emergencies. Adrenalin speeds up the heart rate and tones up the muscles. It makes us alert and ready for action. Adrenalin is released when we are frightened or excited. Next time you become scared or excited see if you notice your pounding heart and clear mind. These are effects caused by your adrenalin.

The ovaries

These, of course, are only found in females. They produce *oestrogen* and *progesterone,* which control the menstrual cycle (Figure 6.15). Oestrogen controls when an egg is released from an ovary; progesterone makes the uterus wall grow a thick lining to prepare for a fertilised egg. When both hormones stop being produced because the egg has not been fertilised, the thick uterus lining is shed during the menstrual period.

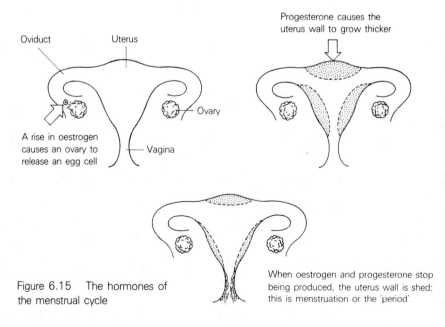

Oviduct   Uterus

Progesterone causes the uterus wall to grow thicker

Ovary

A rise in oestrogen causes an ovary to release an egg cell

Vagina

Figure 6.15   The hormones of the menstrual cycle

When oestrogen and progesterone stop being produced, the uterus wall is shed: this is menstruation or the 'period'

Oestrogen also controls the changes at *puberty* when a girl develops into a woman. Changes such as the development of breasts, the growth of hip bones, and the growth of hair around the entrance to the vagina.

Contraceptive pills are made of different amounts of oestrogen and progesterone. They work by disrupting the menstrual cycle so that an egg is released from the ovary only when it is dead. In this way fertilisation can never occur.

The testes These are found only in males. They produce the hormone *testosterone,* which controls the changes from boy to man at puberty. Such changes include the deepening of the voice and the broadening of the chest. Other changes are the growth of a beard and the growth of hairs on the chest and around the penis.

Hormones and homeostasis

Hormones like insulin, ADH and thyroxin are involved in keeping body conditions stable. This is homeostasis (see Chapter 4). All hormones work by *negative feedback*. That is, the changes which the hormone produces in some way stops the hormone from being produced any more. Thus there cannot be too much hormone.

Figure 6.16 shows negative feedback and describes how thyroxin is controlled.

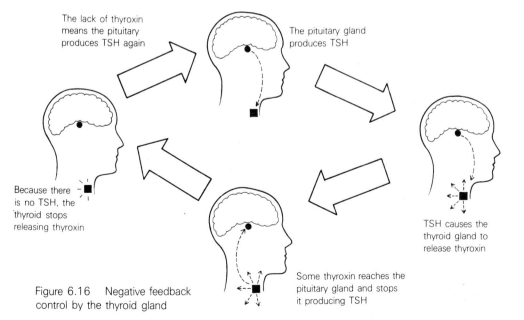

The lack of thyroxin means the pituitary produces TSH again

The pituitary gland produces TSH

Because there is no TSH, the thyroid stops releasing thyroxin

TSH causes the thyroid gland to release thyroxin

Some thyroxin reaches the pituitary gland and stops it producing TSH

Figure 6.16 Negative feedback control by the thyroid gland

Thyroxin is released by the thyroid only when the pituitary releases TSH. When there is lots of thyroxin in the blood, it stops TSH from being made. With no TSH, no thyroxin is released. Gradually all the thyroxin in the blood becomes used up or removed. This lets the pituitary release TSH again and the cycle begins once more.

Summary

1. Chemical control of the body is by hormones produced by endocrine glands.

2. Hormones travel to all cells in the blood.

3. Hormones control slower, more long term reactions in the body, like growing.

4. Hormone production is controlled by negative feedback.

Questions on Chapter 6

1. What is the job of the nervous system?

2. Copy out the following and fill in the blanks.
   _____ nerve cells carry impulses from sense cells to the _____ _____ _____ . _____ nerve cells carry impulses from here to the _____ . The long strand of membrane in a nerve cell is called the _____ . It sometimes has a wrapping of a _____ material called the _____ _____ . The job of this wrapping is to _____ _____ the impulse, but no one is sure how it does this.

3. A nerve cell transmits an _____ impulse. This cannot cross the gap between nerve cells called the _____ . To do this a _____ has to be made. These gaps are necessary because they only let an impulse pass _____ _____ . They also allow one nerve cell to connect to _____ _____ .

4. Why do we have reflexes?

5. In Pavlov's experiment with dogs, what reflex action did he want to change? What change did he make to this reflex action?
   Training animals in this way is known as _____ .

6. A drug is a chemical which interferes with the normal working of our bodies. Give an example of a useful drug and describe how it is useful. Give an example of a harmful drug, stating how it may harm us.

7. Figure 6.17 shows a reflex arc system which includes the spinal cord. The labels are missing. What labels would you use for:

(a)   (b)   (c)
(d)   (e)   (f) ?

Labels g, h, i and j show possible directions for the nerve impulses to take. Only two labels are correct. Which are they?

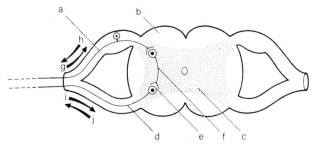

Figure 6.17   A reflex arc

8. Copy out the following and fill in the blanks.
Chemicals called _____ are used to control the body. They are produced by _____ glands and released into the _____ . This carries them all over the body. The pituitary gland makes _____ which controls how much water is in the body. The _____ gland makes thyroxin. _____ is an illness caused when the pancreas stops making _____ . The _____ glands just next to the kidneys make _____ , which makes us alert when we are excited or scared. The ovaries in females produce _____ and _____ , but in males the testes make _____ .

9. Why do we have two control systems, one nervous and the other chemical?

10. What is negative feedback control? Give an example of how this works.

Crossword on Chapter 6

Across

1 See 8 across

3 It produces insulin (8)

8, 1 across The simplest form of 4 down pathway (6, 3)

10 Drugs like heroin give people strange ideas about what is _____ (4)

11 Gap between 4 down cells (7)

12 Pavlov's dogs were fed at the same _____ 20 down day (4)

13 The spinal _____ is found inside the backbone (4)

15 Liquid pumped around the body (5)

18 In FSH, the F stands for this (8)

19 Sensitive part of the leg in a reflex arc (4)

22 2 down are too _____ to see without a microscope (4)

23 Growth hormone controls _____ of growth (4)

25 Pavlov made his dogs salivate even though they had nothing to _____ on (4)

26 _____ meddle with drugs! (4)

27 Some matter in the spinal 13 across is _____ (5)

Down

1 This chemical crosses from one 4 down cell to another (13)

2 See 4 down

4, 2 down Another name for neurons (5, 5)

5 An 8 across is a fast _____ (8)

6 In CNS, S stands for _____ (6)

7 This part of a neuron can be up to a metre long (4)

9 It travels along 7 down (7)

14 The _____ neuron forms the connection in the 8, 1 across (5)

15 An area of your body you cannot see? (4)

16 The sort of animal Pavlov experimented with (3)

17 Adrenalin may be released when you are _____ (6)

20 _____ sense cell in your toes is connected to the 13 across by a single sensory 4, 2 down (4)

21 A pleasant emotion in the brain, not the heart (4)

24 Animals normally produce saliva when they _____ (3)

(Teacher, please see special note in front of book.)

Copy this grid, then fill in the answers. Do not write on this page.

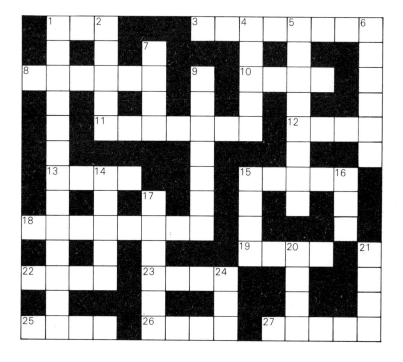

7. Responding to the environment (animals)

Animals respond to their environments by moving towards favourable conditions and away from unfavourable ones. They move to search for food, mates and shelter. They also move to avoid being eaten by other animals.

7.1 How animals move

Muscles

All animals, except the very simplest ones, move by using *muscles*. These are made of fibres which can *contract* (get shorter). To do this, muscles need energy which they get by *respiration*.

When you eat meat or fish, it is the muscle of the animal you are eating. Muscles form most of an animal's flesh.

Some human muscles are shown in Figure 7.1(i) and (ii).

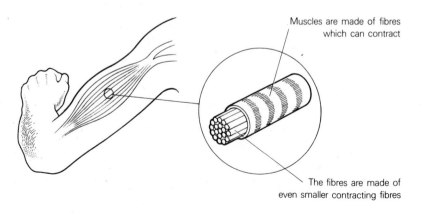

Muscles are made of fibres which can contract

The fibres are made of even smaller contracting fibres

Figure 7.1(i)   Muscle fibres

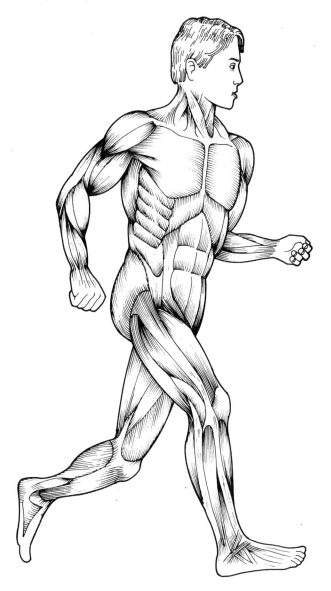

Figure 7.1(ii)   Muscles in the human body

Skeletons   Muscles work by pulling, but they must have something to pull against if the animal is to move. The stiff structures which muscles pull against are called *skeletons*. Not all animals have the same sort of skeleton.

A worm does not have a rigid skeleton. It is made stiff by the liquid inside it. As a worm's muscles contract they squeeze this liquid. This pushes out against other parts of the body. To help it move, a worm can anchor parts of its body to its burrow using the tiny bristles on its underside (Figure 7.2).

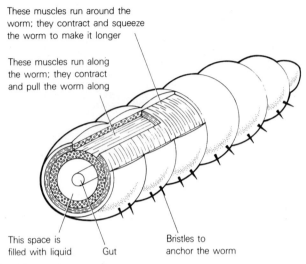

These muscles run around the worm; they contract and squeeze the worm to make it longer

These muscles run along the worm; they contract and pull the worm along

This space is filled with liquid

Gut

Bristles to anchor the worm

Figure 7.2   Muscles in an earthworm

An insect has a rigid skeleton. However, unlike ours, the insect skeleton is on the outside. It is called an *exoskeleton.* Muscles pull against the exoskeleton from the inside (Figure 7.3). An exoskeleton is very useful because it also protects the insect. However, for its size it is very heavy. Insects could never grow very large because the exoskeleton would weigh them down.

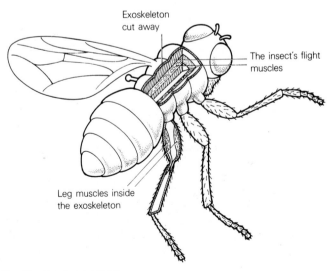

Exoskeleton cut away

The insect's flight muscles

Leg muscles inside the exoskeleton

Figure 7.3   Muscles in an insect

Our skeleton is inside and is called an *endoskeleton*. It is made of rigid bones which are strong and light. Figure 7.4 shows a human skeleton. You should try to remember the names of some of the bones.

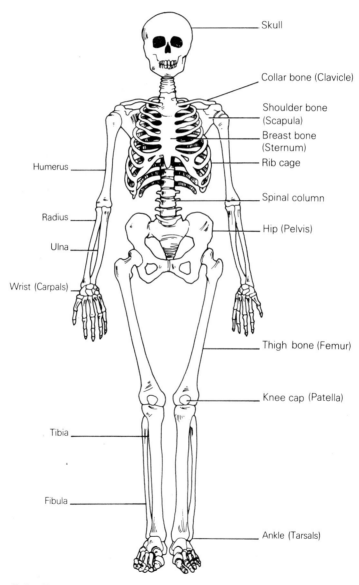

Figure 7.4   The skeleton

Experiment 7.1

Investigating movement in animals

1. Begin with a worm. Place a live worm on a sheet of newspaper. Be careful not to damage it.

2. Watch how it moves. Watch how its segments change when the muscles contract. Listen carefully for any noises it makes.

3. How does the worm appear to move?

4. Did it make any sound? If so, what could have caused it?

5. What effects did its muscles appear to have?

6. Return the worm to the soil.

7. Try to observe other animals. You may find snails in the grass. You can watch these moving on a glass plate.

8. You can find insects in the grass or in the leaf litter under trees and bushes. You may need a hand lens to watch them and a petri dish to stop them from running away.

9. For any animals you can find, try to answer questions 3, 4 and 5 above.

Joints   The point where two rigid parts of a skeleton meet is called a *joint*. The human skeleton has three sorts of joint:

(a) The *fixed joint*, where the bones meet and join solidly together. This happens in the skull so that the bones form a strong box to protect our brain.

(b) The *hinge joint*, where the two bones meet but can move. The ends of the bones are shaped so that they can move like a hinge against each other. The elbow and the finger joints are examples.

(c) The *ball-and-socket joint*, where the end of one bone is shaped like a ball and the other bone has a socket. The bones fit together and can move freely in several directions. The hip and the shoulder joints are like this.

Some different human joints are shown in Figure 7.5 (opposite).

Insects have only hinge joints, which means that to get circular movement they need several joints. This is why insect legs have lots of joints. (See Figure 7.6 (opposite).)

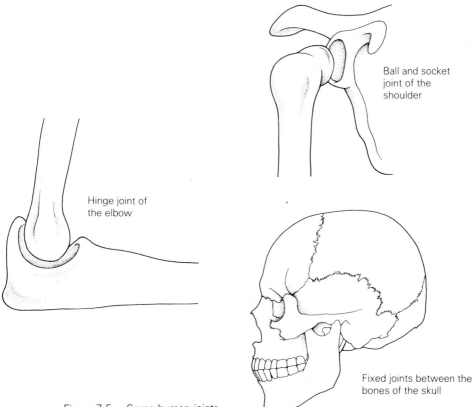

Ball and socket joint of the shoulder

Hinge joint of the elbow

Fixed joints between the bones of the skull

Figure 7.5   Some human joints

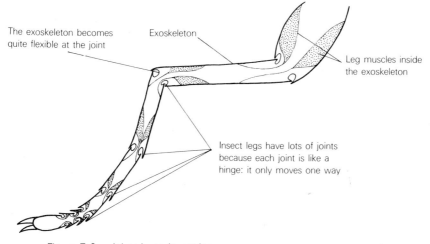

The exoskeleton becomes quite flexible at the joint

Exoskeleton

Leg muscles inside the exoskeleton

Insect legs have lots of joints because each joint is like a hinge: it only moves one way

Figure 7.6   Joints in an insect leg

Ligaments and tendons

At a joint the ends of the bones are held together by strong, flexible *ligaments.* These have to be strong enough to stop the bones from pulling apart but they must still allow the bones to move.

Muscles are attached to bones by *tendons,* which are strong and not stretchy. When a muscle contracts, it pulls the tendon, which in turn pulls the bone.

Experiment 7.2

Investigating muscle and tendon

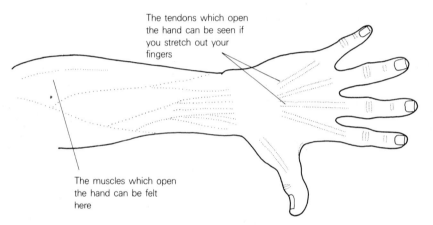

The tendons which open the hand can be seen if you stretch out your fingers

The muscles which open the hand can be felt here

Figure 7.7   Muscles and tendons of the hand and arm

1. When muscles contract, they get shorter, fatter and quite hard. You can feel your own muscles through your skin.

2. Look at the back of your hand. Stretch out your fingers. Can you see the tendons which run to each finger? (See Figure 7.7.)

3. Move each finger in turn. The muscles which move the fingers are in your forearm. As you move each finger try to find the muscle which is contracting.

4. Now find the tendons and muscles which close the hand.

5. Study your elbow. Can you find the tendons on the inside of the elbow? What muscle are these attached to? Move your arm up and down to feel muscles working.

7.2 What happens at a joint?

Figure 7.8 shows the muscle and bones of the elbow joint. You can feel the muscles, bones and tendons if you squeeze your arm. At all moving joints, the ends of the bones are covered in tough, shiny *cartilage*. This is much smoother than bone and allows the joints to move freely. Cartilage, being smooth, does not wear out as quickly as bone would. To make the joint even more slippery it has an oily liquid called *synovial fluid*. This is made by the *synovial membrane*. Ligaments hold the bones together.

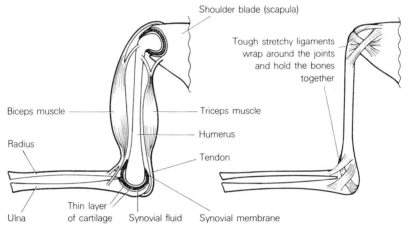

Figure 7.8   Bones, joints and muscles of the arm

At the elbow, when the *biceps* muscle contracts, it pulls the ulna bone upwards. When the *triceps* muscle contracts, it pulls the ulna down again. Pairs of muscles which work like this are called *antagonists*. Muscles always work in pairs in this way. One muscle makes a movement in one direction, and the other makes the opposite movement.

7.3 Damaging muscles and bones

Bones will break, or *fracture*, if too much force is put on them. Broken bones heal themselves, but to make sure the bones heal in the correct position they are often held in place by a plaster cast. In young children, bones do not break cleanly. Instead they bend and crack. Fractures like this are called *greenstick fractures*, because they are like a break in a fresh green twig.

Joints can become *dislocated*. This means the two bones become pulled apart because the joint has been twisted too far the wrong way. Dislocated joints usually mean that the ligament has become stretched or torn. A dislocated joint can quite easily be put back again. The ligament, however, may take a long time to heal. The joint may have to be set in plaster to avoid pulling the ligament. Ligaments can become torn or stretched without the joint being dislocated. A stretched ligament is called a *sprain*. Tendons may tear away from the bone or from the muscle. This happens when the muscle tries to do too much work — for instance, if a weight lifter tried to lift too much weight. To heal a torn tendon the joint and muscle may have to be set in plaster.

Summary

1. Muscles work by contracting using energy from respiration.

2. Muscles pull against a stiff skeleton.

3. Muscles work in antagonistic pairs.

4. For movements, a skeleton has to have joints.

5. Tendons attach muscles to bones. They are not at all stretchy.

6. Ligaments hold the bones together at joints. They stretch to allow movement.

7.4 How animals behave towards the environment

Any change in the environment is called a *stimulus* (plural: *stimuli*). Any movement that an animal makes to a change is called a *response*. Behaviour is what sort of response animals make to different stimuli.

Not all animals behave in the same way. In general, they avoid unpleasant or unfavourable conditions and try to find pleasant or favourable ones.

It is easiest to study simple behaviour in simple animals. Woodlice or fly larvae (maggots) are useful animals to study. Woodlice are found in dark corners under wood or stones. Maggots are found in or under rotting material, especially rotting meat. You can make an intelligent guess as to what sort of environment they find favourable. A guess like this is called a hypothesis. You must then investigate whether your hypothesis was correct.

A *choice chamber* is a large dish which can be used to give simple animals the choice between two environments. (See Figure 7.9.) By offering animals only a simple choice you can build up a picture of how they behave.

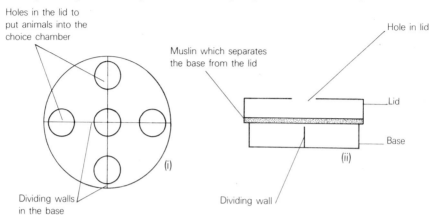

Figure 7.9   A choice chamber seen from above (i) and from the side (ii)

Experiment 7.3

Investigating behaviour in animals

Hypothesis: that woodlice prefer damp conditions to dry

1.   Take a choice chamber, and ten woodlice in a small beaker.

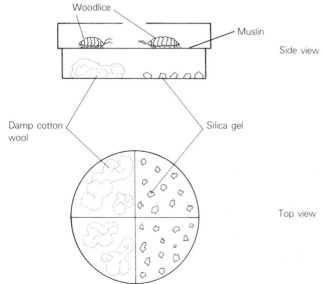

Figure 7.10   A choice chamber and its contents

2. On one side of the choice chamber, under the muslin, place some damp cotton wool.

3. On the other side place some silica gel which will dry the air. Assemble the choice chamber but be very careful not to let any water get into the dry side. (See Figure 7.10 (on the previous page).)

4. Draw up a results chart like the one below.

5. Start the clock and put all ten woodlice into the choice chamber through the middle hole.

6. Every half minute, count the number of woodlice on the dry side and the number on the damp side.

7. Stop the experiment after 5 minutes. This will give you ten sets of results.

8. You may like to repeat the experiment with ten different woodlice. The more results you get, the more sure you can be that they are correct. To be certain that, in general, woodlice prefer one environment to the other, at least two-thirds (67%) of your results should be for one of the environments. Add up all your results to see if woodlice show a preference.

Time in minutes	Number of woodlice on dry side	Number of woodlice on damp side
½		
1		
1½		
2		
2½		
3		
3½		
4		
4½		
5		
Total		

9. Did woodlice prefer damp or dry conditions?

10. Is this the result you expect from the hypothesis?

11. Did you do the experiment accurately? For example, was the temperature the same on both sides of the choice chamber?

Movement towards stimuli

The choice chamber tells us whether animals spend more time in one environment than another. It does not tell us whether animals can move towards one environment or away from others. Most animals do not just wander around until they happen to find a favourable environment. They generally need some stimulus to guide them.

Experiment 7.4

Investigating the effects of light on the direction of maggot movement

1. You must work in a room which can be completely blacked out. Get the apparatus shown in Figure 7.11 and arrange it as in the diagram.

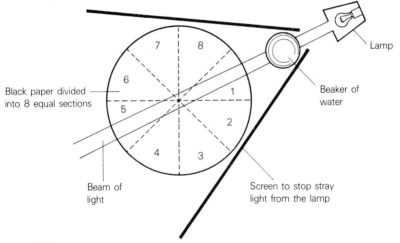

Figure 7.11   Investigating how light affects maggot movement

2. The lines on the black paper should be drawn lightly in white chalk so that they show up during the experiment.

3. Move the beaker of water until it produces a narrow beam of light across the middle of the circle and through segments 1 and 5. Arrange books to block out any light other than this single beam.

4. Write out a results chart like the one below.

5. *Before you begin,* write down your hypothesis. You will put the maggots on the middle of the black paper and watch how they move.

6. Get ten maggots in a beaker.

7. Switch on the lamp and switch the room light off. Put the maggots on to the paper and let them crawl off it.

8. Record how many maggots crawled off the paper through each segment.

9. Repeat this experiment at least twice to get a lot of results.

Segment	Number of maggots which crawl off the paper			
	Experiment 1	Experiment 2	Experiment 3	Total
1				
2				
3				
4				
5				
6				
7				
8				

10. Which segment had the most maggots crawling off it?

11. Which segment had the least?

12. Which half of the circle had the most maggots crawling off it?

13. Which half of the circle had the least?

14. Do maggots seem to crawl towards light or away from it?

15. In general, do maggots seem to respond directly to the light? That is, do they move directly towards or away from it? Or do the maggots just wander about?

Experiment 7.5

Further investigation into animal behaviour

Now you know how a choice chamber is used you should be able to do your own investigations. First think of a hypothesis and then investigate it. You may study maggots, woodlice or any other small animal which is available. Some choices you can offer include: dark/light warm/cold food/no food different coloured backgrounds.

You may be able to think of others. For each investigation the method is exactly the same as for Experiment 7.3.

Maggot behaviour

Even a simple animal like a maggot does not always have simple behaviour. Maggots hatch from eggs laid by flies on rotting material. As soon as the maggot has hatched, it burrows into the material. This means it goes towards food and moisture and away from light where it could be seen and eaten by birds. The maggot will eventually become a pupa and, after a while, a fly will emerge from the pupa. It is no good the fly emerging inside rotting material — it would be trapped. The pupa has to be on or very near the surface. Thus when a maggot is about to pupate it has to move towards the light and not away from it. If the results of Experiment 7.4 showed some maggots crawling towards the light and some crawling away from it, this could be the reason (Figure 7.12).

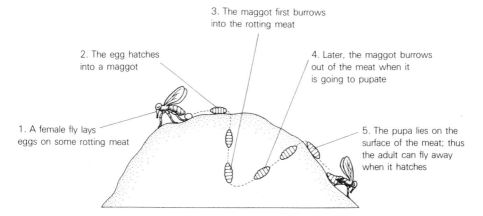

3. The maggot first burrows into the rotting meat

2. The egg hatches into a maggot

4. Later, the maggot burrows out of the meat when it is going to pupate

1. A female fly lays eggs on some rotting meat

5. The pupa lies on the surface of the meat; thus the adult can fly away when it hatches

Figure 7.12   Maggot behaviour

7.5 Courtship behaviour

Much study has been made of the behaviour of animals at mating time. Courtship behaviour is the actions of one animal to attract a mate. Very often courtship behaviour seems quite unusual and elaborate. This is important since it means that the behaviour of one type of animal is not likely to be the same as another. In this way an animal will not be attracted to the wrong kind of mate by mistake.

Courtship behaviour is often made more obvious by bright colours. At mating time, many animals develop colours which they do not have for the rest of the year. Bright colours and special behaviour all tend to make sure an animal finds the correct mate.

Stickleback courtship

In a very famous study a scientist called Tinbergen studied the courtship and mating of sticklebacks. He discovered that the courtship and mating had several stages as shown in Figure 7.13 (parts i–vi). These are as follows:

(a) The male develops a red underside. Males will fight off any other males which they recognise by the red colour. Males can be made to fight all sorts of models, provided they are painted red underneath.

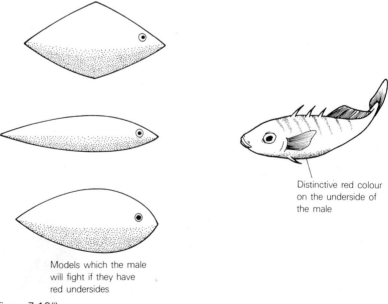

Distinctive red colour
on the underside of
the male

Models which the male
will fight if they have
red undersides

Figure 7.13(i)

(b) The male builds a nest on the bottom of a stream.

Figure 7.13(ii)

(c) A female becomes swollen with eggs. She swims into a male's territory where his nest is.

(d) The male swims towards the female. He then performs a zigzag 'dance' around her and may bump into her.

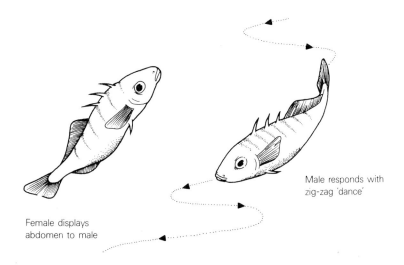

Female displays
abdomen to male

Male responds with
zig-zag 'dance'

Figure 7.13(iii)

(e) The male leads the female to his nest. He shows her the nest by pointing at it and turning on his side.

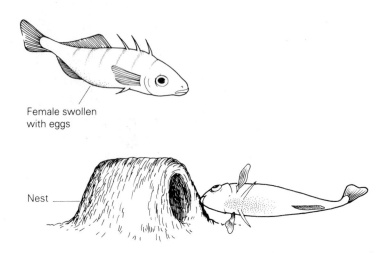

Female swollen with eggs

Nest

Figure 7.13(iv)

(f) The female enters the nest and the male prods her so that she will lay her eggs.

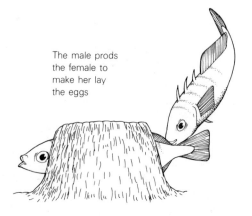

The male prods the female to make her lay the eggs

Figure 7.13(v)

(g) The female leaves the nest. The male quickly goes into it. He sheds sperm over the eggs to fertilise them.

The male fertilises the eggs as the female swims off

Figure 7.13(vi)   Sticklebacks mating

The male looks after the eggs and guards the nest. Once the eggs hatch the father looks after the young until they are big enough to swim off.

7.6 Human behaviour

Human behaviour is complicated because there are so many possible responses. For example, if your teacher sets you some homework, you are expected to do it properly. However, you know that sometimes you do it well, and not so well at other times. Some people in your class will work harder at their homework than others. Some pupils may even not do the homework at all. You should ask yourself: Why are there so many different responses to the same task?

There are many reasons why human behaviour varies; so many that often only a highly trained person can begin to understand them. It is possible, however, to see some behaviour patterns which most people share.

Take human courtship, for instance. A sideways glance and raised eyebrows are signs that you will recognise (Figure 7.14).

Figure 7.14   Human courtship signals

When two people begin to fight, they will take a deep breath and stand upright. This is a common behaviour pattern among animals. Each individual tries to make his body as large as possible to scare his opponent. In this way, the fight itself may be avoided. (See Figure 7.15.)

Figure 7.15   Human aggression signals

In situations where you feel uncomfortable (perhaps when your teacher tells you off), you will perform a *displacement activity*. Some examples of displacement activities are shown in Figure 7.16. You might fiddle with your hair or scratch your ear or look away and tap the ground with your feet. All behaviour like this helps us to release the tension that we feel. If you watch people, you will see other examples.

Twiddling
moustache

Scratching
ear

Playing with
hair

Looking away and
gazing around
the room

Figure 7.16   Displacement activities

Summary

1. A stimulus is a change in the environment.

2. A response is an action taken as a result of one or more stimuli.

3. Many animals have very specific sorts of behaviour, especially courtship behaviour. This ensures that they find the correct type of animal for a mate.

4. Human behaviour is complex and sometimes very hard to understand, but common patterns can be seen.

Questions on Chapter 7

1. Copy out the following and fill in the blanks.
   Muscles work by _____ . To do this they use energy from _____ .
   When a muscle _____ it gets shorter and _____ .

2. There are many sorts of skeleton. Using your own words, describe what sort of skeleton each of the following animals has:
   (a) fly   (b) snail   (c) tortoise   (d) crab
   (e) goldfish   (f) woodlouse (g) grass snake   (h) chicken

3. The following results were obtained in a choice chamber experiment with woodlice. What conclusions can you come to about woodlouse behaviour?

Time in minutes	Number of woodlice			
	Dry	Wet	Dark	Light
½	6	4	5	5
1	3	7	6	4
1½	3	7	7	3
2	2	8	6	4
2½	0	10	8	2
3	5	5	9	1
3½	4	6	8	2
4	1	9	9	1
4½	2	8	7	3
5	3	7	5	5
Total				

4. Describe three animals you know which develop special colours or behaviour at mating time. Explain what makes their behaviour special.

5.   Where in the body would you find (a) a fixed joint, (b) a hinge joint, (c) a ball-and-socket joint?

6.   Describe in your own words how two bones are able to move freely and easily at a joint without wearing out.

7.   What are the differences between a ligament and a tendon?

8.   The biceps and triceps muscles are said to be antagonists. What does this mean?

9.   The following table lists some reactions. For each, there is a stimulus, a sense organ and a response. Copy the table out and fill in the blanks. (The first one has been done for you.)

Stimulus	Sense organ	Response
(a) Large dog growling	Eyes/ears	You run away
(b) Mouse runs past	_____	Cat pounces on mouse
(c) Fisherman's float bobs under water	_____	_____
(d) A girl looks and smiles at a boy	_____	_____
(e) You are sunbathing and something slides over your back	_____	_____
(f) _____	Nose	_____

Wordfinder on Chapter 7

1   Animals need them to move (7)
2   Chemical action to produce energy (11)
3   Your 4 is made of this (4)
4   A supporting structure found inside animals (8)
5   Courtship behaviour is used by animals to attract a _____ (4)
6   An animal may have to find this for protection (7)
7   Where two rigid parts of a skeleton meet (5)
8   The elbow is a _____ 7 (5)
9   The shoulder 7 is a ball and _____ 7 (6)
10 A _____ is strong but not stretchy (6)
11 _____ is shiny and allows 7s to move freely (9)
12, 13 It makes the oily liquid which helps 7s to move (8, 8: 2 words in separate places)

14 A muscle in the upper arm (6)
15 A _____ is an over-stretched ligament (6)
16 A fly larva is also known as a _____ (6)
17 He studied the courtship of sticklebacks (9)
18 10s can be _____ from 1s when the 1 tries to do too much work (4)
19 A detectable change in the environment is called a _____ (8)
20 19 produces a _____ in an organism (8)
21 The male stickleback develops a _____ underside when courting (3)
22, 23 _____ (12, 8)

The answer to 22, 23 may be formed from the unused letters taken from left to right row by row top to bottom. Please write a clue.

(Teacher, please see special note in front of book.)

Copy or photocopy the wordfinder, then solve the clues and put a ring around the answers. The answers go in any direction backwards and forwards, up and down, and diagonally. Do not write on this page.

D	R	M	U	S	C	L	E	S	I	S	N
M	E	M	B	R	A	N	E	N	N	O	P
L	S	T	N	I	O	J	E	I	T	E	A
S	P	E	C	I	B	G	A	E	E	G	C
B	I	E	D	E	R	R	L	G	N	A	S
O	R	M	M	E	P	E	M	N	D	L	T
N	A	A	B	S	K	S	A	I	O	I	I
E	T	N	E	S	O	P	G	H	N	T	M
E	I	N	O	C	T	O	G	A	C	R	U
T	O	D	K	S	Y	N	O	V	I	A	L
T	N	E	I	V	I	S	T	T	Y	C	U
E	T	O	R	N	R	E	T	L	E	H	S

8. Responding to the environment (plants)

8.1 What can plants detect?

When you plant some seeds, they will germinate and grow. Fairly soon shoots will appear and grow upwards out of the ground. Underground the roots will be growing downwards. All seeds do this, no matter which way up they are planted. This means that the seedlings must have some way of detecting which direction is up and which is down.

We know which way is up and which is down by detecting the pull of gravity. Plants can detect this and also the direction from which light comes. Climbing plants like beans and peas can detect *touch*. They use this to twist around objects to help them climb. Plant roots can detect *water*. (See Figure 8.1.)

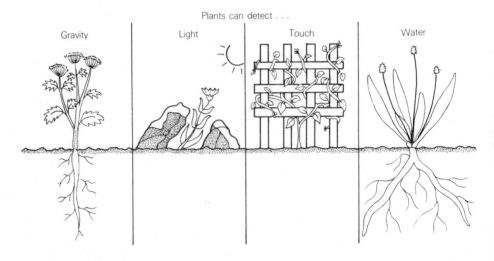

Figure 8.1   What plants can detect

Some plants, like the vinegar plant (*Oxalis acetosella*), detect day and night. Their leaves are raised in the morning and drop down at night (Figure 8.2). The Livingstone daisy flower opens only on sunny days and not on dull ones.

Figure 8.2   Vinegar plants during the day (i) and at night (ii), showing leaf reactions

Many plants also have ways of detecting the season. You may have noticed that all the daffodils in your area flower within a couple of weeks of each other. They are adapted to flower at one particular time of year and have a way of detecting when this is. Daffodils flower early, but poppies flower later. Michaelmas daisies do not flower until the autumn.

Thus you can see that plants are able to detect, and to respond to, a lot of changes in their environment.

8.2 Plants and gravity

The easiest way to see how plants respond to gravity is to confuse the plant so that it cannot detect which way is down. You can do this with a *clinostat* (Figure 8.3). This is a machine which spins a cork pad at about four revolutions per hour. Any plants attached to the cork pad will be gently rotated. This means that downwards will always be in a different position for the plant.

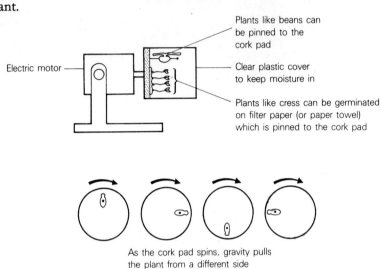

Plants like beans can be pinned to the cork pad

Electric motor

Clear plastic cover to keep moisture in

Plants like cress can be germinated on filter paper (or paper towel) which is pinned to the cork pad

As the cork pad spins, gravity pulls the plant from a different side

Figure 8.3   The clinostat

Experiment 8.1

Investigating the effects of gravity on the growth of cress

Cork pad

Paper towel with germinated cress seeds

Stand

Clinostat

Clear plastic cover

Control

Figure 8.4   Investigating how gravity affects the growth of cress

1. Cut about six discs of paper towel and pin them to the cork pad of a clinostat. Do the same for a second large cork. This will be the control for the investigation.

2. Arrange the clinostat and the control so that the paper towels are horizontal. Damp the towels and sprinkle them with cress seeds. Put on the covers and leave them for two days to give the seeds time to germinate. The roots will grow into the towels to stop the seedlings from dropping off.

    Make sure that the clinostat and the control are placed next to each other and in plenty of light. Conditions must be the same for both sets of apparatus.

3. After two days, turn the apparatus so that the paper towels are upright as in Figure 8.4 (opposite). Make sure both sets of apparatus are in the same conditions. Switch the clinostat on.

4. Leave the apparatus for a few days until the cress has grown several centimetres. During this time make sure that the seeds do not dry out.

5. Did the control plants react normally to gravity?

6. Did the clinostat plants react normally to gravity?

7. Explain what happened to the clinostat plants.

Experiment 8.2

Investigating the effects of gravity on root growth

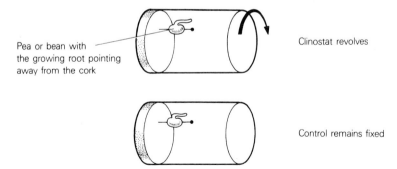

Pea or bean with the growing root pointing away from the cork

Clinostat revolves

Control remains fixed

Figure 8.5   Investigating how gravity affects the growth of roots

1. This experiment uses the same apparatus as the last one, but instead of cress, germinating peas or beans are used.

2. Pin a pea or bean to the clinostat and the control. The plant should have germinated so that a root of 1 – 2 cm has grown (Figure 8.5).

3   Make sure the clinostat and the control have exactly the same conditions. Switch the clinostat on.

4.   Leave the apparatus for a couple of days, but make sure the plants do not dry out.

5.   Did the control root react normally to gravity?

6.   Did the clinostat root react normally to gravity?

7.   Explain what happened to the root of the plant on the clinostat.

8.3 Plants and light

Experiment 8.3

Investigating the effects of light on cress growth

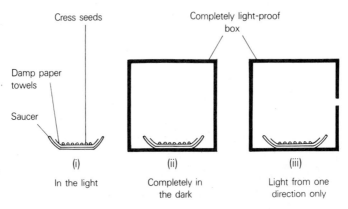

Figure 8.6   Investigating how light affects cress growth

1.   Take three small dishes (saucers will do). Lay several layers of paper towel in the dishes. Soak these and sprinkle them with cress seeds. (See Figure 8.6.)

2.   Treat each of the dishes as follows:
     Dish (i). Leave this open to the light.
     Dish (ii). Cover this with a light-proof box. This must be at least 10 cm taller than the dish. Make sure no light gets in around the bottom of the box.
     Dish (iii). Cover this with a similar light-proof box to dish (ii). Make a small hole about 5 mm across, in one side of the box.

3. Leave the cress in a warm, well-lit place to grow. Make sure the seedlings do not dry out. Check them every day. *Note:* If you remove the box from dish (iii), make sure you replace it with the hole always in the same place.

4. After five days or so, when the cress has had a chance to grow, take the results. Measure ten seedlings in each dish and calculate the average height. Copy out and fill in a results table like the one below.

	Dish (i)	*Dish (ii)*	*Dish (iii)*
Direction of cress growth			
Average height of cress			
Colour of cress			

5. Dish (i) was the control. The cress should have grown normally in this. What does growing cress in the dark do to it?

6. Why do you think plants might react in this way to the dark?

7. How does cress react to light from one direction?

8. Why should plants react in this way?

9. Why did you take the average height of the cress plants?

Plant roots and water

Experiment 8.4

Investigating the effects of water on plant root growth

1. Soak some peas for 24 hours.

2. You will need a wooden frame with a floor made of metal mesh. Put a layer of compost into the frame.

3. Plant a number of peas into the compost.

4. Arrange the frame so that it is sloping and supported above the ground as in Figure 8.7.

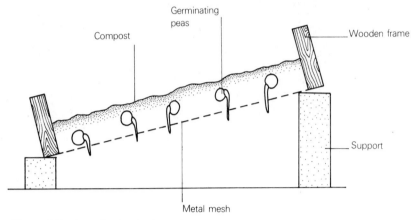

Figure 8.7   Investigating hydrotropism

5. Leave the apparatus until the peas have germinated. Water them occasionally. The roots should grow through the holes in the metal mesh.

6. Leave the apparatus until the roots have grown to 2–3 cm.

7. Did the roots grow straight down as you would expect?

8. Explain the reason for the root behaviour.

8.4 How plants respond — tropisms

The behaviour of the plants in the previous experiments involves them growing in certain directions. Growth movements like this are called *tropisms*. They are permanent changes in the shape of the plant. They cannot be altered once they have taken place. If, for example, a plant grows towards the light in one direction and the light is moved, then the plant will have to grow some more to face the light again. (See Figure 8.8, (opposite).)

There are a number of different sorts of tropism:

(a) *Positive phototropism* — growing towards the light.
(b) *Negative phototropism* — growing away from the light.
(c) *Positive geotropism* — growing towards gravity.
(d) *Negative geotropism* — growing away from gravity.
(e) *Positive hydrotropism* — growing towards water.

(*Photo* denotes *light; geo* denotes *gravity; hydro* denotes water; *positive* denotes *towards; negative* denotes *away from.*)

Once a plant has grown towards
light in one direction . . .

. . . it will have to grow more to
change direction to a new
light source

Figure 8.8   Plant response to light

Plant shoots are positively phototropic and negatively geotropic. Plant roots are negatively phototropic and positively geotropic. They are also positively hydrotropic.

What causes tropisms?

Tropisms are brought about by chemicals which make plant cells grow. These are called *auxins*. One of the most common auxins is IAA. Actual growth takes place only at the tips of roots and shoots (Figure 8.9). If a plant is to grow in a different direction, it is the cells in this area that must cause the change.

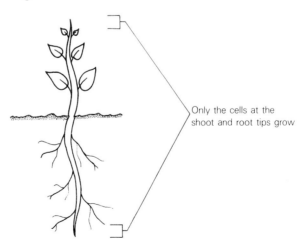

Only the cells at the
shoot and root tips grow

Figure 8.9   Growing points in a plant

The next experiment gives an idea of how IAA affects these cells.

Experiment 8.5

Investigating how IAA affects plant growth

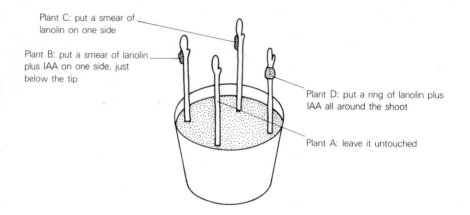

Plant C: put a smear of lanolin on one side

Plant B: put a smear of lanolin plus IAA on one side, just below the tip

Plant D: put a ring of lanolin plus IAA all around the shoot

Plant A: leave it untouched

Figure 8.10   Investigating the effects of IAA on plant growth

1. Germinate at least four peas in a tub of soil or compost. Allow the plants to grow until they are 3–5 cm tall (Figure 8.10).

2. Select four plants and label them A, B, C, D. Measure their lengths and record these in a results table like the one opposite.

3. Treat each of the plants as follows:

    Plant A. Do nothing at all.

    Plant B. Put a tiny smear of IAA dissolved in lanolin on to one side of the shoot just below the tip. Be careful to keep the IAA to one side only. Make a note of which side the IAA was put on.

    Plant C. Put a tiny smear of lanolin without IAA on to one side of the shoot just below the tip. Make a note of which side the lanolin was put on.

    Plant D. Put a smear of IAA in lanolin in a ring right around the shoot just below the tip.

4. Leave the plants for at least 24 hours.

5. Observe any changes in the growth of the plants. Measure their lengths. Fill in your results table.

	Length in millimetres at start of experiment	Length in millimetres at end of experiment	Did the shoot change its direction of growth?
Plant A			
Plant B			
Plant C			
Plant D			

Plant A is the control. It tells you how a plant grows normally.

6. Does IAA on one side of a shoot affect the direction it grows in?

7. Does lanolin on one side of a shoot affect the direction it grows in?

8. Does IAA all around a shoot affect how much it grows?

9. Can you tell what effect the IAA has had on the growth of the shoot cells?

IAA and phototropisms

IAA works by making plant cells grow longer (Figure 8.11). If the cells on one side of a plant grow longer than the cells on the other side, the plant will bend. IAA is made by the cells at the very tips of shoots.

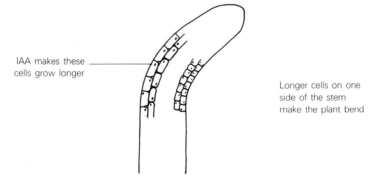

IAA makes these cells grow longer

Longer cells on one side of the stem make the plant bend

Figure 8.11   One effect of IAA

Light on a plant tends to stop IAA from moving down that side. This means that the plant will grow less on the light side than on the dark side.

Thus the plant will bend towards the light. It bends until the light affects the IAA on both sides by the same amount (Figure 8.12).

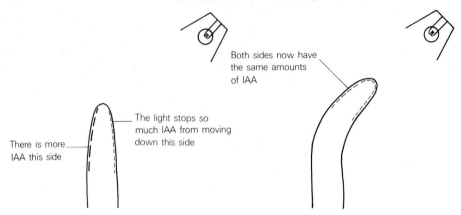

Both sides now have the same amounts of IAA

The light stops so much IAA from moving down this side

There is more IAA this side

Figure 8.12   IAA and phototropism

Other auxins

Other auxins are responsible for making fruits like apples and strawberries ripen. When a plant egg is fertilised, it develops into a seed. This produces an auxin which makes the fruit ripen so that the seed may be dispersed by an animal which eats the fruit. We sometimes use artificial auxins to ripen fruit before it is sold. This allows the seller much more control over the condition of the fruit. A farmer can send unripe fruit all over the world and know that it can be ripened and sold in perfect condition.

Dilute auxins also make root cells grow. Rooting compounds, which are used by gardeners to make cuttings grow, contain auxins. Although a cut stem would produce them naturally, root growth is often quicker if a rooting compound is used.

Summary

1. Plant behaviour can be complex and plants can respond to many changes in their environment.

2. Many plant responses involve growing in certain directions. These growth movements are called tropisms.

3. Tropisms can be caused by light (phototropism), gravity (geotropism) and water (hydrotropism).

4. Growing towards a stimulus is a positive tropism. Growing from it is a negative tropism.

Questions on Chapter 8

1. In an experiment, two lots of wheat plants were grown. Group A were grown in normal conditions and group B were grown in a completely dark cupboard. The following measurements were taken.

Length of shoot	
Group A	Group B
6.5 cm	8.3 cm
5.4 cm	9.0 cm
6.5 cm	7.6 cm
7.0 cm	8.0 cm
7.5 cm	6.5 cm
4.5 cm	7.5 cm
5.0 cm	8.2 cm
5.3 cm	8.7 cm
7.6 cm	7.8 cm
5.7 cm	8.4 cm

   (a) What is the average length of shoot in each group?
   (b) What does the experiment tell you about the effect of growing plants in the dark?

2. Which part of a plant would be positively phototropic?
   Which part of a plant would be positively geotropic?
   Which part of a plant would be negatively phototropic?

3. Copy out the following and fill in the blanks.
   _____ are growth movements brought about by chemicals called _____ . One of the most common of these is _____ . It makes plant cells grow _____ . Only the cells near the _____ of a shoot or root can grow.

4. Copy out the following and fill in the blanks.
    When a seed is planted, the shoot grows _____ but the root grows
    downwards. The whole plant is responding to _____ and this re-
    sponse is called _____ .

5. (a) What would be a control for the experiment seen in Figure 8.13?
    (b) What would the control tell you?

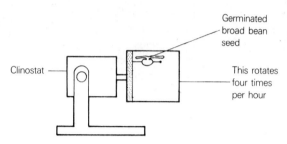

Figure 8.13   Arrangement of experiment

6. Explain how IAA makes plants grow towards light.

Acrostic on Chapter 8

(Teacher, please see special note in front of book.)

Copy or photocopy the acrostic. Do not write on this page. Solve the clues and fill in the spaces. This will give you a 12-letter word going across from 13. Write your own clue for this word.

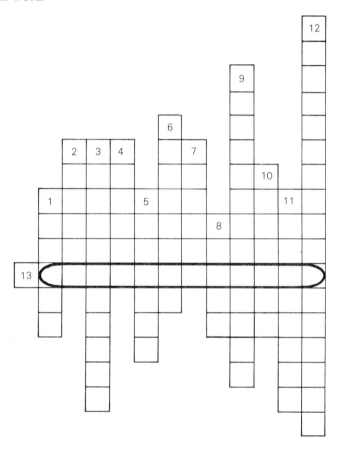

1   Some 10 help fruits to _____ (5)
2   Beans and peas can detect _____ (5)
3   A machine for showing how plants respond to 7 (9)
4   Plants can detect the direction of _____ (5)
5   _____ movements are called tropisms (6)
6   Plants can detect the pull of _____ (7)

7   Plant 8s can detect _____ (5)
8   It grows underground (4)
9   Another name for *Oxalis acetosella* (7, 5)
10 Chemicals involved in plant growth (IAA is an example of one) (6)
11 Growing towards 7 is called _____ hydrotropism (8)
12 They contain 6 and help cuttings grow (7, 9)

Section 2

HOW ORGANISMS GROW, REPRODUCE AND EVOLVE

9. How organisms grow

Since you were born you have grown. You have got bigger, which means you have made more cells. You have also become more complex which means you have made different sorts of cell. (See Figure 9.1.)

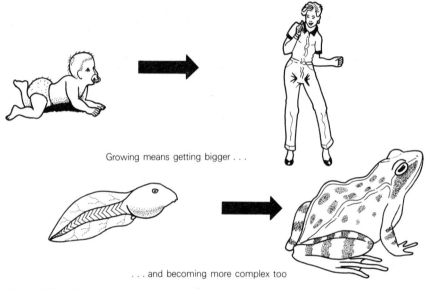

Growing means getting bigger . . .

. . . and becoming more complex too

Figure 9.1   The meaning of growth

You began your life as a single cell and now you are made of many millions of cells. Clearly then, growing new cells is very important. (See Figure 9.2.)

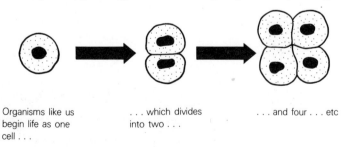

Organisms like us begin life as one cell . . .

. . . which divides into two . . .

. . . and four . . . etc

Figure 9.2   Growth by cell division

9.1 Growing new cells

All living organisms grow new cells in the same way. One cell divides and becomes two new cells. This process is called *mitosis*. It happens in your body several hundred thousand times each day. What happens first is that the *nucleus* of the cell divides into two. Then the rest of the cell separates around each new nucleus. The cell nucleus controls all the activities of the cell. It is essential that any new cells get enough of the substances in the nucleus for them to work properly.

What is the nucleus?

The nucleus in a cell is a roundish structure that is easily coloured to make it show up clearly (Figure 9.3). It is made up of lots of a chemical called DNA (deoxyribonucleic acid). This chemical controls everything that a cell does. DNA can do this because it controls all the chemical reactions that go on inside a cell. In every cell there are hundreds of reactions taking place all the time. Each reaction needs an enzyme to make it work. DNA controls what enzymes will be made in each cell (Figure 9.4).

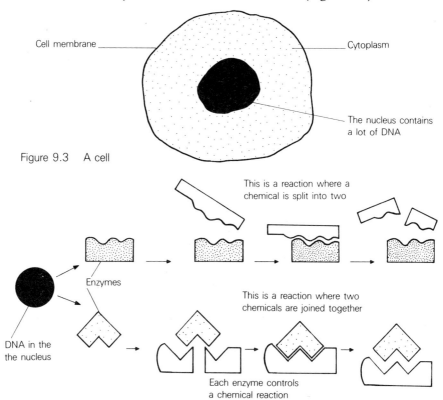

Cell membrane

Cytoplasm

The nucleus contains a lot of DNA

Figure 9.3   A cell

This is a reaction where a chemical is split into two

Enzymes

This is a reaction where two chemicals are joined together

DNA in the the nucleus

Each enzyme controls a chemical reaction

Figure 9.4   DNA controls the chemical reactions in each cell

What is DNA?

DNA is a very long chemical. It has a spiral structure and it looks a little like Figure 9.5. Usually the DNA is very stretched out, but sometimes it coils up quite tightly. When it does this, we can see it separate from the other DNA in the nucleus. When it is like this, it is called a *chromosome*. Human cells have 46 chromosomes. Other organisms have different numbers. Members of one type of organism always have the same number of chromosomes.

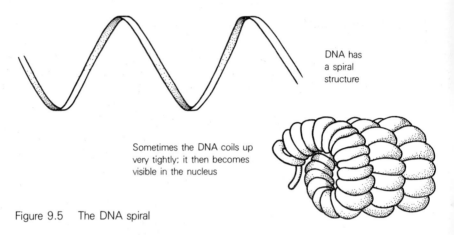

DNA has a spiral structure

Sometimes the DNA coils up very tightly; it then becomes visible in the nucleus

Figure 9.5   The DNA spiral

We can see chromosomes only when a cell is about to divide. You can see chromosomes if you look at a tissue which has lots of dividing cells in it. The tips of plant roots are like this. Figure 9.6 shows some chromosomes under the microscope.

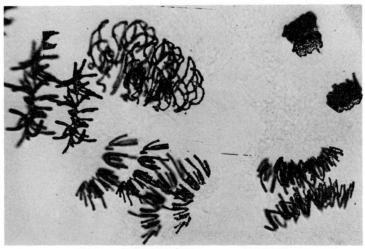

Figure 9.6   A light microscope preparation of a cell stained to show the chromosomes

Experiment 9.1

Experiment to see chromosomes

1. Take a microscope and a prepared slide of a root tip. The roots must have been cut lengthways (longitudinal section) and should look like Figure 9.7(ii).

(i)

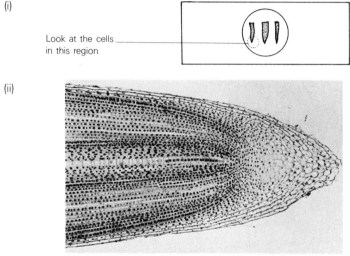

Look at the cells in this region

(ii)

Figure 9.7   Slide of longitudinal sections of root tips (i); Photograph of root tip (ii)

2. You need only study the cells in the first 3 mm behind the root tip. Focus the microscope with the low-power lens. Search the root tip until you find a cell which has obvious chromosomes in it.

3. You may wish to look more closely at this cell. Arrange for it to be exactly in the centre of your field of view. Swing the high-power lens into position: it should automatically be just about in focus. *Do not* focus this lens too far because it is very close to the slide. By moving the focus knob more than 2 mm you may push the lens through the slide.

4. Draw a large labelled diagram of the cell you are looking at.

5. Now switch back to the low-power lens. Search for another cell and draw this. Repeat until you have drawn at least four different cells.

6. Were chromosomes easy to find?

7. Were the chromosomes arranged the same in each cell?

8. Did any cells show the chromosome having separated into two groups?

What is special about DNA?

DNA controls what enzymes are made in a cell. It also has one ability which no other chemical in the body has. DNA can organise the cell to make *exact copies* of itself. This process is called *replication*. By replicating, DNA can make sure that any new cells get exactly the same DNA as the cell they developed from. This is what happens during *mitosis*. It makes sure that all the cells in an organism have the same DNA. (See Figure 9.8.)

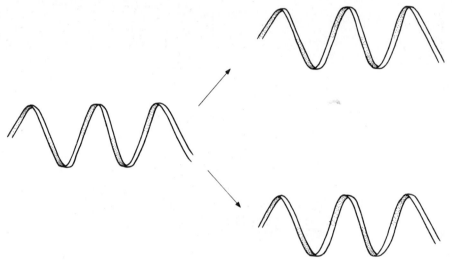

Figure 9.8   DNA can make exact copies of itself

Mitosis   Mitosis is a series of events which happen in a cell. The DNA in the nucleus replicates and is shared out into two new groups. Each new group has exactly the same DNA as the original cell had. You can follow the events of mitosis in an imaginary cell which has only two strands of DNA. That is, the cell has *two chromosomes* (Figure 9.9).

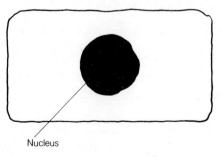

Nucleus

Figure 9.9(i)

(a) The cell before it is about to divide. In the nucleus the DNA is already replicating so that the two chromosomes become four.

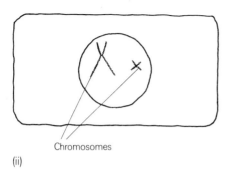

Chromosomes

(ii)

(b) The DNA coils up to become shorter and fatter. This makes the chromosomes visible. They show up as pairs of chromosomes joined together. Each pair contains two identical strands of DNA.

Pairs of DNA strands line up across the centre of the spindle

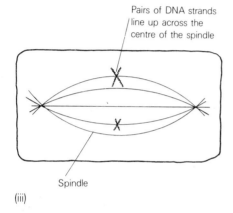

Spindle

(iii)

(c) The cell makes a structure called a *spindle*. This is a network of microscopic fibres. The pairs of DNA strands move about until they become attached to the spindle across the centre.

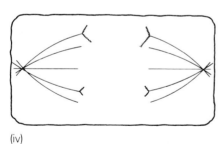

(iv)

(d) The pairs of DNA strands seem to pull apart and are pulled to either end of the spindle.

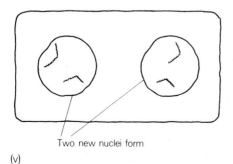

Two new nuclei form

(v)

(e) A nucleus forms around the new group of chromosomes. Each new nucleus now has two chromosomes exactly like the original cell nucleus.

(f) The chromosomes uncoil and become invisible again. The cell divides in two around each nucleus.

(vi)

Figure 9.9   Stages in mitosis

Experiment 9.2

Experiment to see the stages of mitosis

1. Look at the root cells again exactly as in Experiment 9.1.

2. Remember that each plant cell will have many more than two chromosomes. Different cells will have been stopped at different stages of mitosis. Identify and draw as many of the stages of mitosis as you can.

Summary

1. Growing means making more cells and different sorts of cell.

2. The activities of a cell are controlled by DNA.

3. DNA can make exact copies of itself.

4. DNA forms long strands called chromosomes.

5. The number of chromosomes is the same for all members of the same species. All humans have 46 chromosomes per cell.

6. Mitosis is when a cell divides to produce two identical new cells.

7. During mitosis, the DNA replicates and is then shared out to produce two nuclei. Each one has exactly the same DNA as the nucleus of the original cell.

9.2 Human growth

A body as complex as ours does not grow evenly all the time. Cells in different parts of the body grow and divide at different speeds and at different times. You can see this in the stages of growth and development which happen *before* a baby is born (Figure 9.10 (opposite)).

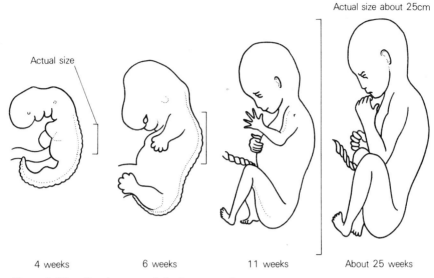

Actual size about 25cm

Actual size

4 weeks   6 weeks   11 weeks   About 25 weeks

Figure 9.10   Development of the human embryo

Figure 9.11 (on the next page) is a graph showing how boys and girls get taller as they get older. The figures used to draw the graphs are averages of lots of boys and girls. To be a little taller or shorter than average is quite normal. It is also normal to grow at slightly different ages to the ones on the graph.

The steepness of the graph tells us how quickly height is changing. The steeper the graph, the more rapid the growth. Each line on the graph has been labelled with letters for you to follow.

Boys and girls both grow most quickly just after they are born. A → B and A → G are the steepest parts of the graph. A baby needs to grow rapidly in the first year after it is born so that it can quickly begin to move around and take on a more normal way of life.

From about 1 year old both boys and girls grow steadily. Boys grow a little taller than girls on average. At around 9 years old boys' growth slows down to almost nothing. The graph between C and D is almost flat. Girls of 9, on the other hand, grow very quickly up to about 13 years (H → I). They overtake boys in height. Boys do not begin to grow rapidly until they are about 13 years old. Then they grow quite quickly until they end up taller than girls.

Girls grow only a little after about 13 years. Boys start to grow more slowly after about 16 years. Eventually at around 20 years old both boys and girls stop growing altogether. On average boys end up a little taller than girls.

The very rapid growth shown by sections H → I and D → E is called *puberty*. At this time not only do our bodies get taller but they also change.

The reproductive organs begin to work. A boy's body will change shape to that of a man. A girl's body changes shape to that of a woman.

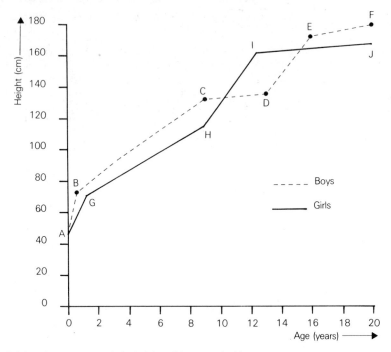

Figure 9.11   Average growth in height of boys and girls

How growth is controlled

How quickly a body grows is controlled by chemicals called *hormones*. These are produced by glands and released into the blood. They are carried to all the cells in the body. In this way all the body's cells can grow at much the same rate. The most important hormones which control growth are:

(a) *Thyroxin* — produced by the thyroid gland in the neck. It controls the speed of all the body's chemical reactions. If a child produces too much thyroxin it will grow very large. If a child produces too little thyroxin it will be small and often mentally retarded.

(b) *Growth hormone* — produced by the pituitary gland. Too much growth hormone leads to a child growing too big, and vice versa.

(c) *Testosterone* — produced by the testes in boys. This causes the boy's body to grow taller and his chest to broaden. It also starts the sperm production in the testes.

(d) *Oestrogen* — produced by the ovaries in girls. This causes the body to grow, the hips to get broader and the breasts to develop. It also helps to control the menstrual cycle.

Other factors affecting growth

One of the most important factors affecting how quickly we grow is the food we eat. A growing child needs a lot of protein to make new cells. Without this the child will not grow so well. In severe cases this can lead to a disease which is common in Third World countries, called *kwashiorkor*. A child suffering from this will not grow well and may become seriously ill. Often kwashiorkor leads to death.

Figure 9.12 shows three young boys. The one in the middle is just over 2-years-old and he weighs 11.5 kg. He is quite normal in size for his age. The boy on his left has kwashirkor. He is 2½-years-old but weighs only 6.8 kg. The lack of protein in his diet has caused his muscles to waste away as you can clearly see around his shoulders and arms.

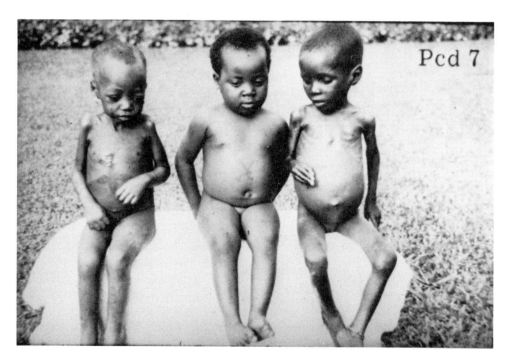

Figure 9.12   The effects of not eating enough

The boy on the right is actually 4-years-old. He weighs only 7.5 kg and is a little bigger than the healthy boy in the middle. This boy is suffering from *marasmus*. This is caused by simply not having enough to eat. It leads to poor growth and often to disease. We would call this starving but in Third World countries it is often called marasmus. Children with marasmus do not get enough protein for cell growth or calorie foods for energy to help growth. They usually catch diseases very easily.

Figure 9.13 shows two girls from South East Asia. The girl on the right is suffering from marasmus, although in Asia this is just called malnutrition. Both girls are similar in age, around 3½-years-old. You can clearly see the effects of not getting enough food. The girl on the right is much smaller and lighter. Overall, she has grown much less than the other girl.

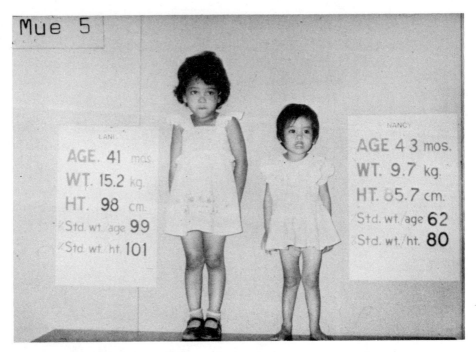

Figure 9.13   The effect of marasmus

Neither kwashiorkor nor marasmus are conditions we often see in this country. Two hundred years ago, however, they would have been fairly common. In those days, very few people ate proper balanced diets. Many people did not grow as large as they should have done. You can see this if you visit old houses or stately homes. The beds are much shorter than modern beds because the people who slept in them did not grow so tall as they do nowadays.

Among other animals (and plants) the temperature may affect how quickly they grow. The chemical reactions inside all organisms do not work so quickly in the cold. Thus, for most animals (and plants) a lower temperature means less growth or slower growth.

Plants will not grow successfully without enough light or water. They need light for photosynthesis to make the food they need to grow. Animals need water, too, but in most cases a lack of water will kill the animal rather than slow its growth.

Microbes do not grow without water, which is why we dry some foods to preserve them. The microbes may not die, however, and may begin to grow again as soon as they get water.

9.3 Growth in a butterfly

Growth in humans is generally quite smooth. The rate of growth is different at different stages of our life, but there are no sudden changes. In insects, however, growth takes place in spurts. It sometimes involves enormous changes to the shape and structure of the insect. This can easily be seen in the butterfly.

Insects have a skeleton on the outside called an *exoskeleton*. It is hard and rigid, and once formed it cannot grow. If an insect is to get bigger it must shed its exoskeleton and grow a larger one (Figure 9.14). The cabbage white caterpillar does this several times as it grows.

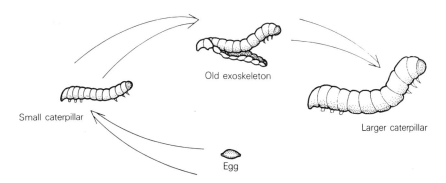

Figure 9.14   Insects must shed their exoskeleton to grow

Shedding the exoskeleton is called *moulting*. The caterpillar grows a soft exoskeleton inside the old one. Then, once it is large enough, it cracks open the old exoskeleton and wriggles out of it. The caterpillar then expands its body with air for a couple of hours until the new exoskeleton hardens.

The caterpillar, however, is only an eating machine. It is a simple organism which needs to change a great deal to become a butterfly. The caterpillar stops feeding about a month after hatching. It finds a sheltered spot and spins a silk pad to cling on to. It spins more silk to attach its body to the surface. The caterpillar exoskeleton splits and a *pupa,* or *chrysalis,* emerges (Figure 9.15).

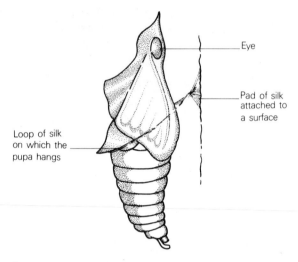

Figure 9.15   A pupa

The pupa is the stage where the body inside turns into the adult butterfly. The pupa does not move whilst this is happening. It takes about two weeks; then the pupa exoskeleton splits and the adult butterfly wriggles out (Figure 9.16). It stretches its wings by pumping them full of blood and after an hour or two they harden. The butterfly can then fly away.

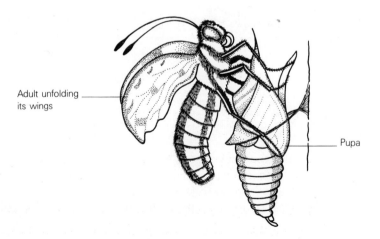

Figure 9.16   Adult butterfly emerging from pupa

A complete change like this, from caterpillar to butterfly, is called *metamorphosis*. Other animals which show metamorphosis include the housefly, which changes from maggot to fly, and the frog, which hatches from the egg as a tadpole. (See Figure 9.17.)

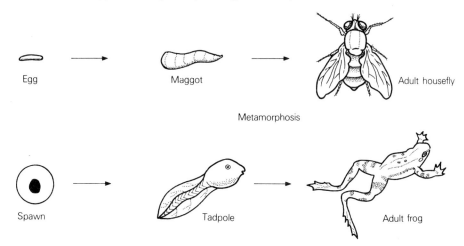

| Egg | | Maggot | | Adult housefly |

Metamorphosis

| Spawn | | Tadpole | | Adult frog |

Figure 9.17   Metamorphosis in other animals

Summary

1. In animals with an endoskeleton, growth is smooth. Animals with an exoskeleton grow in stages as they shed their rigid exoskeleton and grow a new one.

2. In all animals growth is controlled by hormones.

3. Some animals have a two-stage life. The first is simple and grows quickly. The second is the more complex adult. The change from the first stage to the second is called metamorphosis.

4. How quickly an animal grows depends on its food supply. Some animals also grow more slowly when it is cold.

9.4 Growth in plants

Germination

New plants often grow from seeds. Seeds contain a plant *embryo* and a store of food for the embryo to grow. Seeds are quite tough and can be spread around by wind or animals. In this way plants can reach new ground. The stage when a plant embryo starts to grow into a new plant is called *germination*. (See Figure 9.18.)

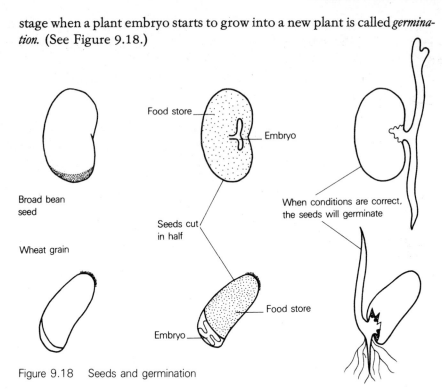

Figure 9.18   Seeds and germination

For a seed to germinate, it needs warmth, water and oxygen. Remember that most seeds germinate under the ground where it is dark, so light is not needed. Now you have been told this, could you show it to be true? Experiment 9.3 may help.

Experiment 9.3

To show that seeds need warmth, water and oxygen to germinate

Petri dish lid

All the conditions for germination: water, warmth, air

Peas

Cotton wool

Choose your own conditions for these three beakers

Figure 9.19   Apparatus investigating germination of peas

1. Take 20–25 dried peas and four beakers with plastic Petri dishes as lids. Use the cotton wool inside the beaker to support the peas.

2. Set up one beaker with 5–6 peas and all the conditions necessary for germination (Figure 9.19 (opposite)).

3. Set up the other beakers each with slightly different conditions. Choose your conditions so that the whole experiment will show whether it is essential for seeds to have warmth, water and oxygen for germination.

4. Leave your beakers for about a week to give the peas time to germinate.

5. Do your results prove that peas need warmth, water and oxygen to germinate?

Plant growth

Animals grow evenly all over their bodies. Plants, however, only grow at the tips of their roots and shoots (Figure 9.20). At the tips the cells are actively dividing by mitosis. The new cells then expand until they reach their full size. Once they have done this, their cell walls become quite rigid and the cells cannot then change their shape.

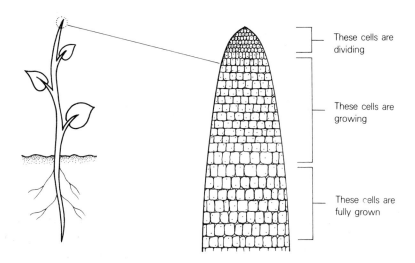

Figure 9.20   Cell growth takes place at root and shoot tips only

Experiment 9.4

To show that plants grow at their shoot and root tips only

1. Set up the apparatus as in Figure 9.21. If the bean is kept in a warm place it will germinate and grow in about a week.

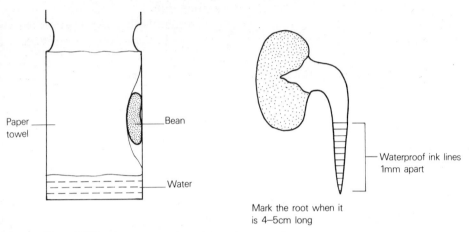

Figure 9.21   Apparatus to investigate plant growth

2. Wait until the root is about 4–5 cm long. Then mark lines on the root 1 mm apart. Begin at the root tip and work backwards. You will have to use a waterproof ink and a pen with a fine point.

3. Wait 5–7 days and check the markings.

4. In which part of the root are the markings still 1 mm apart? Can you explain how this happened?

5. In which part of the root are the markings more than 1 mm apart? Can you explain how this happened?

6. Is there any part of the root which has no marks at all? Can you explain how this happened?

7. You can do the same experiment on the shoot when it has grown. Do you get the same results?

Tree growth

Woody plants like trees grow at the tips of their roots and branches. However, tree trunks also grow; they get wider year by year. Each year the xylem cells around the outside of the trunk become strengthened with lignin. These cells become the wood of the tree trunk. Each year new xylem and phloem grow around the old. Each new layer of xylem leaves a visible ring on the tree trunk. By counting these rings you can tell how many years the tree has been growing (Figure 9.22).

Figure 9.22   This tree is several hundred years old

Buds

In the autumn, most twigs and branches on a tree end in buds. Inside the bud are lots of leaves all crinkled up. These are protected by the black or brown scales which form the outside of the bud. These bud scales are thick, tough, very small leaves. (See Figure 9.23.)

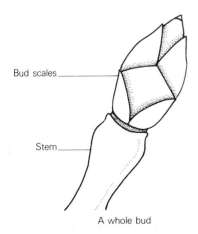

A whole bud

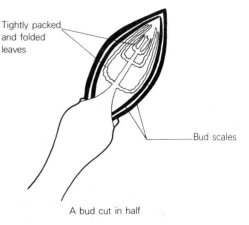

A bud cut in half

Figure 9.23   A bud

When spring comes, the stem inside the bud grows very rapidly. As it does, the bud scales are pushed open and the stem with its new leaves pushes out. The leaves do not take many days to open out and become spaced as the stem continues to grow. In this way a tree can quickly have lots of photosynthesising leaves. It would take much longer if the leaves had to grow from the very beginning instead of being already formed. You may have noticed that in spring it takes only a few weeks for trees and bushes to become covered in leaves. The sudden growth marks the end of winter, and signals that the more pleasant spring and summer days are not far off (Figure 9.24).

The bud scales fall off, leaving tiny scars to mark where they were attached. You can easily see these rings of scars on a twig and can tell its age by counting them. Each ring marks a year's growth (Figure 9.25).

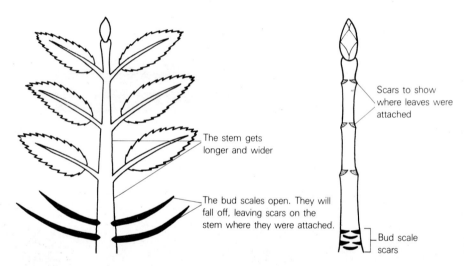

The stem gets longer and wider

The bud scales open. They will fall off, leaving scars on the stem where they were attached.

Scars to show where leaves were attached

Bud scale scars

Figure 9.24   Growth of a bud in spring

Figure 9.25   Twig showing bud and leaf scars

What controls plant growth?

Plant growth — like animal growth — is controlled by chemicals. In plants these chemicals are called *auxins.* IAA is one of the most common ones (see Chapter 8). There are other chemicals called *kinins* and *gibberellins* which also help control growth.

The rate at which plants grow depends on the temperature, the amount of light, the supply of minerals like nitrates from the soil, and the amount of water.

(a) *Temperature.* The warmer it is, the faster plants will grow. However, when temperatures get too high, a plant will lose so much water that its growth is slowed down.

(b) *Light.* Plants need a good supply of light, which is why few plants grow on the ground in thick woodland. The trees absorb so much light that there is not enough light for other plants.

(c) *Minerals.* Plant roots take in water and minerals. Substances like nitrates, sulphates and magnesium compounds are essential for plant growth. Without nitrates, plants cannot make the proteins needed to make new living cell material. For a plant to take in minerals, it needs to use energy. It gets this by respiration using glucose made by the leaves, and oxygen in the soil. If a soil becomes waterlogged, then there is no oxygen left in it. The roots cannot respire and may eventually die.

(d) *Water.* Water is needed for photosynthesis, transport, keeping cells turgid (swollen), and to allow all the chemical reactions to take place. Without a good supply of water all these things slow up and the plant will not grow so well.

Summary

1. The stage at which a seed begins to grow into a plant is called germination.

2. Seeds need warmth, water and oxygen to germinate.

3. Plants grow only at the tips of their roots and shoots.

4. Trees grow wider each year. Each new growth produces a new layer around the trunk. By counting the layers or rings you can tell the age of a tree.

5. Buds are very short stems with leaves. They grow rapidly in spring.

6. Plant growth is controlled by chemicals called auxins, kinins and gibberellins.

Questions on Chapter 9

1. A cell nucleus contains the chemical DNA. What does DNA do?

2. Why is DNA such a special chemical?

3. What is a chromosome?

4. Copy out and complete the following sentence.
   Mitosis is the process by which a cell divides _____ .

5. What is a bud? How is it that trees can develop leaves in only two or three weeks in the spring?

6. The drawings in Figure 9.26 show cells in different stages of mitosis. They are not in the correct order. Write down what the correct order should be.

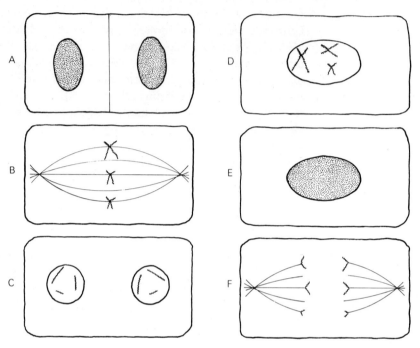

Figure 9.26 Cells at different stages of mitosis (in jumbled order)

7. You are given ten baby mice and asked to investigate how food affects their growth. You are given two diets for them. One is normal mouse food (diet A) and the other is chocolate, cream cakes and peanuts (diet B). How exactly would you set about investigating the effects of these two diets on mouse growth?

8. Copy out the following and fill in the blanks.
Animals like _____ have a hard exoskeleton which is rigid and does not _____ . When the animal gets too big, it must shed its exoskeleton and grow a new one. This process is called _____ . Some _____ have a two-stage life. The change from one stage to the other is called _____ . In the butterfly, the stage when this change happens is called the _____ .

9. Germinating seeds need _____ , _____ and _____ . Once they have germinated, plants only grow at the _____ of their roots and shoots.

10. A farmer cut down three trees. His son said that tree C was the oldest because it had been the tallest. Look at the drawings of the sawn tree trunks in Figure 9.27. Was the son correct? How do you know?

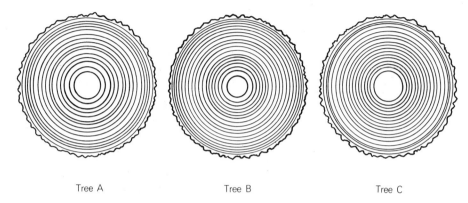

Tree A   Tree B   Tree C

Figure 9.27   Measuring the ages of trees

11. The table below shows the average mass of a sample of boys and girls up to 16-years-old.

Age	Mass in kilograms	
	Boys	Girls
0 (birth)	3.5	3.3
1	10.0	9.5
4	16.5	16.5
8	27.5	25.5
12	38.0	40.0
16	59.0	53.5

(a) Draw a line graph of these results. Label clearly which line shows boys' growth and which shows girls'.
(b) At what three ages are boys, on average, the same weight as girls?
(c) In between which years do boys grow most quickly?
(d) In between which years do girls grow most quickly?
(e) Is the slowest growth period for boys faster or slower than the slowest growth period for girls? How can you tell?

'Mitosis' Crossword on Chapter 9

(Teacher, please see special note in front of book.)

Copy this grid, then solve the clues. The answers to each clue have been split into two *equal* parts (mitosis!). Do not write on this page.

1+4	These chemicals control plant growth (6) . . .
3+14	. . . so do these (12)
5+2	DNA (16, 4)
10+8	Seeds contain a plant _____ (6)
11+9	You can only see it when a cell is about to divide (10)
12+6	Thyroxin and oestrogen are _____ (8)

13+19	General term meaning not having enough to eat or eating the wrong sorts of food (12)
17+16	A condition caused by not having enough to eat (8)
18+15	These chemicals also control plant growth (6)
20+7	This causes a boy's chest to broaden (12)

10. Reproduction and genetics

There are two sorts of reproduction:

(a) *Asexual* reproduction, in which one parent organism reproduces by itself.

(b) *Sexual* reproduction, in which two parents are needed to produce offspring.

Asexual reproduction is easier because an organism does not need to find another one to mate with. However, it does mean that the offspring will only *inherit* the features of one parent. It will be identical to its parent. Sexual reproduction is more difficult since two organisms need to come together in some way. The offspring of sexual reproduction inherit some of their features from both parents. This means that these offspring are always different to the parents in some way. These differences are called *variation*.

10.1 Asexual reproduction

Microbes and one-celled animals and plants reproduce *asexually*. The parent cell simply divides into two and becomes two new organisms.

Larger animals cannot reproduce asexually, but many larger plants can. In fact, many plants can reproduce both sexually and asexually. These plants reproduce sexually using their flowers, and asexually using one of several methods.

For example, strawberries can reproduce by runners, which are long, thin stems that grow across the ground. In certain places, runners grow roots and leaves to become new plants. In this way, one strawberry plant can grow lots more. Potato plants produce potatoes underground. Each potato can, if it is left, grow into a new plant. Both strawberries and potatoes have flowers, which reproduce sexually to produce seeds.

Plants like daffodils and tulips can reproduce asexually by bulbs. A bulb contains stored food which is used to feed the plant as it grows. Later on, the fully grown plant stores food in a new bulb for next year. Quite often one plant will store food in two or more bulbs so that more plants can grow the following year.

You may have taken cuttings from house plants by removing and planting a small piece of stem. The cutting will grow roots and become a whole plant. This is asexual reproduction too. Because a plant will not normally take cuttings from itself, reproduction like this is called *artificial propagation*. (See Figure 10.1.)

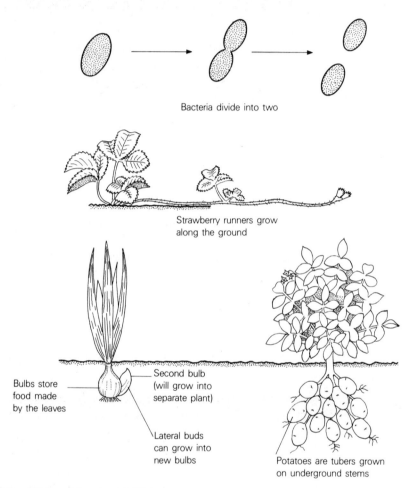

Bacteria divide into two

Strawberry runners grow along the ground

Bulbs store food made by the leaves

Second bulb (will grow into separate plant)

Lateral buds can grow into new bulbs

Potatoes are tubers grown on underground stems

Figure 10.1   Asexual reproduction

Cloning is another form of artificial propagation. It is becoming common where flowers are grown in large quantities. The *grower* takes a plant which produces the sort of flower he wants. He cuts this plant up into hundreds of small groups of cells. Each group is then grown in carefully controlled conditions. Eventually, each group of cells grows into a whole new plant. The plants produced like this are identical to each other and to the plant they came from. They are called *clones*.

In this way, a grower can produce hundreds of the same sort of flower. He can thus guarantee the types he will produce and be more certain of selling them.

Cloning animals is much more difficult. Scientists are investigating whether it is possible to clone new organs rather than whole animals. If, for instance, a new kidney could be grown from a few cells, a diseased human kidney could be replaced with one which is identical but healthy. Kidney donors would no longer be necessary.

Asexual reproduction means that the cell or cells of the offspring have exactly the same DNA as the parent. This means that the offspring will have exactly the same enzymes as the parent and will carry out exactly the same chemical reactions. This is why the offspring will be identical to the parent.

10.2 Sexual reproduction

Most living organisms reproduce sexually. The two parents each produce a cell called a *gamete*. The male parent produces a male gamete and the female parent produces a female gamete. The two gametes join together to produce a cell called a *zygote*. The joining of gametes is called *fertilisation*. Once the zygote has been formed, it grows into an embryo and eventually into an independent new organism. (See Figure 10.2.)

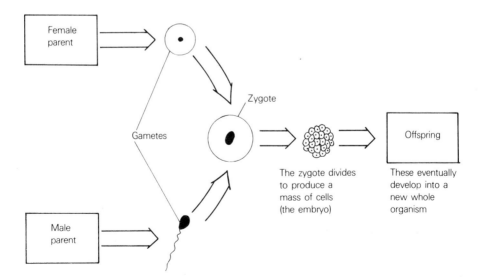

Figure 10.2   Outline of sexual reproduction

Sexual reproduction in animals

In animals, the male gamete is called a *sperm* and the female gamete is called an *egg-cell* or *ovum*. In humans, fertilisation happens when a sperm cell is passed into the reproductive organs of the female. It swims to the egg cell and fertilises it. The zygote develops for nine months inside the uterus of the female. The embryo gets food and oxygen from its mother through the *placenta*. When the baby is born it still needs several years of growing and developing before it is a completely independent organism. (See Figure 10.3.)

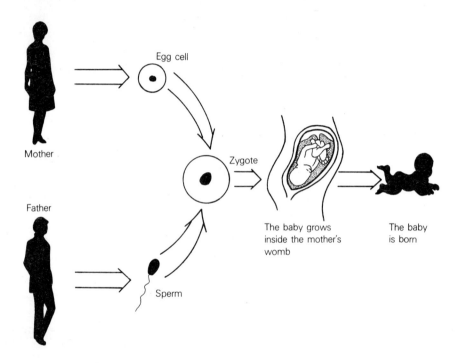

Figure 10.3   Sexual reproduction in humans

Although there are differences, this process is much the same for all animals. The embryo may take more or less time to develop and be born. Elephants take two years, gerbils take three weeks. Many animals lay eggs with the embryo and its food supply inside. The embryo does most of its growing and developing in the egg. Some water animals, like frogs and fish, just pass their sperm and eggs into the water. The sperm then swim to the eggs to fertilise them. Occasionally animals have both male and female reproductive organs. Worms and snails do. These animals still need to mate but each one passes sperm to the other for fertilisation. (See Figure 10.4 (opposite).)

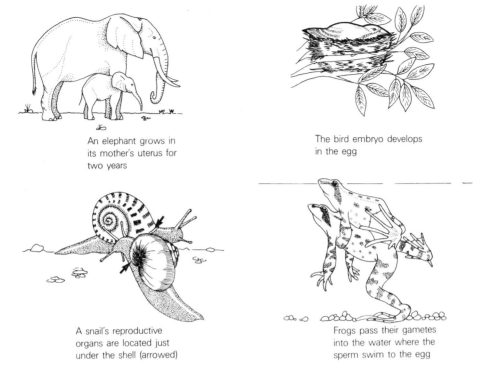

An elephant grows in
its mother's uterus for
two years

The bird embryo develops
in the egg

A snail's reproductive
organs are located just
under the shell (arrowed)

Frogs pass their gametes
into the water where the
sperm swim to the egg

Figure 10.4   Sexual reproduction in animals

Sexual reproduction in plants

Many plants have both male and female reproductive organs in the same
flower. The *anthers* produce *pollen,* which contains the male gamete. The
ovary produces the female gamete called the *ovule,* or plant egg. Pollen is
blown by the wind or carried by insects from one flower to another (Figure
10.5).

Figure 10.5   A bee pollinating a flower

Pollen lands on the stigma and grows a tube through the female organs to the ovule. The male gamete passes through the tube to fertilise the ovule. The zygote and then the embryo develop inside the ovary. A food store grows with the embryo. Eventually, a seed is formed which, when planted, will grow into a new plant. (See Figure 10.6.)

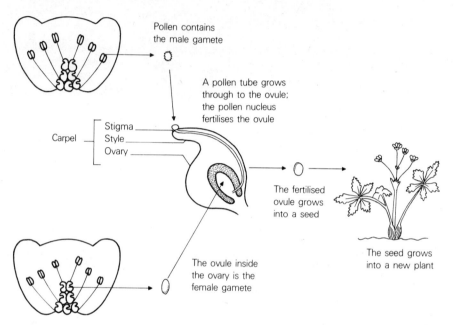

Figure 10.6   Sexual reproduction in plants

This process is the same for most plants. Some, however, have flowers with only male or female reproductive organs. Some have one ovary which produces lots of ovules. Some have lots of ovaries each containing one ovule. Many plants have their pollen carried by insects. These plants have coloured petals and may have nectar and a scent to attract insects (see Figure 10.7(i).

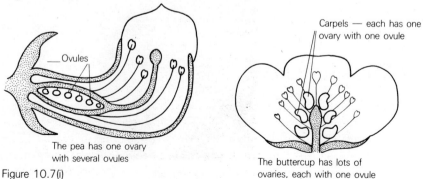

Figure 10.7(i)

The pollen of other plants is blown by the wind. These plants have small petals or none at all. They are not coloured and have no scent or nectar. Grass flowers are like this and so are hazel and plantains (see Figure 10.7(ii)).

(ii)

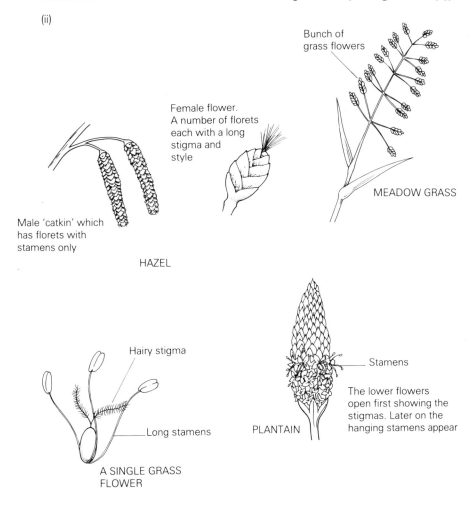

Figure 10.7   Different plant reproductive systems

10.3 Gametes and chromosomes

Different members of the same type of organism have the same number of chromosomes in their cells. Thus all humans have 46 chromosomes per cell. For a human baby to have 46 chromosomes in its cells the zygote must have had 46. The zygote was made by the joining of two gametes. Clearly, then, the gametes had to have only 23 chromosomes each. This is an important feature of all gametes. They have only half the number of chromosomes found in the normal body cells. (See Figure 10.8.)

The process of producing gametes with only half the number of chromosomes in their cells is called *meiosis.*

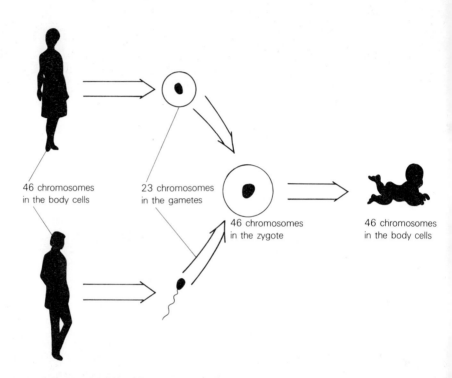

Figure 10.8   Keeping the chromosome balance

46 chromosomes
in the body cells

23 chromosomes
in the gametes

46 chromosomes
in the zygote

46 chromosomes
in the body cells

Meiosis   The sharing of chromosomes needs to be carefully organised if the zygote is to end up with the correct number and sort. In fact, to make sure that the zygote gets the correct number and sort of chromosomes, each cell in an organism has not one but two sets of chromosomes. Thus human cells have two sets of 23 chromosomes and not one set of 46.

Imagine an organism with six chromosomes in each cell. They form three pairs which we can call A,A; B,B; C,C. A and A are exactly the same size and shape. So too are B and B and C and C. Figure 10.9 (opposite) shows a simplified version of what happens during meiosis.

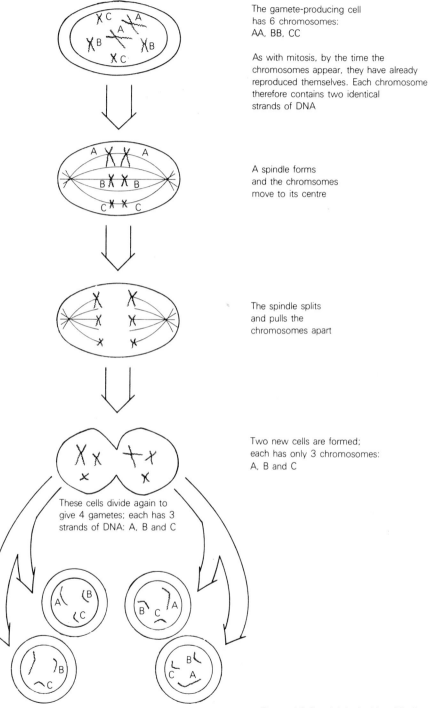

The gamete-producing cell
has 6 chromosomes:
AA, BB, CC

As with mitosis, by the time the
chromosomes appear, they have already
reproduced themselves. Each chromosome
therefore contains two identical
strands of DNA

A spindle forms
and the chromsomes
move to its centre

The spindle splits
and pulls the
chromosomes apart

Two new cells are formed;
each has only 3 chromosomes:
A, B and C

These cells divide again to
give 4 gametes; each has 3
strands of DNA: A, B and C

Figure 10.9   Meiosis (simplified)

Gametes produced by meiosis end up with half the normal number of chromosomes. In this case, each gamete has A,B,C. When two gametes like this join together during fertilisation the zygote gets a full set of chromosomes — AA, BB, CC. (See Figure 10.10.)

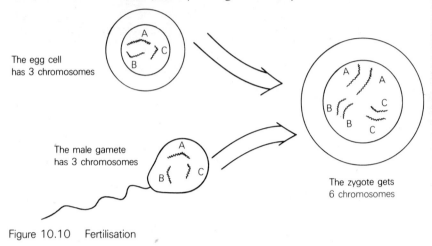

The egg cell has 3 chromosomes

The male gamete has 3 chromosomes

The zygote gets 6 chromosomes

Figure 10.10   Fertilisation

Summary

1. There are two sorts of reproduction — asexual and sexual.

2. Most organisms reproduce sexually, although many plants can reproduce asexually as well.

3. In asexual reproduction, one parent produces offspring by itself. These offspring get all their chromosomes from one parent. This means they are identical to the parent.

4. Sexual reproduction needs two parents. Each produces gametes. A male gamete joins with a female gamete and fertilises it. This produces a zygote which grows into a new organism.

5. The normal cells in an organism have two sets of chromosomes. Gametes have only half as many, i.e. one set.

6. Meiosis is the division of a cell to produce gametes with only half the normal number of chromosomes.

7. At fertilisation, two gametes join to produce a zygote with the normal number of chromosomes again. Since half of the zygote's chromosomes came from one parent and half from the other, it will grow into an organism which has features from both parents but is not exactly the same as either.

10.4 Chromosomes and genes

A chromosome is a very long strand of DNA (Figure 10.11).

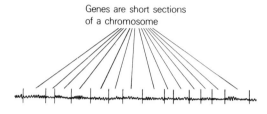

Figure 10.11   A chromosome consists of many genes

A gene is a short section of the DNA strand. A chromosome may be made up of hundreds of genes. Each gene contains enough DNA to allow the cell to make one protein, usually an enzyme. Each gene, therefore, allows a cell to perform one chemical reaction. We say that a gene controls a single *characteristic* of the organism. Some genes control characteristics which are easily visible. Others control characteristics which are not so obvious. In humans, one visible characteristic is the ability to roll the tongue. People either have the gene that controls this or they do not (Figure 10.12). You may like to try to see if you have it.

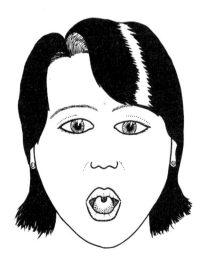

Figure 10.12   Tongue-rolling: some people find it impossible

If you look around your class you will see that some people can roll their tongues while others cannot. Clearly some people have the tongue rolling gene and others do not. The study of why there are differences in the genes that different organisms have is called *genetics*. We will look at some simple examples.

Genetics   We have already seen that every normal cell in an organism has two sets of chromosomes. We also know that a gene is a small piece of one chromosome. It follows, therefore, that every normal cell must have two sets of genes. This means that for *each characteristic* there must be two genes per cell. Pairs of genes like this are called *alleles*. (See Figure 10.13.)

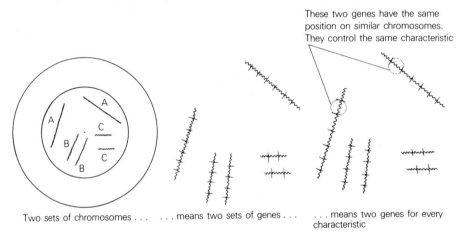

These two genes have the same position on similar chromosomes. They control the same characteristic

Two sets of chromosomes . . .   . . . means two sets of genes . . .   . . . means two genes for every characteristic

Figure 10.13   Every characteristic has two genes

Now let us consider a woman called Janet who can roll her tongue. In this case, Janet has two genes for tongue rolling; we can call these genes R and R (R for Rolling). A man called Mark cannot roll his tongue. He has two genes for not being able to roll. We can call these r and r.

A person studying genetics would want to know whether Mark's and Janet's children could or could not roll their tongues. This is easy to predict.

Janet's cells all have the genes R and R (along with many others). Janet produces gametes by meiosis. Each gamete can have *only one* gene for each characteristic. Each of Janet's gametes (egg cells) get a single R gene.

Mark's cells all have the genes r and r (along with many others). Mark produces gametes by meiosis. Each of Mark's gametes (sperm) has a single r gene. When Janet's egg cell is fertilised by Mark's sperm the zygote gets one R gene and one r. Thus the children end up with two genes to control tongue rolling, just like their parents. Follow this process in Figure 10.14 (opposite).

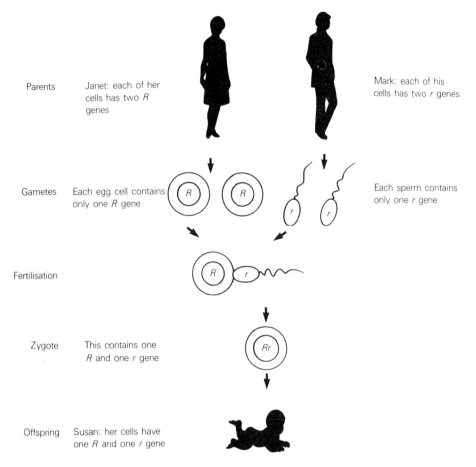

Parents   Janet: each of her
           cells has two *R*
           genes

Mark: each of his
cells has two *r* genes

Gametes   Each egg cell contains
           only one *R* gene

Each sperm contains
only one *r* gene

Fertilisation

Zygote   This contains one
           R and one *r* gene

Offspring Susan: her cells have
           one *R* and one *r* gene

Figure 10.14   Passing genes from parents to child

You can see that no matter how many children Janet and Mark have, every child will have the same genes to control tongue rolling. They will all have one *R* gene and one *r* gene in every normal cell.

Since nobody can only half roll their tongue, can these children roll their tongues or not? The answer is yes, they can. In this case the *R* gene takes control and allows the person to roll the tongue. The *r* gene seems to have no effect at all. This is what usually happens when different genes which control the same characteristic (different alleles) are mixed together.

The gene which takes control is known as the *dominant* gene. The other gene is called the *recessive*. This is why the gene for tongue rolling was given the capital letter R. It shows it is the dominant gene. Recessive genes are always given the smaller letter. Dominant genes always cover the effects of recessive genes.

Some genetics definitions

(a) *A cross.* This is a mating between a male and a female to produce offspring.

(b) *Alleles.* These are genes that control the same characteristic.

(c) *Pure-bred.* The two genes in a cell for any one characteristic are the same (the alleles are the same). Both Janet and John were pure-bred as far as tongue rolling was concerned.

(d) *Hybrid.* This describes an offspring with two different genes in a cell for any one characteristic (the alleles are different). Janet's and John's offspring were hybrid as far as tongue-rolling was concerned. In a hybrid, one gene is usually dominant and the other recessive.

(e) *Dominant.* A gene which always produces an effect. In a hybrid, the dominant gene will decide the characteristic of the organism. John was pure-bred dominant for tongue-rolling.

(f) *Recessive.* A gene which can have its effects hidden. In a hybrid, it has no influence over the characteristic. Its effects can be seen only in a pure-bred individual. Janet was pure-bred recessive for tongue-rolling. She could not roll her tongue.

(g) *Genotype.* What genes an organism has. For instance, a tongue-roller may have the genotype RR or Rr.

(h) *Phenotype.* The appearance of an organism. For instance, for tongue-rolling the phenotype is either able to roll the tongue or not able to roll it. The genotypes RR and Rr produce the same phenotype.

Most living organisms have thousands of different genes, and it is unlikely that an organism will be pure-bred or hybrid for them all. Most organisms are pure-bred for some and hybrid for others.

A hybrid cross

What happens if two people who are hybrid for tongue-rolling have children? Will the children be able to roll their tongues or not?

Both parents have the genes R and r in their cells. Reproductive cells will divide by meiosis to produce gametes. Each gamete will have R or r in it. Because of meiosis, half the gametes will have R and the other half will have r. (See Figure 10.15 (opposite).)

When it comes to fertilisation, there is no way of predicting which sperm will fertilise the egg cell. Both the R sperm and the r sperm have an equal chance of getting to the egg cell first. Similarly, there is no way of telling

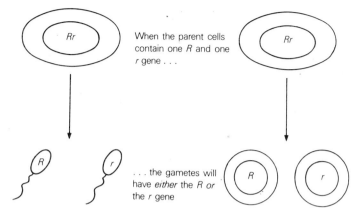

Figure 10.15   Random distribution of genes

whether the egg cell will contain *R* or *r*. Because of this, it is much more difficult to predict what sort of offspring will be produced.

There are two possible sorts of sperm and egg. They can fertilise in four different ways to produce four offspring. Each of the four fertilisations has the same chance of happening (Figure 10.16).

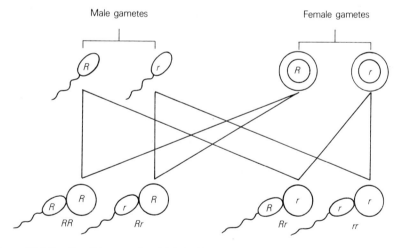

Figure 10.16   Possible ways in which fertilisation could happen

Of the four different offspring one will be *RR,* two will be *Rr* and one *rr.* Since both *RR* and *Rr* produce the ability to roll the tongue then there is a 3 to 1 chance that any children of a hybrid cross like this could roll his or her tongue. This is the same as saying that if there were four children born to *Rr* parents, three would probably be able to roll their tongue and one would not be able to.

Experiment 10.1

Making a model to investigate a hybrid cross

1. Take two beakers each containing 15 red and 15 blue beads (you may choose different colours). The red beads represent gametes containing the gene *R* for tongue rolling. The blue beads represent the gametes containing the genes *r* for non-rolling. Each beaker represents the gametes of one hybrid parent.

2. Close your eyes and take out one bead from each beaker. Put the beads together. This represents the random fertilisation of two gametes.

3. Record the results in a table like the one below. Put a tick in the box under the sort of offspring you obtained.

4. Repeat this until all the beads are used up.

5. Add up the total offspring in the separate groups *RR, Rr, rr,* by adding the ticks.

Type of offspring	RR	Rr	rr
Number of offspring produced			
Total			

6. Did you find a 3:1 ratio of tongue rollers to non-rollers?

7. Add up all the class results. Do these give a 3:1 ratio?

Other examples

So far we have looked only at the genes for tongue rolling, but we could have chosen many other examples. Exactly the same rules would apply. We have used sperm and eggs as the gametes, but the same results would have occurred if we had used pollen and ovules. The rules of genetics apply to all organisms which reproduce sexually.

Other examples we could have used include:

(a) *Tallness and dwarfness in pea plants.* Some of the very first genetics experiments were done on pea plants by a monk called Gregor Mendel. He found that the gene for tallness (T) was dominant over the gene for dwarfness (t). (See Figure 10.17.)

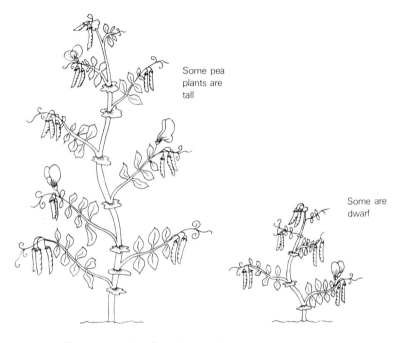

Some pea plants are tall

Some are dwarf

Figure 10.17   Tallness and dwarfness in pea plants

(b) *Smooth and wrinkled peas.* The gene for smoothness (S) is dominant over the gene for wrinkledness (s). (See Figure 10.18.)

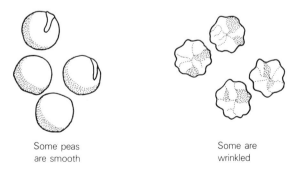

Some peas are smooth

Some are wrinkled

Figure 10.18   Smoothness and wrinkledness in peas

(c) *Complete wings and small or vestigial wings in the fruit fly.* This tiny animal has been used for many years for genetics experiments. It is small and reproduces in only a few weeks. Complete wings are dominant over vestigial ones. (See Figure 10.19.)

Other examples, like eye colour in humans, are controlled not by one pair of genes but by several. As you can imagine, it becomes more difficult to understand and follow when more genes are involved.

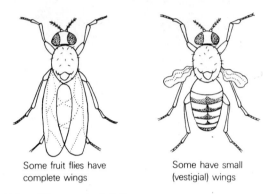

Some fruit flies have complete wings

Some have small (vestigial) wings

Figure 10.19   Wing differences in fruit flies

Chromosomes and sex

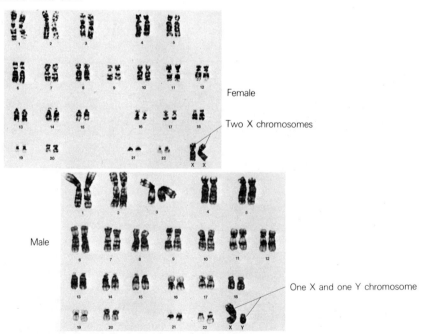

Female

Two X chromosomes

Male

One X and one Y chromosome

Figure 10.20   The chromosomes in a boy and a girl

Whether you are a boy or a girl is controlled by a pair of chromosomes. As you can see in Figure 10.20, a girl has two X chromosomes and a boy has one X and a much smaller Y chromosome.

All the egg cells produced by a female will have one X chromosome. In males, however, half the sperm will have an X and half will have a Y. This means that if fertilisation is random half the babies born will be boys and half girls. (See Figure 10.21.)

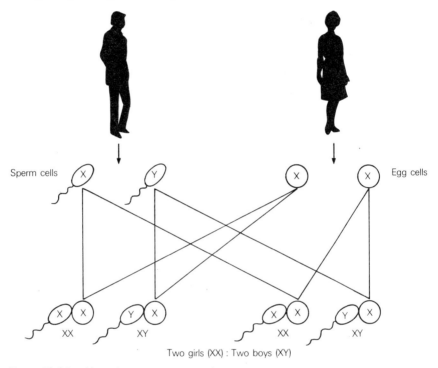

Figure 10.21   How chromosomes control sex

10.5 Why study genetics?

The study of genetics is important for a number of reasons. For example, it has helped enormously in agriculture. By understanding a little genetics it has been possible to breed better plants and animals. Modern wheat and barley both produce much more corn than earlier varieties. Because farmers no longer use horses, straw is not so useful. It has been possible to breed shorter plants which means there is less straw to get rid of. Modern cattle produce much more milk than cattle used to. Our chickens put on weight more quickly, and our pigs produce less fat for leaner meat. Genetics and careful breeding have achieved this.

The study of genetics has allowed scientists to produce crops which will resist disease. They have been able to interbreed crops to produce varieties which will grow better and produce more food.

Recently it has even become possible to move genes from one bacterium to another. The new strains this has created have been successful in producing substances such as drugs for medicine. This is called *genetic engineering*. It is likely that this will become more and more important in the future.

There is also a branch of genetics called *genetic counselling*. Some human diseases are caused by genes. Haemophilia, the condition where a person's blood will not clot, is one of them. Couples where one or both partners have a family history of certain diseases like this can get advice on how likely they are to pass them on to their children. (They may decide to adopt children rather than have any of their own.)

Summary

1. A gene is a small piece of DNA. A chromosome is made up of hundreds of genes.

2. A gene contains enough information to allow the cell to make (or not make) one protein, usually an enzyme. This allows one chemical reaction to take place in a cell. The gene is said to control one characteristic of the organism.

3. In normal cells, there are two genes for each characteristic. In gametes, there is only one gene for each characteristic.

4. Genes are usually dominant or recessive.

5. An organism can be pure-bred for one characteristic if both genes are the same. If the two genes are different, the organism is said to be hybrid for that characteristic.

6. In a hybrid, the dominant gene controls the characteristic. The recessive gene plays no part at all.

7. If an organism which is pure-bred dominant for a characteristic is crossed with one which is pure-bred recessive, all the offspring will be hybrid for that characteristic.

8. If two hybrid organisms are crossed, there is always a 3 to 1 chance that the offspring will show the dominant characteristic.

9. In humans, sex is controlled by two chromosomes. A person with two X chromosomes (XX) will be female. Someone with one X and one Y will be male.

Questions on Chapter 10

1. What is the difference between asexual and sexual reproduction?

2. Copy out the following and fill in the blanks.
    There are many types of asexual reproduction. Microbes simply _____
    into _____ and become two new organisms. The strawberry plant
    produces _____ . These are _____ which grow away from the
    parent plant and develop _____ and _____ to become whole
    new plants. Daffodils reproduce asexually by _____ . These remain in
    the _____ over the winter and produce new plants the following year.

3. Use this list of words in a paragraph which explains what the words mean:
    male gamete, female gamete, fertilisation, zygote, embryo, organism.

4. A reproductive cell of an animal is about to undergo meiosis. Its chromo-
    somes are shown in Figure 10.22. Draw the gamete cells to show the
    chromosomes they would have.

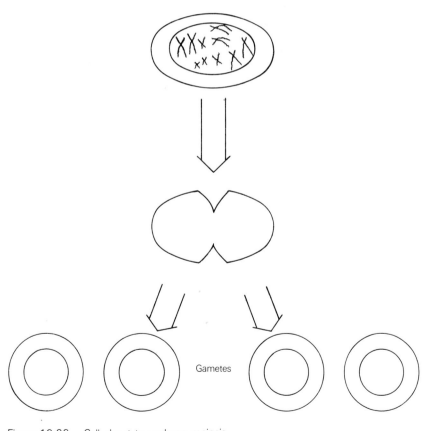

Figure 10.22   Cell about to undergo meiosis

5. If an animal has 30 chromosomes in its normal body cells, how many would it have in its gametes? How many chromosomes would a zygote of this animal have?

6. What is a gene? What does a gene do?

The next few questions involve doing genetics crosses. To make them easier, there is a standard way of working through these questions. Two examples are given. The first is a cross between a pure-bred tongue roller (*RR*) and a pure-bred non-roller (*rr*). The second is between two hybrid tongue rollers (*Rr* and *Rr*). In your answers you will use different genes but you should follow the same system.

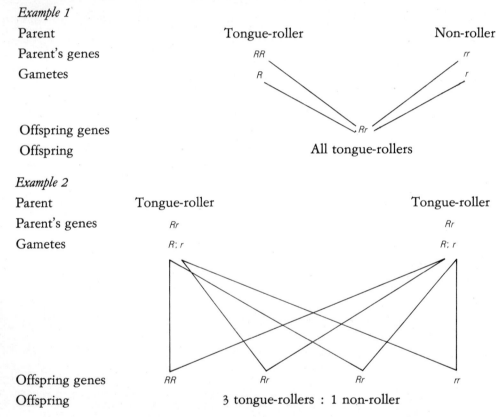

Example 1

Parent   Tongue-roller   Non-roller

Parent's genes   *RR*   *rr*

Gametes   *R*   *r*

Offspring genes   *Rr*

Offspring   All tongue-rollers

Example 2

Parent   Tongue-roller   Tongue-roller

Parent's genes   *Rr*   *Rr*

Gametes   *R; r*   *R; r*

Offspring genes   *RR*   *Rr*   *Rr*   *rr*

Offspring   3 tongue-rollers : 1 non-roller

7. (a) In mice, black coat (*B*) is dominant over brown coat (*b*). What genes will a pure-bred black mouse have and what genes will a pure-bred brown mouse have?
    What would be the colour of the offspring if these two mice were mated?

    (b) What colour would the offspring be if one parent was pure-bred black and the other hybrid black?

    (c) What colour would the offspring be if one parent was hybrid black and the other was pure-bred brown?

8. In pea plants, tallness (*T*) is dominant over dwarfness (*t*).
   (a) What genes would a pure-bred tall pea plant have?
   (b) What genes would a pure-bred dwarf pea plant have?
   (c) What genes would a hybrid tall pea plant have?
   (d) What would the offspring of two hybrid tall pea plants look like?

9. In pea plants smooth pea seeds (*S*) is dominant over wrinkled pea seeds (*s*). Two hybrid smooth peas were crossed and they produced between them 200 peas.
   How many of these would you expect to be smooth and how many wrinkled?

10. Two pea plants produced a hundred peas. Fifty of them were smooth and 50 were wrinkled. One of the parent plants had been grown from a smooth pea and the other from a wrinkled pea. What genes do you think each parent had?

11. A fruit fly with complete wings was crossed with one which has vestigial wings. All their offspring had complete wings. What would be the genotypes of each parent and of the offspring?
    If two of these offspring were crossed what sort of wings would the next generation of fruit flies have?

12. Five classes in a school were counted. The results were listed as numbers of boys and girls.

Class	Boys	Girls
1	10	19
2	14	16
3	16	9
4	11	13
5	17	11
Total		

(a) What was the overall ratio of boys to girls?
(b) A person's sex is controlled by two chromosomes.
What chromosomes would a girl have and what chromosomes would a boy have?
(c) What would you expect the ratio to be of boys to girls? Why would you expect this?

Crossword on Chapter 10

(Teacher, please see special note at front of book.)

Copy this grid, then solve the clues. Do not write on this page.

	Across		*Down*
1	A gene may be dominant or _____ (9)	2	A zygote is a special form of _____ (4)
8	A male has just one (1, 10)	3	A person's _____ is determined by a pair of chromosomes (3)
10	It may store food for a daffodil (4)	4	All of us will have _____ certain characteristics from our parents (9)
12	An important chemical in organisms (1, 1, 1)	5	The number of 8 across a female has (3)
14, 11 down	In a _____ - _____ organism, the two genes in a cell for any one characteristic are the same (4, 4)	6	A mating to produce an off-spring is called a _____ (5)
15	See 19 across	7	The number of 8 across a human egg cell has (3)
17	They control characteristics (5)	9	An experimenting monk (6)
18	A _____ is produced when the two genes in a cell for any characteristic are different (6)	11	See 14 across
19, 15 across	The total number of chromosomes in a human 2 down (5, 3)	13	Where eggs are produced (5)
		14	A plant well known to 9 down (3)
		16	The _____ type tells us what 17 across an organism has (4)

11. Similarities and differences — why they are important

11.1 Variation

If you look around you will see that all humans have one head, two arms, two legs and a body. Obviously all human beings are similar, but there are differences which make it easy to recognise one person from another. These small but important differences are called *variation*. It is variation that allows us to tell one individual from another of the same *species*.

A species is a group of organisms which can breed with each other. A member of one species cannot successfully breed with a member of another species because the differences are too great. For example, cats and dogs are different species and will not interbreed.

Variation, then, is the differences between members of the same species. There are two sorts of variation:

(a) *Discontinuous* variation.
(b) *Continuous* variation.

Discontinuous variation

This occurs when the differences fall into two or more easily recognisable groups. For example, a person either can or cannot roll their tongue. Thus, there are two separate groups, tongue-rollers and non-rollers. Pea plants produce either smooth seeds or wrinkled. Again, there are two separate groups.

In humans, blood groups fall into four types, A, B, AB and O. A person will have one of these blood groups. Human eye colour was thought to be an example of discontinuous variation. Generally people have one of four eye colours, brown, blue, grey or green.

However, if you look at enough eyes it becomes hard to decide when, for example, blue/grey becomes grey. The categories are not as distinct as you might imagine. Eye colour is probably an example of continuous variation.

Continuous variation

This occurs when there are no distinct groups of variation. There is a continuous spread from one end of the variation right through to the other. Trying Experiment 11.1 may help you to understand this.

Experiment 11.1

Investigating continuous variation

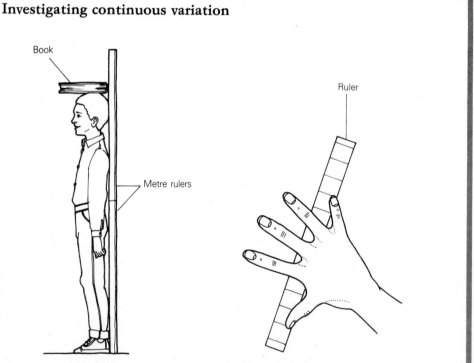

Figure 11.1   Apparatus to measure height and hand span

1. Fix two metre rulers to a convenient piece of open wall.

2. Stand upright with your heels against the wall. One member of the class will use a book on your head to measure your height. Remember that the book must be kept level (Figure 11.1).

3. Record all the class results on the blackboard.

4. Measure accurately the span of your right hand, as shown in Figure 11.1 (opposite).

5. Record the class results for hand span on the blackboard, too.

6. Copy the class results into your book.

7. Working entirely on your own, separate the results into groups. Fill in a results chart like the one below with the number of people in the class which you think should go into each group. Remember — it is up to you to decide where one group ends and another begins.

Height		Hand span	
Group	Number of people	Group	Number of people
Tall		Wide span	
Fairly tall			
Medium		Medium span	
Fairly short		Small span	
Short			

8. Now compare your results table with others in the class.

9. How did your results chart compare with others in the class?

10. Was it easy to decide the sizes for each group?

11. If you did this experiment again would you change the sizes for each group?

From this experiment you should be able to see that it is impossible to separate continuous variation into obvious groups.

Examples of continuous variation in humans include weight, height, hair colour and probably eye colour. There is continuous variation in plants too. In apple trees, for example, there is continuous variation in height, apple size and colour.

11.2 What causes variation?

Variation is caused by the genes an organism has and by the environment it lives in. Very often these two act together.

If two friends are brought up in similar environments and each is given as much food as they need, eventually they will reach their maximum heights. Quite likely one person will be taller than the other. This is due to his or her genes.

Since humans have millions of genes, we will all have different dominants and recessives. The different ways dominant and recessive genes can be combined leads to a great deal of genetic variation (Figure 11.2).

Figure 11.2   Genetic variation

Now suppose that one of the two friends was shipwrecked on a desert island with little food or water. This unfortunate person would gradually lose weight. The friend, meanwhile, might be living at home eating large quantities of food — and getting very fat by doing so. In this case it would be the environment and not the genes which caused the variation. With so many different sorts of environment in the world a lot of variation will be caused this way (Figure 11.3, opposite).

It is not easy to understand how genes and the environment influence each other. It is sometimes said that the children of criminals are likely to become criminals. This would be *either* because of their genes, or the way they were brought up. However, many children of criminals grow up into honest people. Similarly, the children of honest people sometimes grow up to be criminals. We do not know why this happens and we are unable to control it in any way. There is still much about genes and the environment that we do not understand.

Sometimes we can find out what causes a particular type of variation. Discontinuous variation is often caused by one or two genes only — the environment has little effect. For example, the environment plays no part in whether or not you can roll your tongue.

Figure 11.3   Variation due to the environment

Occasionally a new discontinuous variation appears quite suddenly in a group of organisms. There seems to be no cause for it. One organism just suddenly appears with one feature quite different from the other organisms. We call this a *mutation*.

Mutations   A mutation is caused when one or more genes change for some reason. There are different sorts of mutation. A gene may change slightly, which causes a different effect in the organism. A mutation like this causes *haemophilia* in humans. This is where the gene which controls blood clotting changes so that it no longer works. The blood does not clot or it clots very slowly. A person with haemophilia must be careful not to get cuts or bruises. Red/green colour blindness is also caused by a change in one gene.

Some mutations are caused when one or more genes get lost or where extra genes are added. This upsets the balance of the body and may produce drastic changes in the organism. The most extreme case of this is where a whole chromosome is lost or added. *Mongolism* or *Down's syndrome* is such a mutation (Figure 11.4). One extra chromosome causes the person to be mentally retarded and to have a typically 'Mongol' appearance.

Mutation can be inherited in the normal way. Harmful mutations may kill the organism or prevent it from reproducing. In this way the mutation becomes lost. Useful mutations, however, may be passed to offspring and may lead to an improved type of organism.

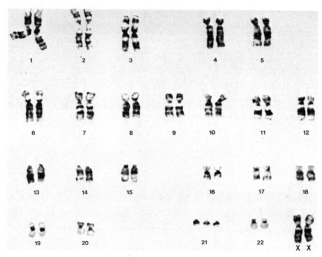

Figure 11.4   An extra number 21 chromosome causes Down's syndrome

What causes mutation?

Mutations are quite natural. They occur quite steadily but not very often in all groups of living organisms. Some mutations are useful, some are harmful, and some have no effect at all. In humans it has been estimated that you can find one mutated gene in every 40 000 gametes.

Mutations can be caused if the chromosomes or genes are damaged. Atomic radiation will do this. So too will X-rays and ultra-violet light. Remember, though, that these do not produce mutations which would not occur naturally. They simply speed up the number of mutations which occur.

It is because of the risk of mutations that people are concerned about atomic radiation. Small amounts of radiation may have no immediate effect on our bodies. However, they may produce mutations which will eventually lead to disease or to changes in our offspring. Effects like these have been seen in the people of Hiroshima in Japan who received radiation from an atomic bomb during the Second World War. However atomic radiation is caused we must be very careful whenever we use it.

11.3 How variation is useful

Variation leads to a whole range of differences among organisms; some of these are useful, and some are not. Some organisms may be better at surviving than others. Some variations may just be sufficiently different for the organisms to survive better in slightly different conditions. They may go on to live more easily and produce more offspring than others of their type.

Conditions change slightly. For example, the temperature may fall a little. This may be harmful to some organisms and may kill them. There are, however, almost always variations which will not die. They survive and so the species does not become extinct.

You may think that conditions do not seem to change much. The weather may have been much the same as far as you can remember. But animals and plants have been on Earth for millions of years. There have been ice ages and times of very high temperature. Today, some areas of the world suffer droughts which go on for years; others seem to have constant rain. The tilt of the Earth changes slowly all the time: probably this affects our climate.

Without variation, plants and animals would have died out long ago. In fact some species did. Dinosaurs could not survive the changes, but relatives of theirs, like crocodiles and alligators, did survive (Figure 11.5).

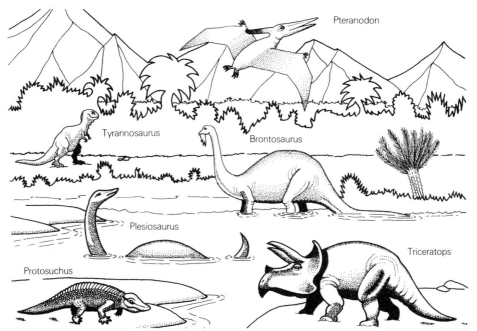

Figure 11.5   Dinosaurs died out but some of their relatives survived

Variation among organisms and changes in conditions have led to the vast range of plants and animals we see today. Each animal or plant is well suited to one particular way of living. For example: bluebells live in woodland; when the trees are in leaf there is not enough light for other plants to grow well. Bluebells, however, grow and flower before the trees come into leaf (Figure 11.6). In this way, they have survived. Later flowering variations will die because of lack of light.

Figure 11.6   Bluebells flower before the trees come into leaf

Owls feed on mice and voles, which move and feed mostly at night. Only owls which can see well at night, or have sharp hearing can catch enough prey to survive. Owls with good daylight vision may not survive. Kestrels, too, feed on mice and voles. They hunt during the day when small animals are not usually so active. Kestrels can hover and wait to catch some prey, but owls cannot. Both owls and kestrels are well suited to their different ways of life. (See Figure 11.7.)

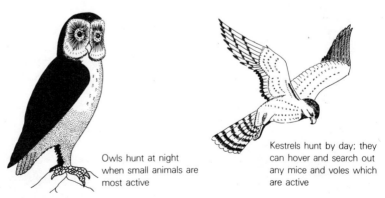

Owls hunt at night when small animals are most active

Kestrels hunt by day; they can hover and search out any mice and voles which are active

Figure 11.7   Hunting behaviour

Variation occurs and some varieties survive better. This leads to slight changes as some other types of variation begin to die out. Mutations occur which produce new variations. Sometimes these survive better and sometimes not. Slowly, as conditions change, so organisms change too. This process of constant change is called *evolution*. It has been happening for millions of years and is still happening today.

11.4 Evolution

Charles Darwin was the first man to describe evolution — in 1859. Before that time it was generally believed that God made the world exactly the way it is today. Many people still believe this to be true and it is not possible to prove that they are wrong. Darwin spent five years travelling around South America and the Pacific, where he studied many different organisms. He found that a particular organism in one area was sometimes very similar to one in another area. He thought that this could have happened only if both came from the same ancestor.

Although many organisms were similar, they did show differences. Darwin thought that the organisms must have changed slightly to suit the conditions in the different areas. 'Changing to suit the conditions' is what we call *evolution*.

How does evolution happen?

Darwin thought that the process of evolution happened like this:

(a) A group of organisms reproduce. They produce many more offspring than could possibly survive. There is not enough food or shelter or light or groundspace for them all. The offspring all show variation.

(b) Depending on conditions, some offspring survive better than others. The others are killed or die off. Those that do not die reproduce and pass their genes to their offspring.

(c) The second generation tend to show the variation that their parents had. Some show other variations. Once again, only some survive and reproduce — only those that are best able to do so.

(d) Gradually, over many generations, all the organisms tend to resemble one type of variation. The less successful variations become rarer and rarer. They never quite die out but the population as a whole tends to be one sort. Only if conditions change will the process start to happen again, because variation is occurring all the time. Darwin thought that in this way all the different organisms in the world gradually evolved. The process took millions and millions of years. Darwin called his idea the 'survival of the fittest'. By 'fittest' he meant those best suited to their environment and so best able to survive (Figure 11.8).

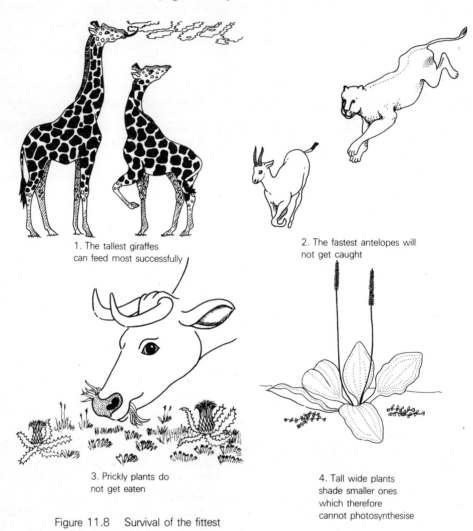

1. The tallest giraffes can feed most successfully

2. The fastest antelopes will not get caught

3. Prickly plants do not get eaten

4. Tall wide plants shade smaller ones which therefore cannot photosynthesise

Figure 11.8   Survival of the fittest

11.5 How do we know evolution has happened?

One way of showing that evolution may have happened is to look for traces of plants and animals which have died out. Very often these traces can be found as fossils in rocks. Plants and animals died and became covered with mud. Gradually the mud hardened to rock, with the plant or animal inside.

Eventually the organism decayed to nothing, leaving its imprint in the rock. This imprint is a fossil. You can see how one is formed in Figure 11.9.

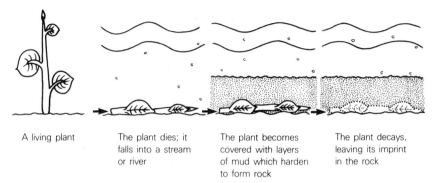

| A living plant | The plant dies; it falls into a stream or river | The plant becomes covered with layers of mud which harden to form rock | The plant decays, leaving its imprint in the rock |

Figure 11.9   How a plant fossil is formed

Sometimes skeletons or parts of skeletons may be found. These may be from animals which no longer exist. It may be possible to show that the skeleton belonged to a creature which was part-way between two modern animals. This may show that the two animals had a common ancestor. For instance, Darwin thought that humans had the same ancestor as the apes. Ancient human skulls have been found all over the world, and some examples are shown in Figure 11.10. These have been shown to be human and yet they are not like ours. In some ways they are like the skull of an ape.

Figure 11.10   Some ancient human skulls

So far, no one has yet found a skull which proves beyond doubt that humans and apes had the same ancestor. What the skulls do show is that humans have changed over millions of years. This shows that evolution has happened to some extent.

A modern example of evolution

The peppered moth (*Biston betularia*) has been widely studied in the United Kingdom as an example of evolution. The colour of the moth varies from being quite light with dark speckles to dark all over. The two extremes of colour are known as the light and dark forms (Figure 11.11).

Figure 11.11   The two forms of the peppered moth against a light lichen covered background

In woodland the light form is well camouflaged against the bark of trees when it comes to rest. The dark form, however, is highly visible. Birds feeding on the insects are therefore more likely to eat the dark form than the light. Under normal circumstances, then, the dark form was very rare.

It was found, though, that in grimy, smoky, industrial towns the dark form of peppered moth became common. With trees and buildings covered in dark staining, the light form of moth became more visible than the dark one. Thus, by around 1900, it was almost impossible to find a light peppered moth in cities. However, in the last thirty years our cities have been cleaned considerably. We no longer burn as much coal as we used to and there is less smoke to stain trees and buildings. The dark form of moth is becoming rarer again because it is no longer so well camouflaged. By changing colour over many generations, the population of moths has adapted to the environment. This is an example of evolution.

11.6 Natural and artificial selection

When one type of variation makes an organism better able to survive then we say that this variation is being *selected*. Normally, nature selects the varieties which are best suited to conditions because all the other variations die off. This is *natural selection*. In the peppered moth example birds do the selecting by eating the moths which are not camouflaged.

We can, however, choose to breed certain animals or plants. We may wish to breed plants which produce good crops, or flowers of a certain colour. We may want animals which give good meat, milk or wool. Whatever the purpose, we select the organisms we want. Those with qualities which are not wanted are prevented from breeding.

This process is called *artificial selection,* and we have been doing it for many centuries. It has led to the different varieties of dogs which we now have. It has also produced the huge range of roses which grow in our gardens. It has allowed farmers to produce more food by using better crops and livestock. Artificial selection has played an important part in the development of agriculture. It will continue to be important in the field of biotechnology. Here, microbes are being bred for industrial processes, such as the manufacture of drugs. Scientists have even succeeded in breeding a strain of bacteria which can make plastic. Some examples of controlled breeding are shown in Figure 11.12.

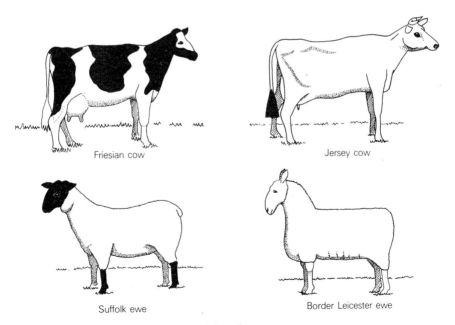

Friesian cow

Jersey cow

Suffolk ewe

Border Leicester ewe

Figure 11.12   Selection by controlled breeding

Summary

1. Variation is the differences between members of the same species of organism.

2. Discontinuous variation occurs when the differences between organisms can be easily separated into quite distinct groups.

3. Continuous variation occurs where there are no easily separated groups of differences. The organisms vary in a continuous spread from one variation to the other.

4. Variation is caused by genes, or the environment, or a combination of both of these.

5. A mutation is a sudden change in an organism. It is caused by a sudden change in the genes or chromosomes.

6. Mutations occur naturally all the time. They can be made to happen more quickly by X-rays, atomic radiation, ultra-violet light and some chemicals.

7. Variation leads to differences which may mean one variation survives better than the others. If this leads to a change in the type of organism, it is called *evolution*.

8. Darwin said that evolution happens by natural selection — that is, nature selects those which will survive. The others are either killed or they die.

9. We can select the organisms we want to breed. This is called artificial selection. We can use this to breed more useful or more attractive animals and plants.

Questions on Chapter 11

1. Which of the following differences are examples of variation?
    (a) Different feather colours in budgerigars.
    (b) The different beak shapes of a sparrow and a kestrel.
    (c) The different types of coat of an alsatian and a poodle.
    (d) The differences in colour between a goldfish and a herring.
    (e) The differences in wing structure between birds and bats.

2. Which of the following are examples of continuous variation and which are examples of discontinuous variation?
    (a) Hair colour in humans.
    (b) Colour blindness in humans.
    (c) Albinism in rabbits.
    (d) Body weight in rabbits.
    (e) Running speed in greyhounds.

3. Which is the more important influence on the way you work — your genes or your environment? Give one or two examples to support your view.

4. Copy out the following and fill in the blanks.
    A mutation is a _____ change in the _____ or _____.
    Some examples of mutation in humans include _____ , where the blood does not clot very well and _____ syndrome or _____ .
    This second example is caused by having one too many _____ . Mutations do occur naturally but they can be speeded up by _____ and
    _____ .

5. Charles Darwin said that evolution happened by the process of survival of the fittest.
    What does 'the fittest' mean?
    How could their survival lead to evolution?

6. A and B in Figure 11.13 are two modern plants. You believe that they evolved from the same ancestor. Draw a simple sketch of the fossil that you would like to find to help you prove this.

A

B

Figure 11.13   Do they have a common ancestor?

7. What is the difference between natural selection and artificial selection? Give three examples of artificial selection.

Wordfinder on Chapter 11

(Teacher, please see special note in front of book.)

Copy or photocopy this wordfinder. Do not write on this page. You know how to solve wordfinder puzzles by now. This time the letters left over spell out a very famous book and its author. What was the book about?

A	O	N	T	L	O	G	N	O	M	H	E	C
O	R	S	E	I	C	E	P	S	U	R	I	O
E	G	T	I	E	V	O	L	U	T	I	O	N
V	A	R	I	A	T	I	O	N	A	D	N	T
I	O	F	S	F	P	E	C	H	T	O	M	I
V	I	E	S	C	I	H	A	R	I	W	L	N
R	E	S	E	L	E	C	T	I	O	N	S	U
U	D	T	S	E	T	T	I	F	N	S	A	O
S	Y	N	D	R	O	M	E	A	R	W	I	U
N	H	A	E	M	O	P	H	I	L	I	A	S

1   Someone with _____ must try to avoid cuts and bruises (11)

2   A _____ is caused when one or more genes change (8)

3, 4   This 2 produces a mentally retarded person (5, 8: 2 words in different places)

5   ... who has a _____ appearance (6)

6   The differences between one person and another are examples of _____ (9)

7   The difference in height between people is an example of _____ 6 (10)

8   All cats belong to the same _____ (7)

9   The process by which a particular 8 changes (9)

10   A famous 19th century biologist put forward the idea that only the _____ (7) ...

11   ... would be able to _____ (7)

12, 13   Horse breeders would use _____ _____ to produce fast runners (10, 9: 2 words in different places)

14   The peppered _____ is an example of 9 that we can study (4)

Section 3

HOW ORGANISMS LIVE TOGETHER IN THE ENVIRONMENT

12. Relationships among organisms

12.1 Sharing the environment

No organism lives alone. Plants and animals live together and react with each other in many different ways. Perhaps the most obvious form of reaction is feeding. Some animals feed on other animals. Some plants get food from dead animals and plants.

Feeding is not the only way plants and animals react together. Some plants provide shelter for animals. Some animals help plants reproduce. Animals often disperse plant seeds. Animals trample plants. They also produce waste products which are useful to microbes and then to plants. (See Figure 12.1.)

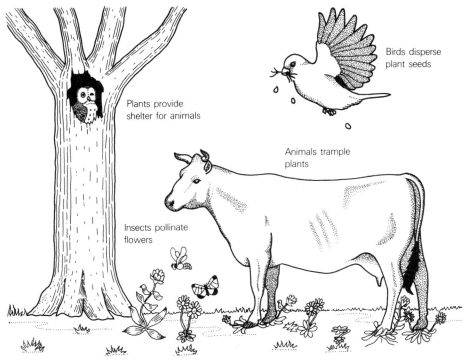

Birds disperse
plant seeds

Plants provide
shelter for animals

Animals trample
plants

Insects pollinate
flowers

Figure 12.1   Sharing the environment

There are always too many organisms for them all to survive. This means that they must *compete* with each other. Plants often compete with each other for groundspace. Seeds which germinate early, or seedlings which grow tall, will get most light. Other plants may then not be able to get enough light to survive (Figure 12.2).

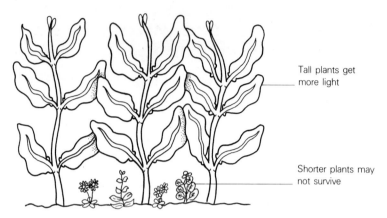

Tall plants get more light

Shorter plants may not survive

Figure 12.2   Survival in plants

Several animals may feed off the same type of plant. Only the animals which can find enough plants to eat will survive. If there is not enough food to go around, then some animals will die.

Competition happens when there is not enough of any resource to supply all the organisms wanting it. Organisms compete with others of the same type and with others of different types. Competition leads to survival of the fittest.

Plants may compete for:
   (a) light.
   (b) water.
   (c) space.
   (d) insects (for pollination).

Animals might compete for:
   (a) food.
   (b) water.
   (c) shelter.
   (d) mates.
   (e) territory.

Experiment 12.1

Experiment to observe competition

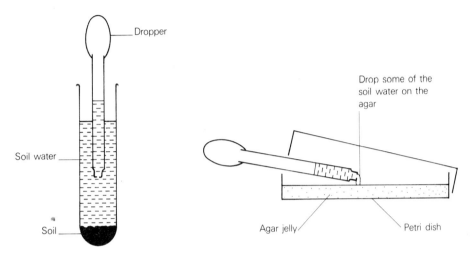

Dropper

Drop some of the
soil water on the
agar

Soil water

Soil

Agar jelly

Petri dish

Figure 12.3   Apparatus investigating growth of soil microbes

1. Obtain or pour an agar plate.

2. Put a few spatulas of soil in a test-tube. Shake the soil up with a few cubic centimetres of water.

3. Use a dropper to add a few drops of the soil water to the agar in the Petri dish (Figure 12.3).

4. Swish the dish so the water runs over the surface of the agar. Do not add so much water that the agar becomes flooded. The water will transfer microbes from the soil to the agar.

5. Tape the lid on to the Petri dish. Write your initials on one side of the lid. Incubate at 25 °C for a few days.

6. Observe the microbe colonies which have grown. Make an accurate sketch of the size and position of each colony. You may find it helpful to draw a cross on the lid. This, plus your initials, will help fix the position of each colony. Do not remove the Petri dish lid.

7. Return the dish to the incubator for a few more days.

8. Repeat step 6 again. Are there any changes in the size and position of the colonies?

9. Leave the dish in the incubator for a few days further and then repeat step 6 again.

10. When you compare your drawings of the microbe colonies, is there any evidence of competition?

11. What happened when two different colonies grew together?

12. What might the microbes have been competing for?

Ecology   As you can imagine, the relationships between organisms can become very complex. When dozens of different organisms all live in the same area they react with one another in many ways. The study of the way organisms react in a community is called *ecology*. You can get some idea of what ecology is like in the following experiment.

Experiment 12.2

An ecological investigation

1. Select a small area of plants. A hedgerow or piece of waste ground are very useful for this. Your area should not be more than 2 m long if it is a piece of hedge, or 2 m^2 if it is a piece of ground.

2. Identify as many plants and animals as you can. This is not always easy, so do not try to identify every organism precisely. It is often good enough to identify the type of organism. Do not pick the flowers or you will start to change the ecology of your area.

3. Many of your animals will be insects, so you might need to catch them and take them back to the lab for identification. You can use a pooter like the one in Figure 12.4 (opposite). Suck the correct pipe and the animal will be drawn into the test-tube. Once you have caught a few animals, do not suck the wrong pipe. In the lab tip the animals into a Petri dish. With the lid on you can observe them more easily and they will not escape. Remember to put them back when you have finished.

4. Draw up a list of what organisms are in your area.

5. Now try to explain why those organisms were there. This is not easy, but you should be able to make some suggestions. What do you know about what the animals feed on? Do the plants give each other shelter, or do they shelter the animals? Are some plants fast growers? Do they produce lots of seeds so that each year they have more chance of growing?

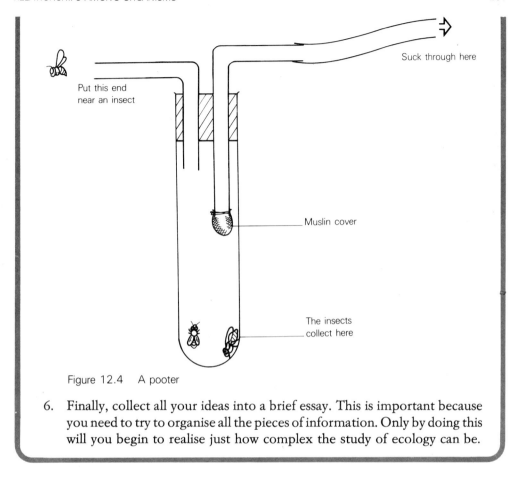

Figure 12.4   A pooter

6. Finally, collect all your ideas into a brief essay. This is important because you need to try to organise all the pieces of information. Only by doing this will you begin to realise just how complex the study of ecology can be.

12.2 Feeding relationships among organisms

A plant may be eaten by an animal. This in turn may be eaten by another animal. Such a feeding relationship is known as a *food chain* (Figure 12.5 (overleaf)).

Green plants produce food by photosynthesis, so they are called *producers*. Animals which eat those plants are called consumers. In fact, they are called the first or *primary consumers*. The next animals in the chain are called the *secondary consumers*, and so on.

A feeding relationship like a food chain is sometimes written out in this way:

Plants ⟶ Insects ⟶ Birds ⟶ Buzzard

The arrows show that each organism is feeding on the previous one.

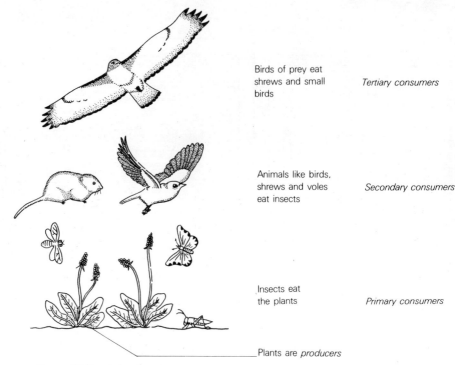

Birds of prey eat
shrews and small   *Tertiary consumers*
birds

Animals like birds,
shrews and voles   *Secondary consumers*
eat insects

Insects eat
the plants   *Primary consumers*

Plants are *producers*

Figure 12.5   A food chain

Food chains of three or four organisms are quite easy to find but only rarely
can you find one with more organisms. This is because of the numbers of
organisms each animal needs to feed on. In our example, the insects will
have to visit many plants to get enough nectar. The bird will have to catch
many insects to stay alive. If the buzzard fed only on birds, it would have to
catch at least one per day. There would only be enough birds to feed a
few buzzards in any one area. There would not be enough buzzards for
some other animal to survive by eating them. This relationship is often
drawn as a *pyramid of numbers*. An example is shown in Figure 12.6.

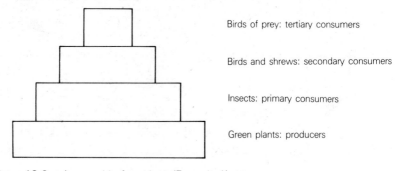

Birds of prey: tertiary consumers

Birds and shrews: secondary consumers

Insects: primary consumers

Green plants: producers

Figure 12.6   A pyramid of numbers (Example 1)

The size of each box is an approximate guide to the number of organisms which are needed if the organism above is to survive.

Not all pyramids of numbers are pyramid-shaped. Figure 12.7 shows the pyramid for the food chain

Rose bush ⟶ Aphids ⟶ Ladybirds

You can see part of the food chain in Figure 12.8.

Of course, hundreds of aphids can feed on one rose bush and several ladybirds can feed on them.

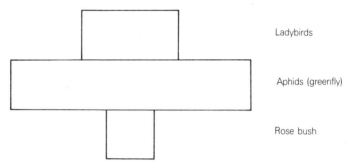

Ladybirds

Aphids (greenfly)

Rose bush

Figure 12.7   A pyramid of numbers (Example 2)

Figure 12.8   A ladybird eating an aphid — one stage in a food chain

Food chains are simple to follow. However, as you can imagine, nature is not usually so simple. Most animals have several sources of food, and some eat both plants and animals. This builds into more complex feeding relationships which can be drawn out as a food web (Figure 12.9).

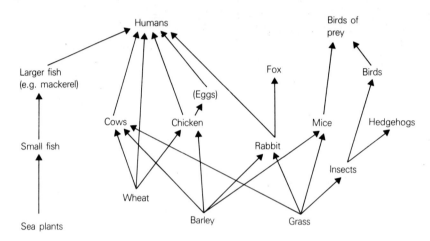

Figure 12.9   A simplified food web

Energy flow

A food chain or web is an example of how energy flows from one organism to another. The Sun's energy is trapped by plants in photosynthesis. Plants use the Sun's light to build chemicals like starch which act as an energy store. Animals which eat plants can release that energy by digestion and respiration. Some of the energy will be used by the animal for activities like movement. Some energy however, will be used to build chemicals like fats and protein.

When another animal eats the first one, the process is repeated. Some energy is used and some is stored. Eventually, all the original energy is used. It is lost either as heat or in movement in animals and cannot be recaptured. The energy system relies on a constant energy input from the Sun and on plants being able to trap it.

Summary

1. Living organisms share the environment.

2. There are too many organisms to survive so all compete with one another for resources.

3. Competition leads to survival of the fittest. The organisms which survive are well adapted. Those which are not so well adapted are more likely to die out.

4. Ecology is the study of the way organisms live together.

5. A food chain is a simple feeding relationship where one organism feeds on the previous one.

6   Green plants are called producers. Animals which feed on them are called primary consumers. Animals which feed on animals are called secondary consumers or tertiary consumers.

7. A food web shows a more complex feeding relationship.

8. There is an energy flow between organisms. The Sun supplies the energy. Plants and then animals use it, and it is eventually lost.

12.3 Parasites and saprophytes

A parasite is an organism which feeds on another organism while it is still alive. The food organism is called the *host*. Parasites often harm their host but do not usually kill it. If they did, they would, of course, probably kill themselves too. There are many different sorts of parasite:

(a) *Plant parasites with plant hosts* — e.g. mistletoe and some fungi. Fungi parasites cause rust diseases of cereal crops such as wheat, and scab diseases on fruit such as apples. They get all their food by growing into the host and digesting it or its food supply. The diseases get their names because infected wheat turns a rusty colour and infected apples grow brown scabs on their surface. The rusty substance and the scab are both ways in which the parasite can reproduce. These produce spores which are blown away to infect other plants. A spore is a tiny cell with a very tough outer coat. It can be carried over long distances without being damaged. If a spore lands on a surface which is moist and supplies the correct food, it will germinate.

The outer coat splits and the cell starts to grow. It multiplies and grows until it becomes a new complete organism.

Mistletoe is only a part-parasite. It is unusual because it has leaves with chlorophyll, and can make some of its own food. It takes water and minerals from its host by growing into the xylem. (See Figure 12.10.)

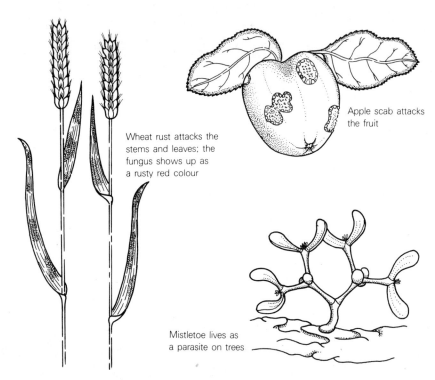

Wheat rust attacks the stems and leaves; the fungus shows up as a rusty red colour

Apple scab attacks the fruit

Mistletoe lives as a parasite on trees

Figure 12.10   Plant parasites

(b) *Plant parasites on animals* — e.g. the fungus which causes ringworm and athlete's foot in humans. Aquarium fish, too, often suffer from fungus parasite diseases. The fungus grows into the skin of the host and takes food from it. The part of the fungus which can be seen on the surface is again the reproductive part. This produces spores which are released to infect other hosts. Diseases like ringworm and athlete's foot are easily spread. Anyone suffering with them must take great care not to allow spores to get from their body to other people.

(c) *Animal parasites on plants.* These are not called parasites but are known as plant pests. There are many thousands of them and some do a great deal of damage to crops. A common example is greenfly (aphids). These are small insects which have tube-like mouthparts. They pierce the stem of plants and suck out the plant juices from the phloem. Aphids can often be found on roses where they may be a nuisance (Figure 12.11). They are, however, more economically important when they attack crops like beans, apples and cereals.

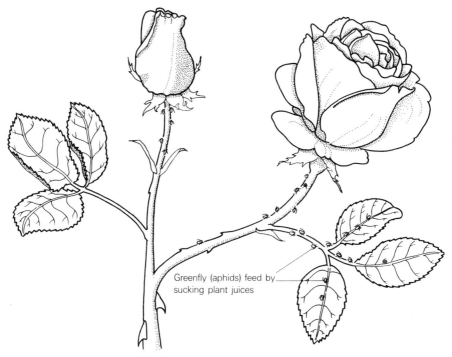

Greenfly (aphids) feed by sucking plant juices

Figure 12.11   Greenfly on roses

(d) *Animal parasites on animals.* There are two sorts of animal parasites. *Ectoparasites* live on the outside of the host. They may not always stay on the host but may move from one host to another. Examples of these include fleas, mosquitoes and head lice. Ectoparasites generally suck blood, although some feed on the skin itself. *Endoparasites* spend a large part of their lives inside the host and pass from one host to another by eggs or larvae. Many live in the gut of the host, although some live in the blood and others in the lungs or liver. Examples of ectoparasites include tapeworms, pinworms, the malaria parasite and *Entaomoeba* (which causes one type of dysentery).

The flea — an ectoparasite

Figure 12.12 shows an adult flea. Fleas suck blood. Their shape lets them move easily through the fur of an animal and they can jump from one host to another. Fleas lay their eggs in dry, dusty corners. The eggs hatch into larvae which are not parasites, but feed on any scraps of food they can find. Fleas like warmth, which is why they thrive in centrally heated homes. The larvae will quite happily live in corners of rooms, hidden in the deep pile of a carpet. A larva grows into a pupa, which is a resting stage between larva and adult. The pupa can survive for a long time. When it is disturbed by a passing animal the adult will quickly emerge, jump on the host and start to feed. The complete life cycle of the flea is illustrated in Figure 12.13.

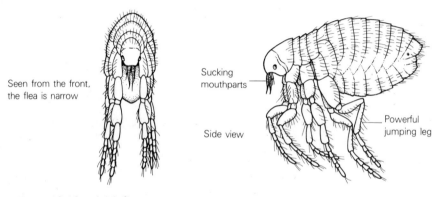

Seen from the front, the flea is narrow

Sucking mouthparts

Side view

Powerful jumping leg

Figure 12.12   Adult flea

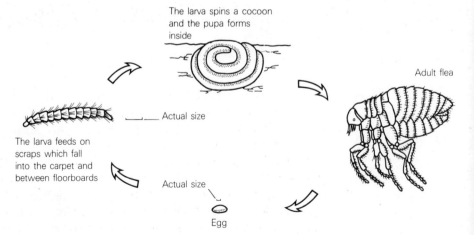

The larva spins a cocoon and the pupa forms inside

Actual size

Adult flea

The larva feeds on scraps which fall into the carpet and between floorboards

Actual size

Egg

Figure 12.13   Life cycle of the flea

Ectoparasites and disease

Ectoparasites themselves may not seriously damage the host. However, they do make the host itch. Scratching scrapes the skin and microbes can then infect the open wound, causing much more harm than the ectoparasite itself. Ectoparasites will often transfer other parasites or microbes which cause disease from one host to another. The flea can carry the virus (a type of microbe) which causes bubonic plague. This disease killed thousands of people as it swept across Europe several times during the Middle Ages. The fleas lived on rats but easily transferred from rats to people. Living conditions were unclean and crowded. The virus was sucked up with the blood of an infected person or rat and injected into the next host.

One of the most widespread diseases in the world today is malaria. It is caused by a tiny parasite which lives in the blood. The parasite attacks and destroys red blood cells and also liver cells. This causes the infected organism to develop a severe fever. The parasite is carried from one host to another by mosquitoes. Like the plague virus the malaria parasite is sucked up with a blood meal. It spends a little time in the mosquito (where it develops from one form to another) and is then injected into a new host. The mosquito's saliva contains chemicals to stop the host's blood from clotting. The mosquito has to inject saliva into the host before it can suck blood. The malaria parasite is injected into the new host with the saliva. (See Figure 12.14.)

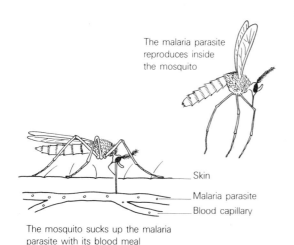

The malaria parasite reproduces inside the mosquito

Skin

Malaria parasite

Blood capillary

The mosquito sucks up the malaria parasite with its blood meal

The next time the mosquito feeds, it injects the malaria parasites into another host

Figure 12.14   The spread of malaria

Malaria occurs in wild animals as well as in humans. It is not possible to get rid of the malaria parasite because there are always wild animals which carry it. The best way to combat the disease has been to kill the mosquitoes. There are several ways of trying to do this, but one of the most successful ways in practice has been to attack the larvae. These live in water and hang just below the surface, breathing through special tubes (Figure 12.15). If the water surface is covered with a thin layer of oil the larvae cannot hang there. They sink and drown. Even though this is an easy way of attacking the larvae, killing *all* of them is not easy — because there are so many remote areas of water which cannot be treated. Scientists are therefore constantly looking for more effective ways of killing mosquitoes.

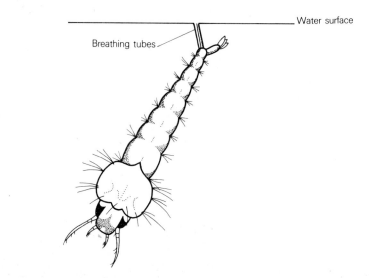

Figure 12.15   Mosquito larvae

The pinworm — an endoparasite

It has been said that almost every child suffers from pinworms at some stage. Happily, they are not very harmful. The pinworm is one of the nematode worms, but it is not at all related to the earthworm. Pinworms live in the gut of the host, feeding on the host's food. Two pinworms mate, and the female produces eggs. These are not laid straight away. It seems that the female can wait until night-time to lay them. This is possibly due to extra warmth when the human host is in bed. The female moves down the gut through the anus and lays her eggs on the skin just outside. The eggs are sticky and stick easily to the skin. The female then goes back through the anus into the gut. Sometimes she does not make it and as she dries out she explodes. This scatters sticky eggs all around the skin and, of course, on to pyjamas or bed-clothes. (See Figure 12.16.)

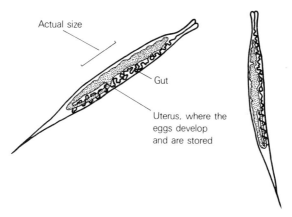

Figure 12.16   Female pinworms

The eggs find their way into a new host by being eaten. The eggs are very light and are easily blown around the house. Sometimes the movement of females causes itching. The host may scratch and collect eggs under the fingernails. In this way they get back into the host's mouth.

Many nematode parasites like the pinworm do not cause much harm to their host. However, very large infections can do damage and this sometimes happens in sheep and pigs. Dogs and cats commonly have worms too, and all puppies and kittens should be treated for them. Worms like these do not transfer to humans.

Tapeworms are completely different from nematode worms. They, too, live in the gut of a host, but their larvae live in a different host. It is not until one host eats the other that the larvae are transferred.

The beef tapeworm is one example. Its larvae live in cattle, but the adults can infect humans. These tapeworms were quite common, but have not been found in the United Kingdom for over thirty years. Strict inspection of meat and treatment of human faeces in sewage works means that it is impossible for the tapeworms to complete their life cycle. Figure 12.17 shows the life cycle of the beef tapeworm.

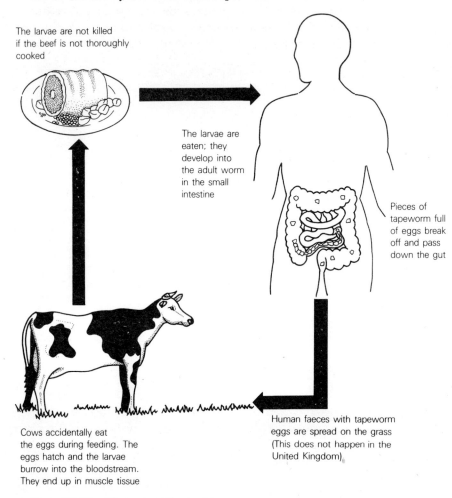

The larvae are not killed if the beef is not thoroughly cooked

The larvae are eaten; they develop into the adult worm in the small intestine

Pieces of tapeworm full of eggs break off and pass down the gut

Cows accidentally eat the eggs during feeding. The eggs hatch and the larvae burrow into the bloodstream. They end up in muscle tissue

Human faeces with tapeworm eggs are spread on the grass (This does not happen in the United Kingdom)

Figure 12.17   Life cycle of the beef tapeworm

Saprophytes

A saprophyte is an organism which feeds on dead organisms. When an animal or plant dies, it rots away. Decay like this is the work of saprophytes.

Most saprophytes are microbes. They exist in huge numbers everywhere. They are an essential part of the recycling system. They feed on dead organisms and, in turn, die and release chemicals to the soil. These are taken up by plants and used to build new tissues. The plants may be eaten by animals or may just die. Whatever happens, at some stage an organism will die and become food for the saprophyte again. (See Figure 12.18.)

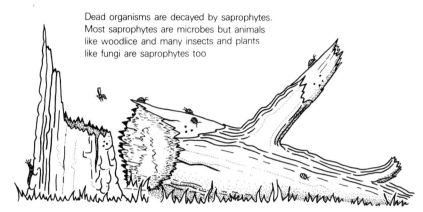

Figure 12.18   The work of saprophytes

Not all saprophytes are microbes. Fungi like mushrooms and toadstools are saprophytes (Figure 12.19). These feed on the dead plant material in the soil. Most of a mushroom plant is under the soil's surface. The mushroom itself is the reproductive part. It produces spores which are blown away to start new plants.

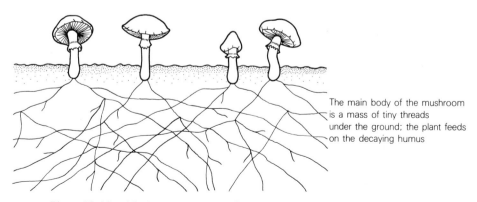

Figure 12.19   Mushrooms are saprophytes

Summary

1. A parasite feeds off a living host. It often harms the host but does not usually kill it.

2. Ectoparasites live outside their host. Endoparasites live inside.

3. Some ectoparasites transfer disease from one host to another.

4. Saprophytes feed off dead organisms. They help recycle essential chemicals.

5. Most saprophytes are microbes.

12.4 Disease — the effects of parasites

Many microbes are parasites. They can infect an organism and begin to feed off it. In the course of their feeding and reproducing they produce poisons called *toxins*. Very often these toxins affect the host and cause a disease.

We all suffer occasionally from diseases. Some can be quite harmful, like pneumonia or tuberculosis (TB). Other diseases are much milder. They make us feel uncomfortable but we usually get over them quite quickly. We may catch colds every year. As children we may catch chicken pox, or measles. The fact that we recover from these infections tells us that our bodies have ways of fighting them.

How we fight infections

Our bodies' most important way of combatting diseases is by keeping microbes out. Microbe spores are everywhere in vast numbers. Because there are so many, any area which offers food, water and a little warmth is likely to become infected. The inside of our bodies is an ideal place for microbes to grow.

We have several ways of keeping microbes out:

(a) *Skin.* This forms a microbe-proof covering all over the body. Microbes cannot pass through it. If, however, the skin is broken then microbes will quickly enter the body. To prevent this from causing too much harm, the skin can be sealed after accidental damage. Our blood forms a clot when it contacts air. When the skin is cut, blood oozes out. It clots to form a sticky plug which hardens into a scab. This keeps microbes out while the cut is healed. When there is no more risk of microbes getting in, the scab falls off.

(b) *Stomach.* All food is covered with microbes. No matter how hard we try, some will always get in. Provided there are not too many, the stomach can deal with them. The acid in the stomach kills many microbes and the enzymes can digest some, but a few microbes are protected against the stomach acid. They pass through the stomach as resistant spores. They emerge and grow in the intestines, where conditions are not so unpleasant.

(c) *Nose and Lungs.* The air we breathe contains many microbe spores. Some of these get trapped in the mucus and hairs in our nose, but others pass into the lungs. The lung tubes have special 'hair' cells which sweep a current of mucus out of the lungs. Many of the spores get swept out in this current. The mucus gets swept up the windpipe and is usually swallowed. This often happens at night when we are lying down. (See Figure 12.20.)

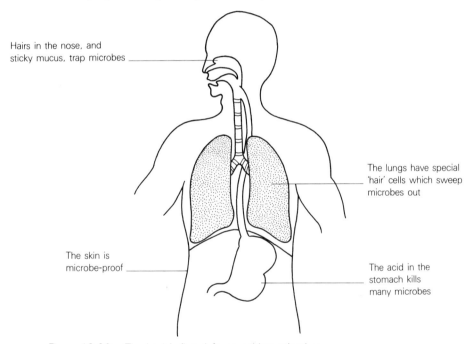

Hairs in the nose, and sticky mucus, trap microbes

The lungs have special 'hair' cells which sweep microbes out

The skin is microbe-proof

The acid in the stomach kills many microbes

Figure 12.20   The body's first defence against microbes

What happens when microbes get into our bodies?

If microbes get into our bodies, then our blood has several ways of dealing with them. All the ways involve white blood cells. Some white blood cells feed on the microbes. They engulf and digest them. Others produce chemicals called *antibodies* which attack microbes. Some antibodies break microbes up; others stick microbes together and stop them from working.

Some chemicals destroy the toxins that the microbes produce. These are called *antitoxins*. (See Figure 12.21.)

Some infections make the white blood cells produce lots of antibodies. More of these antibody-producing cells are made too. After the infection has been cleared up the antibody-producing cells stay in the blood. If the same microbe gets into the body again, it can be destroyed before it has time to cause a disease. This is why we usually catch diseases like chicken pox and measles only once.

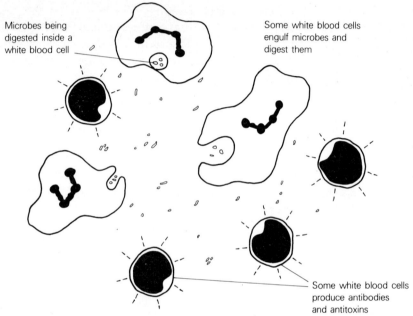

Microbes being digested inside a white blood cell

Some white blood cells engulf microbes and digest them

Some white blood cells produce antibodies and antitoxins

Figure 12.21   White blood cells fight infection

Other ways of controlling diseases

We can help control diseases by reducing the number of microbes which can attack us. This means keeping ourselves and our surroundings as clean and microbe-free as possible. We call this being *hygienic*. As far as possible, we keep microbes off our food and out of our water. Our faeces and urine are treated to prevent microbes which may leave our bodies from getting back again.

Hygiene   We can wash daily and bathe regularly. This reduces the number of microbe spores on our skin. Fewer microbes on our face and hands means fewer can enter our mouths and noses. This is why we should wash our hands after using the toilet. Fewer microbes on the rest of our skin means there is less chance of a cut being infected. (See Figure 12.22 (opposite).)

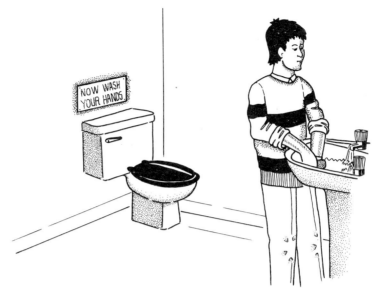

Figure 12.22   Washing removes microbes from the skin, thereby reducing the risk of infection

Our clothes and houses must also be kept clean. We should take extra care in areas like the kitchen where food is prepared. All surfaces should be regularly cleaned with hot soapy water or disinfectant. Microbes will survive in cracks and corners. They will remain stuck to grease spots. We must take care that all grease is removed and cracks are carefully cleaned. (See Figure 12.23.)

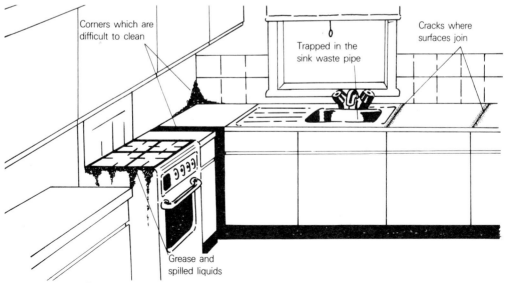

Figure 12.23   Areas where microbes thrive

Experiment 12.3

An investigation into hygiene

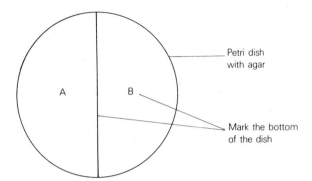

Figure 12.24   Marking
the Petri dish

1. Obtain or pour an agar plate. Remember to keep the lid of the Petri dish on at all times, except when you want to add microbes. Even then, replace the lid as quickly as possible.

2. Draw a line across the *bottom* of the Petri dish and label one side A and the other B (Figure 12.24).

3. Investigate the effects of hygiene by taking swabs from a pair of surfaces. A swab is a piece of sterile cotton wool dipped in sterile distilled water to make it damp. It is wiped over the test surface and then over the surface of the agar.

4. Choose one pair of surfaces from the list below.

Side A	Side B
A bench in the lab	The same bench after it has been cleaned with disinfectant
A finger	The same finger after it has been washed with soap
The skin of your face	The same skin after it has been washed with soap
A dishcloth	The same dishcloth after it has been rinsed through in disinfectant

5. Once you have taken your two swabs, Sellotape the lid on to the Petri dish.

6. Incubate at 25 °C for a few days.

7. Examine the plate for signs of microbe growth. Do not remove the lid.

8. Do unwashed surfaces carry few or many microbes?

9. Does careful washing have any effect on the number of microbes?

Keeping our water clean

All the water which we use is carefully cleaned and purified. Figure 12.25 shows how this is done. The water is collected from rivers, lakes or reservoirs. It passes through filters to remove large pieces of rubbish like leaves and paper. It is then aerated, which helps to remove some of the dissolved substances by turning them into solids. The water then passes into a settling tank where some of these solid particles settle out. This produces water which is quite clear, but it still needs to be filtered. It passes through a gravel and sand filter which removes any solids left. The water is then treated with chlorine which kills all bacteria. This produces pure, clean water. When the water has many bacteria, more chlorine has to be used. As chlorine adds an unpleasant taste to the water, this extra chlorine is removed once it has done its job. The removal of chlorine is done in the chlorine retention chamber.

Put simply: the water is filtered and then treated to kill bacteria. You can investigate how effective this is in Experiment 12.4 overleaf.

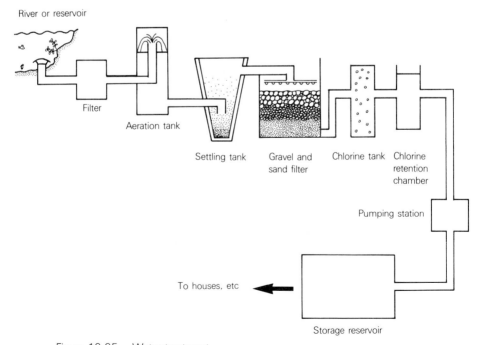

Figure 12.25   Water treatment

Experiment 12.4

Investigating the effectiveness of water treatment

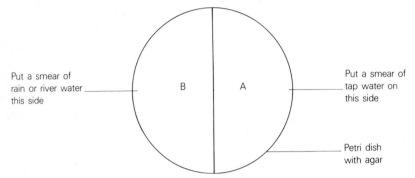

Figure 12.26   Preparing the Petri dish

1. Obtain or pour an agar plate. Remember to keep the lid on the Petri dish at all times, except when you want to treat the agar.

2. Draw a line across the bottom of the dish and label one side A and the other B.

3. Take some sterile cotton wool. Dip it in tapwater and wipe this across the surface of A. Take some more cotton wool and dip this into a sample of rainwater or river water. Wipe this across the surface of B. (See Figure 12.26).

4. Incubate at 25 °C for a few days.

5. Observe and draw the microbes which have grown on side A and side B.

6. Which side had most microbes?

7. Would you say that your tapwater had been efficiently treated?

How the microbes in sewage are treated

All our waste water, faeces and urine are treated at a sewage works. Their job is to remove all the harmful substances from the sewage. The water can be returned to a river and may be used again (Figure 12.27 (opposite)).

The sewage is pumped to the works. It passes through filters to remove odd pieces of rag or plastic or other large objects which somehow pass down our sinks and toilets and into the drains. The sewage then goes into a settlement tank where grit and stones and soil settle out.

The liquid then passes over a biological filter bed, which is a huge tank filled with large pieces of stone. These stones become covered in microbes and insect larvae which feed on the sewage. The liquid sewage is trickled on to the filter bed and it slowly filters through. As it does so most of the harmful substances are digested by the microbes. The process is no different from the decay which happens normally to waste materials. In a biological filter, it is just more concentrated. The microbes have a constant supply of food and air, and they can reproduce rapidly in vast numbers. Under normal circumstances, a biological filter like this needs no attention. The number of microbes rises and falls with the sewage supply. However, a filter bed can be easily poisoned. For example, old car oil poured into the sewers will quickly kill all the microbes in a filter bed. It will then take up to six months to clean and restock the filter.

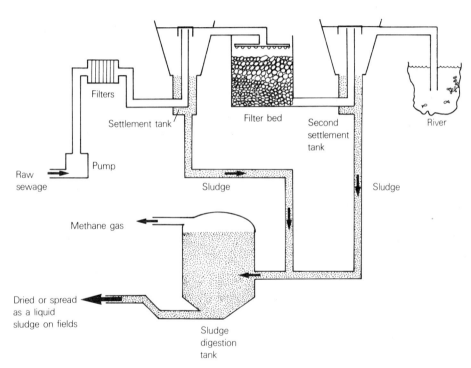

Figure 12.27   Sewage treatment

The liquid which leaves the filter contains the dead bodies of many microbes. These and other solids are removed in the second settlement tank. The liquid which leaves this is clean enough to go back into a river.

The solid material from the final settlement tank is not simply thrown away. It is treated in digestion tanks where more decay and decomposition take place. This finally destroys any harmful bacteria. It also produces large amounts of methane gas which can be collected and used to heat the sewage works or to generate electricity. The solids left after digestion are then often used as fertiliser. They are taken either as a liquid sludge or dried and taken as solids. Spread on farmers' fields, they are a valuable way of returning essential chemicals to the soil.

Summary

1. Diseases are often the result of toxins produced inside our bodies by parasitic microbes.

2. Our bodies control disease by preventing microbes from getting in and by attacking and destroying them if they do.

3. Our skin, our nose and lungs and our stomach all prevent the entry of microbes.

4. White blood cells attack microbes which do get in. Some attack and engulf microbes. These are called *phagocytes.* Other white blood cells produce antibodies to attack microbes, or antitoxins to remove the toxins.

5. We can reduce the number of microbes which could harm us by keeping ourselves and our houses clean. We also purify our water and treat our sewage. We keep our food as free from microbes as possible.

Questions on Chapter 12

1. Below is a list of the organisms found living in a small, disused orchard. Write down all the ways they might react with each other. For instance, sheep eat grass and might trample nettles.

   Grass, dandelions, buttercups, clover, apple trees, mistletoe, bindweed, nettles, wild rose, sheep, aphids, sparrows, ladybirds, ground beetles, grasshoppers, flies, frogs, a grass snake, fieldmice.

2. (a) What is competition?
   (b) If three kestrels lived along the edge of a short stretch of motorway, what might they compete with each other for?

3. Copy out the following food chains and fill in the blanks.
   (a) Grass seeds ⟶ _____ ⟶ Kestrel.
   (b) Leaves ⟶ Earthworms ⟶ _____ .
   (c) Apple tree ⟶ _____ ⟶ Ladybirds.
   (d) Corn ⟶ _____ ⟶ Human being.
   (e) Now write out three food chains of your own.

4. Draw out the pyramids of numbers for the food chains in question 3.

5. You are at the top of a food web. List the food you ate for breakfast, lunch and supper on one day only, then draw an example of your food web.

6. The jar in Figure 12.28 was partly filled with soil and then sown with seeds. What sort of competition would you expect between the plants which grew from these seeds?

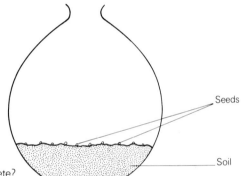

Figure 12.28   How will they compete?

7. What is a parasite? Give three examples of each of the following sorts of parasite:
   (a) A plant parasite of a plant.
   (b) A plant parasite of an animal.
   (c) An animal parasite of an animal.

8. Draw the pyramid of numbers for the following food chain:
   Grass seeds ⟶ Sparrow ⟶ Cat ⟶ Flea.

9. (a) What is an ectoparasite?
   (b) Apart from the damage caused when it feeds on its host, how else can an ectoparasite cause harm?
   (c) Give an example of an ectoparasite which harms its host like this.

10. (a) How does an endoparasite like the pinworm get from one host to another?
    (b) What do you think are the advantages of being an endoparasite like the pinworm?
    (c) What could be the disadvantages?

11. Copy out the following and fill in the blanks.

Human diseases are often caused by parasitic _____ . They live in our
bodies and produce _____ which are poisonous. Our first line of
defence is to stop them from getting into our bodies. Our _____ is
completely _____-proof. If it should become cut or broken our
_____ forms a _____ which seals up the damage. We produce
_____ in our stomachs. Our lungs and our nose have a layer of
_____ and special hair _____ . Together these trap _____
and sweep them out.

12. How do we deal with microbes if they manage to get into our bodies?

13. To prevent the spread of diseases our water is treated to make it pure.
(a) Which part of the treatment actually kills the microbes?
(b) What do the other parts of the treatment do?

14. (a) What is sewage?
(b) In a sewage works, what happens in the filter bed?
(c) Some people describe a filter bed as a 'biological factory'. What do
you think this means?

15. A student drew out Figure 12.29 to show what happens in a sewage works.
He did not manage to finish all the labels. What labels should be used for
1, 2, 3, 4, 5?

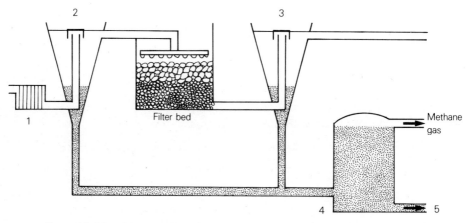

Figure 12.29   Diagram of a sewage works

Crossword on Chapter 12

(Teacher, please see special note in front of book.)

Copy this grid, then solve the clues. Do not write on this page.

Across

5   Animal eats plant, we eat animal. This is an example of a _____ _____ (4, 5)

7   A dead organism will _____ (3)

8   It may stop larvae hanging on a water surface (3)

9, 5 down   A human disease caused by a fungus (8, 4)

11   Malaria sufferers would like mosquitoes to _____ (3)

12   Animals like aphids are often called _____ (5)

14   A study of the way organisms react in a community (7)

15   The hairs in your _____ can trap microbes (4)

Down

1   Clean your kitchen surfaces with _____ water (3)

2   Animals might compete for these (5)

3   _____ parasites live *inside* the host (4)

4   Animals might compete for this (7)

5   See 9 across

6   Malaria is a _____ (7)

10   The organisms a parasite feeds off (5)

11   These pets can have worms (4)

12   The _____ worm is a common nematode (3)

13   Microbes can make us _____ (3)

13. How substances are recycled

13.1 Why recycling is important

Our world is quite big, but it can hold only a limited amount of different chemicals. Take, for example, oxygen. There is only so much oxygen in our atmosphere. There are countless millions of organisms using it up in respiration. Cars and lorries use it, so do factories. It is used wherever a fire is burning. You would imagine that after a time all the oxygen would be used up and the world would end. In fact, this does not happen. The amount of oxygen in our atmosphere stays much the same all the time. This is because oxygen is recycled. Oxygen is used in respiration or in burning and this produces carbon dioxide which plants need for photosynthesis. A waste product of photosynthesis is oxygen, which is released back into the air. (See Figure 13.1.)

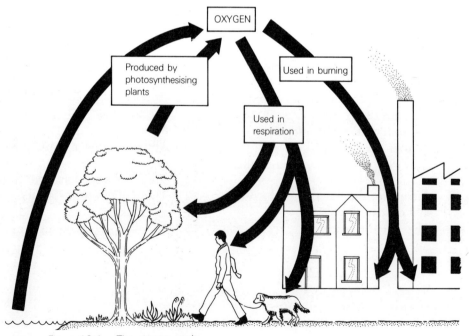

OXYGEN

Produced by photosynthesising plants

Used in burning

Used in respiration

Figure 13.1   The oxygen cycle

The way that substances are recycled is one of the greatest wonders of nature. Every tiny organism plays a part in the system. You can get an idea of this by thinking about your body. Apart from water, it *mainly* consists of protein built from amino acids. Some of these amino acids were part of another animal before you ate it as meat. That animal probably got those amino acids from plants. Those plants made the amino acids using nitrates from the soil. The nitrates came from the decomposition by bacteria of another organism, maybe an animal. So you see that the chemicals which make up your body have already been used in the bodies of many animals and plants. When you die, those chemicals will return into the system again and will be used to build new organisms. (See Figure 13.2.)

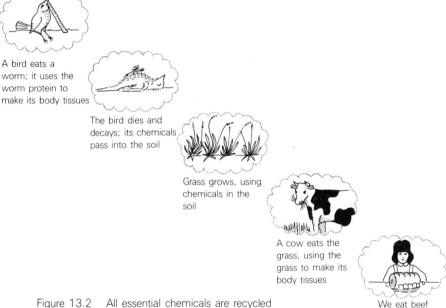

A bird eats a worm; it uses the worm protein to make its body tissues

The bird dies and decays; its chemicals pass into the soil

Grass grows, using chemicals in the soil

A cow eats the grass, using the grass to make its body tissues

Figure 13.2   All essential chemicals are recycled   We eat beef

Recycling links all living organisms together, and it means that no essential substance runs out. Recycling, however, depends on there being a balanced number of organisms in the world. Without this balance the whole system would fail. If, for instance, the number of plants were reduced, the supply of oxygen could get smaller. Much of the world's oxygen comes from tiny sea plants in the plankton. Uncontrolled pollution of the sea could easily kill off many of these plants and seriously affect the oxygen supply.

Many of our activities are on a very large scale. Huge industries can produce lots of pollution. Big fishing fleets can catch enormous numbers of fish. We can chop down millions of trees to supply our wood and paper needs. It is important that we think about the effects that such activities have on the balance of nature.

When we disrupt food chains and interfere with recycling processes, nature can usually cope. However, serious damage is often done and we must guard against this if we want the Earth to survive.

13.2 Soil — a vital part of the recycling process

Soil acts as a store for important chemicals. Plants take some chemicals from the soil. Dead organisms, urine and faeces all put chemicals back. The organisms which live in the soil use these chemicals. In doing so they change them from one form to another and so make them available for plants again.

What is soil?

Soil is a mixture of particles of *rock* (or minerals), and *organic material*. The organic material is called *humus*. It is produced when plants and animals decay. (See Figure 13.3.)

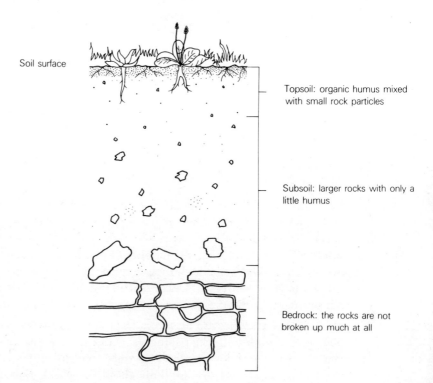

Soil surface

Topsoil: organic humus mixed with small rock particles

Subsoil: larger rocks with only a little humus

Bedrock: the rocks are not broken up much at all

Figure 13.3   Profile of a well formed soil system

Rocks are broken down into small fragments over many years. Summer heat and winter cold help to crack rocks, and rain dissolves some of the chemicals they contain. As organisms die and decompose, the chemicals they produce mix with the rock particles. Sometimes they react together to form larger fragments. Rainwater helps to stick the fragments together, thus making soil. As this happens, organisms begin to live in the soil. They feed on it and burrow through it. Microbes feed on the soil and on other organisms in it.

A layer of soil formed like this is constantly changing. Rocks keep breaking up. Organic material is added at the surface. Animals mix the two as they move about. Chemical reactions take place. Soil, then, is a complex mixture of different sized rock particles and varying amounts of organic material. You can get a good idea of the different particles which make up soil in Experiment 13.1.

Experiment 13.1

Investigating different sizes of soil particles

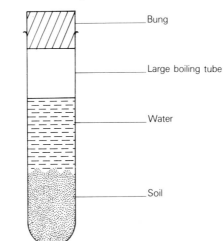

Shake the tube well

Figure 13.4   Investigating soil particles

1. You need a large boiling tube or perhaps a gas jar.

2. Put 2 – 3 cm of soil into the tube and fill the rest with water (Figure 13.4).

3. Put a bung or lid on to the tube and shake it well for about a minute.

4. After you stop shaking, quickly put the tube into a rack or stand it some-where out of the way. Leave it for 10 minutes.

5. Check the way the soil has settled. Compare your results with the ones in Figure 13.5. Notice how the soil has formed layers. The largest particles are at the bottom and the smallest are at the top. The water will probably be a little cloudy. This is because the very tiny particles have not yet settled.

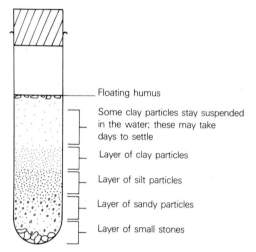

Floating humus

Some clay particles stay suspended in the water; these may take days to settle

Layer of clay particles

Layer of silt particles

Layer of sandy particles

Layer of small stones

Figure 13.5   Possible results of a soil settling experiment

6. Leave the tube undisturbed for several days.

7. Observe the soil again. Have all the particles settled? You can tell if they have because the water will be clear. Draw and label a diagram of your results.

8. How many different layers could you see?

9. Did any material float on the water? What sort of substance would you expect to float?

10. How would you go about measuring the sizes of the soil particles?

Types of soil

Soils are not just dirt. There are many different types of soil. They differ because of the different sorts of rock from which they are formed. They will have varying amounts of humus. Soils which are wet for much of the time will undergo different chemical reactions to soils which are dry. Some sorts of organism live in wet soils, others in dry soils.

There are a whole range of soils but they can be grouped into three main types: *clays, loams* and *sandy soils*. The difference between them is mainly the size of their particles. Soils with tiny particles have only tiny spaces between them. These spaces can fill up with water to form a sticky paste. The particles and the water bind each other together. Soils with large particles have large spaces between them through which water trickles and drains away. The particles, therefore, are not held together and the soil is very dusty when dry. The best type of soil for the farmer or gardener has medium-sized particles, which hold some water but are quite crumbly and easily worked. (See Figure 13.6.)

Clay soils have particles which leave very small spaces in between

Loam soils have medium-sized particles with medium-sized spaces in between

Sandy soils have large particles, which means the spaces between them are also large

Figure 13.6   Particle size in soils

Clay soils   Clay soils have tiny particles. These are the soils which become very sticky when they are wet. They form very hard lumps when they dry out and large cracks appear in the surface. Water does not drain easily through clay soils because it cannot flow between the particles.

When they are wet, clays are difficult to dig or to plough. The soil sticks to the spade or the plough and does not easily break up. Plants do not always grow well in clay soils because the soil space can become waterlogged leaving no room for air. This means the plant roots and other soil organisms cannot get oxygen for respiration.

A farmer or gardener with a clay soil will try to increase the particle size. This can be done by adding humus, which is why manure is good for soil. Lime also helps by reacting chemically with the clay and forming it into larger particles.

Sandy soils   These are the opposite to clay soils. They have large particles which allow water to pass easily through, and any rain quickly drains away. Often it takes dissolved substances with it, removing the minerals which plants need to grow. This is called *leaching*. The minerals are said to have been *leached* from the soil.

Sandy soils, therefore, are also not so good for plant growth. In areas where soils are very sandy, farmers and gardeners have to water their plants continually. In some parts of the world *irrigation* like this is the only way to grow any crops at all (Figure 13.7).

Figure 13.7   An irrigation system

Loams

A loam is an ideal soil for plant growth. Loams contain average-sized particles which hold some water but drain well. There is always plenty of air in the soil. Loams are easy to dig and plough. They break up into small crumbs which allow plants to grow easily. Loams usually contain a mixture of minerals and humus to provide plants with all the chemicals they need.

Analysing soil

A good soil has a balanced amount of minerals, air and water. It is slightly alkaline with a pH of around 7 – 7.5. Soil analysis is important if we are to grow plants as well as we can. The following are a series of simple experiments to analyse soil. You can use them to analyse one soil or you can compare different sorts of soil.

Experiment 13.2

This is a simple test which you can practise anywhere. Some farmers and gardeners become very good at analysing soil in this way.

Investigating soil structure

1. Take a small handful of soil and rub it gently in your hand. Does it crumble to dust? Does it have hard lumps? Does it form soft crumbs? Is it gritty?

    Clay soils often have very hard lumps but also crumble to a fine dust.
    Loam soils have soft crumbs. They do not crush easily to dust.
    Sandy soils easily break up into gritty particles. They have very few crumbs.

2. Take a pinch of soil and wet it. Rub it between your fingers and thumb. Is it gritty or sticky or somewhere in between?

    Clay soils quickly become sticky.
    Loam soils are not very sticky.
    Sandy soils feel gritty and do not stick.

Experiment 13.3

Finding the pH of soil

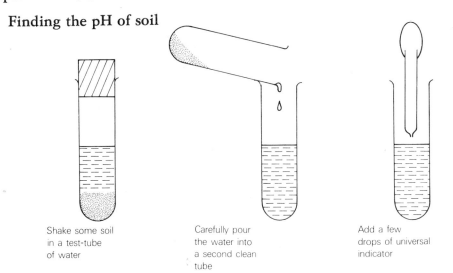

| Shake some soil in a test-tube of water | Carefully pour the water into a second clean tube | Add a few drops of universal indicator |

Figure 13.8   Finding the pH of soil

1. Shake a small amount of soil in a test-tube with 5 cm³ of distilled water.

2. Carefully pour the water off into a second clean test-tube. Add a few drops of universal indicator. (See Figure 13.8.)

3. Check the pH of the soil by comparing the colour with a colour chart.

Experiment 13.4

Finding how much air is in soil

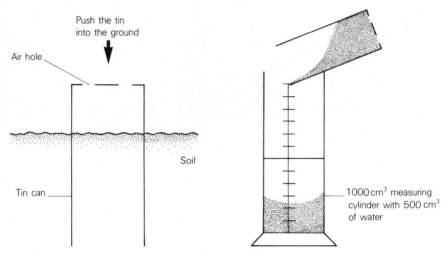

Figure 13.9   Investigating the amount of air in soil

1. Take an old tin can which has had one end removed. Fill it with water. Pour the water into a large measuring cylinder and measure its volume. You now know the volume of the tin (we will call this A). Aim to get a tin with a volume of about 250 cm^3.

2. Punch a hole or two in the bottom of the tin.

3. Press the tin into the soil until the tin is completely full (Figure 13.9).

4. Put 500 cm^3 of water into a 1000 cm^3 measuring cylinder.

5. Carefully tip the soil from the tin into the measuring cylinder. Measure the new volume (we will call this B). Now work out the amount of air in the soil as follows:

    The volume of soil was A cm^3.

    The volume of soil + water in the measuring cylinder should be $A + 500$ cm^3.
    But, because some water in the measuring cylinder filled up the air spaces in the soil, the volume of soil + water was B cm^3.

    The volume of air is therefore $(A + 500) - B$ cm^3

    You can work out the percentage of air in your soil as follows:

$$\text{Percentage air} = \frac{\text{Volume of air}}{\text{Volume of soil}} \times 100$$

Experiment 13.5

Finding the amounts of water, humus and mineral material in a soil

1. To do this experiment successfully you must keep very careful records. Copy out this results chart before you start the experiment. Fill it in as you go along.

Results

Weight of tin lid .... ————— g

Weight of tin lid + soil .... ————— g

∴ Weight of soil .... ————— g

Weight of tin lid + dry soil .... ————— g

∴ Weight of dry soil .... ————— g

∴ Weight of water in soil .... ————— g

$$\text{Percentage water} = \frac{\text{Weight of water}}{\text{Weight of soil}} \times 100 = \underline{\hspace{2cm}} \%$$

Weight of tin lid + soil after burning .... ————— g

∴ Weight of soil after burning .... ————— g

Weight of humus = Weight of dry soil − Weight of soil after burning.

$$\text{Percentage humus} = \frac{\text{Weight of humus}}{\text{Weight of soil}} \times 100 = \underline{\hspace{2cm}} \%$$

Weight of mineral is the weight of soil after burning.

$$\text{Percentage mineral} = \frac{\text{Weight of mineral}}{\text{Weight of soil}} \times 100 = \underline{\hspace{2cm}} \%$$

2. Take a tin lid and weigh it.

3. Place a few spatulas of soil on the lid. Weigh it again.

4. Heat the soil in an oven at just over 100 °C for an hour or so (see Figure 13.10 (overleaf). This will dry all the water out of the soil. Weigh the dry soil.

5. Now put the soil back into the oven for another hour at just over 100 °C. Weigh it again. If both weights are the same, you can be sure that all the water has evaporated.

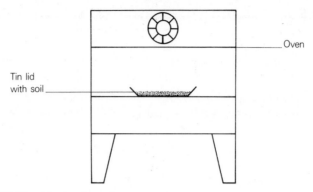

Figure 13.10   Heating the soil

6. Put the tin lid on to a tripod. Heat the soil strongly with a bunsen burner (Figure 13.11). This will burn away all the humus. After 10 minutes, stop. Let the lid cool down and weigh it. Then heat it and weigh it again. If the two weights are the same, you can be sure you have burned off all the humus. What is left is the mineral part of the soil.

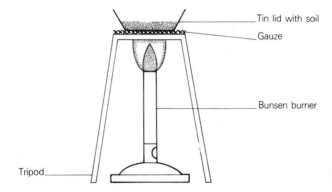

Figure 13.11   Burning the soil

7. Now calculate the percentage water, humus and mineral content of the soil.

The soil and fertilisers

For successful plant growth, soil needs to contain enough of the minerals that plants need. Some of the most important are *nitrates, phosphates* and *sulphates,* which are often added to soil as fertilisers.

Fertilisers are necessary where a soil loses its minerals. Farmers harvest nearly all their crops for sale, so few plants will die and decay back into the soil. Animals can help recycle minerals but they may not be put on the land.

Each year, therefore, more minerals may be taken out than are added. Farmers can restore the balance by adding artificial fertilisers. They can, in fact, increase the yield of their crops by adding extra minerals.

One important way that fertilisers are lost from the soil is by leaching. Rainwater drains through the soil, dissolving the fertilisers and taking them away. Leaching has more effect on sandy soils than on loams and clays. You can see the effects leaching has on different soils in the following experiment.

Experiment 13.6

Investigating how quickly water drains through soil

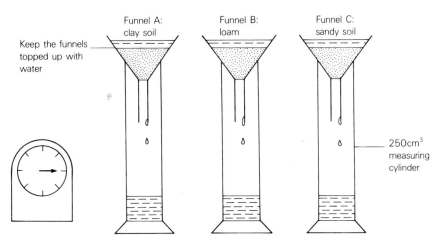

Figure 13.12   Investigating drainage through soil

1. Assemble the apparatus shown in Figure 13.12.

2. Put a small piece of muslin into each of the filter funnels. Then half-fill funnel A with clay soil. Put an equal amount of loam into funnel B and an equal amount of sandy soil into funnel C.

3. Fill the three beakers with water.

4. Copy out a results table like the one overleaf.

5. It is easiest to do the experiment with four people. One records the results; the other three each work with one type of soil.

6. Start the clock and immediately fill the filter funnels with water so that they are full but do not overflow. Keep the funnels topped up throughout the experiment.

7. After exactly one minute, record the volume of water in each of the measuring cylinders.

8. Repeat this every minute for 10 minutes or until one measuring cylinder is completely full.

9. Fill in a results chart like the one below (up to 10 minutes) and then draw a graph of the results.

Time (min)	Volume of water (cm³)		
	Clay soil	Loam	Sandy soil
1			
2			
3			
4			
5			
6			
7			

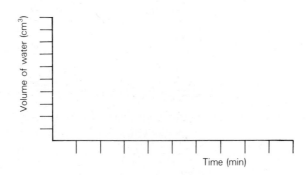

10. Which soil could suffer most from leaching?

11. Which soil could suffer least?

Summary

1. In nature all substances are recycled. Only energy is not. Energy is input from the Sun and is lost as heat to outer space.

2. As long as the balance of organisms remains, the Earth will not run out of essential chemicals.

3. Soil acts as a store for important chemicals and as a place where they can be changed from one form to another.

4. Soil is a mixture of rock material and humus.

5. There are three basic types of soil — *clay, loam* and *sandy soil.*

6. A good soil has medium-sized particles. It drains easily, leaving some water and also enough air for plant roots and soil organisms. It contains plenty of humus and important minerals. Loams are good soils.

7. Fertilisers are needed when soils are short of essential plant materials. This often happens when chemicals are not recycled.

13.3 The nitrogen cycle

Nitrogen is a very unreactive gas, which forms about 80% of the air around us. It is needed to make amino acids which in turn are made into proteins. Proteins are the chemicals which make the living materials in cells. However, very few living organisms can use the nitrogen in the air to make amino acids. For this reason it is extremely important that the nitrogen already in proteins and amino acids is recycled. This recycling is called the *nitrogen cycle,* but very little pure nitrogen is involved in it. The nitrogen is mostly in the form of chemical compounds like nitrates, or amino acids or ammonium compounds. The nitrogen cycle involves changing one compound into another. You can see this in Figure 13.13 (overleaf).

Plants take *nitrates* from the soil and use them to make proteins. Animals that eat plants turn plant protein into animal protein. Animals that eat animals simply change the proteins into the ones they need. Eventually the protein returns to the soil by some means. For example, the plants and animals may die. Also, animal urine contains nitrogen compounds like urea, made when proteins are broken down. Faeces, too, may contain proteins.

All these substances are decomposed in the soil by bacteria and fungi. Much of the nitrogen is turned into *ammonium compounds*. These are used by different sorts of bacteria and are converted into *nitrite* compounds and then, by other bacteria, into *nitrate* compounds. Plants can then use the nitrates again.

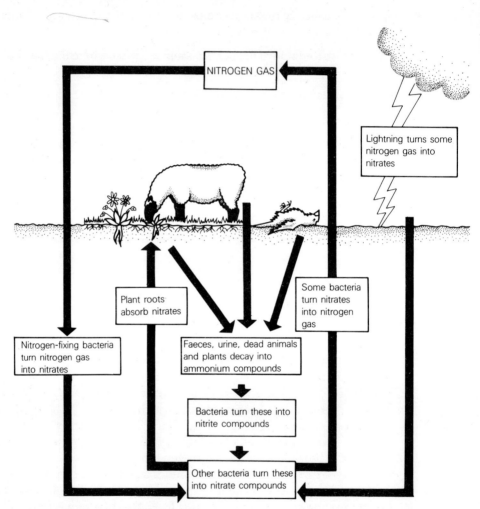

Figure 13.13   The nitrogen cycle

Some bacteria use nitrates and turn them into nitrogen gas which passes into the air. Others can use nitrogen gas and turn it into nitrates. These are called *nitrogen-fixing bacteria*. They are very important because they add nitrate into the nitrogen cycle. Some plants, like clover, have nitrogen-fixing bacteria living in tiny lumps (root nodules) attached to their roots, which gives them their own supply of nitrates (Figure 13.14 (opposite)).

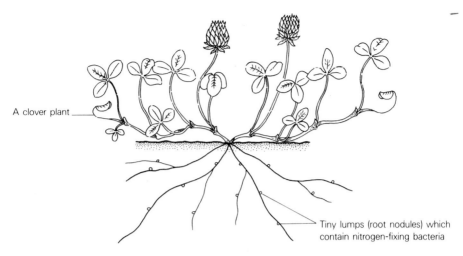

A clover plant

Tiny lumps (root nodules) which
contain nitrogen-fixing bacteria

Figure 13.14   Root nodules on clover

Occasionally, lightning can turn nitrogen gas into nitrates. These dissolve
in rain and fall to the ground.

13.4 The carbon cycle

Pure carbon is a black substance like soot. It is of very little use to living
organisms. Carbon is, however, a major part of nearly all the chemicals
which make up living organisms. These chemicals pass from one organism
to another in a system known as the carbon cycle, but pure carbon is never
involved in it. You can see the cycle in Figure 13.15 (overleaf).

Plants use *carbon dioxide* in photosynthesis to make *carbohydrates* like starch
and glucose, and to make proteins. Animals eat the plants and respire,
using the carbohydrates to produce carbon dioxide again. Other
organisms like bacteria also respire to produce carbon dioxide. This is the
carbon cycle. Put simply, it is the cycle of photosynthesis and respiration. It
allows energy from the Sun to be passed from one organism to another. In
this way all organisms get the energy they need to live.

Burning, too, is part of the carbon cycle. When carbon compounds like
wood, coal and oil are burned, they produce carbon dioxide. This can be
taken up by plants and enters the cycle again.

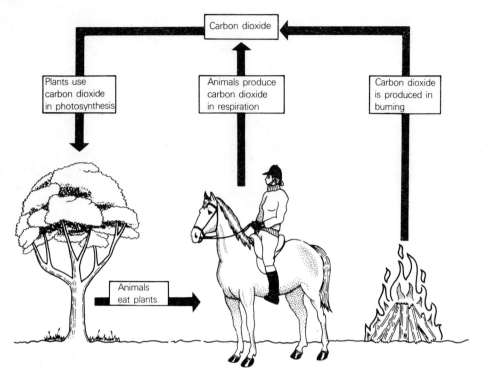

Figure 13.15   The carbon cycle

Summary

1. Nitrogen is needed to make amino acids, which are used to make proteins. Nitrogen is, therefore, essential to life.

2. The nitrogen cycle involves changing one nitrogen compound to another.

3. Bacteria in the soil are an important part of the nitrogen cycle.

4. The carbon cycle can be summarised as:

5. The carbon cycle allows energy to pass from one organism to another.

6. All energy comes from the Sun and is eventually lost as heat to outer space.

Questions on Chapter 13

1. Copy out the following and fill in the blanks.
   All living organisms use oxygen in _____ to provide the _____
   they need to live and grow. _____ _____ gas is produced as a
   waste product which can be used by plants in _____ .

2. Why is recycling so important in nature?

3. Figure 13.16 is a drawing of the nitrogen cycle. Some of the boxes have not
   been filled in. Copy out the drawing and fill in the boxes.

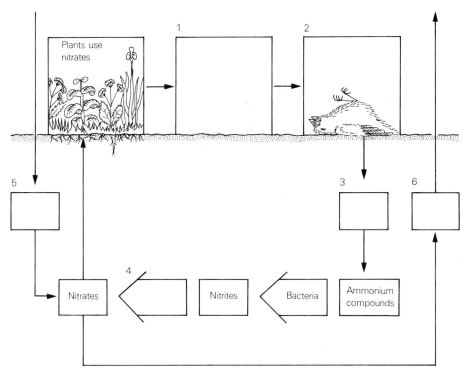

Figure 13.16   Work out the missing words

4. The following were obtained in a soil analysis experiment:

Weight of tin lid	28 g
Weight of lid + soil	53 g
Weight of lid + soil after heating at 100 °C for an hour ...	43 g
Weight of lid + soil after burning with a bunsen burner ...	37 g

   Work out the percentage water, humus and mineral in this soil sample.

5. Copy out the following and fill in the blanks.
   Soil is a mixture of _____ and organic material called _____ .
   The organic material comes from _____ plants and animals.
   Different types of soil are produced by different types of _____ .
   Very often it is the _____ of the particles which is important. Clay
   soils have very _____ particles but _____ soils have very large
   ones. _____ are in between these two.
   Soils act as a _____ for important chemicals. Large organisms like
   _____ live in the soil. So too do millions of microscopic _____ .
   All these organisms help to _____ chemicals from one form to
   another. In this way, essential chemicals can be _____ .

6. (a) How would a gardener know that he had a clay soil?
   (b) What could he do to improve it?

7. (a) How would a gardener know that he had a sandy soil?
   (b) What could he do to improve it?

8. (a) Why is leaching bad for a soil?
   (b) A farmer ploughed up his grass field and started to grow wheat on it.
       Later in the year, he noticed that the stream next to the field was
       overgrown with weed. Can you explain why this was?

9. How are the following substances involved in the carbon cycle: glucose,
   wood, coal, carbon dioxide?

Word pairs from Chapter 13

(Teacher, please see special note in front of book.)

Copy or photocopy the grid below. Do not write on this page.

Find two words jumbled up in *each*.

Write the words in their spaces.

All the words are used in Chapter 13.

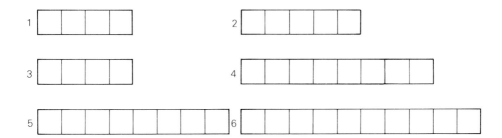

Word group for 1 and 2
LAY US, CHUM

Word group for 3 and 4
LOT IN A STREAM

Word group for 5 and 6
HE'S A TOP ENGLISH CHAP

If you need some extra help, here are some clues:

1 A type of soil (4)   4 Type of minerals (8)
2 Part of soil (5)   5 How a soil loses minerals (8)
3 Another soil type (4)   6 Another mineral type (10)

14. How we are involved with the environment

14.1 The need for a balanced environment

Throughout this book we have seen that organisms live together in this world. On its own, each organism struggles to survive and reproduce. By doing this, all organisms affect each other. Some may become food for others; some provide shelter. Some get crowded out and die. Even this is not an end because dead organisms are food and shelter for others (Figure 14.1).

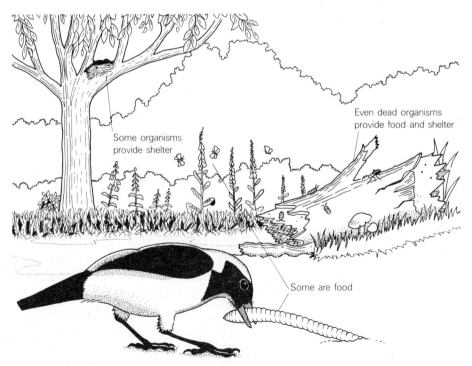

Some organisms provide shelter

Even dead organisms provide food and shelter

Some are food

Figure 14.1   Organisms provide shelter for others

These relationships are often complex and delicately balanced. They have developed over many millions of years. As each type of organism takes its place in a food web, then it relies on all the other organisms in the web. If one organism dies out, the effects will be felt by all the other organisms. A simple example is the food chain shown in Figure 14.2.

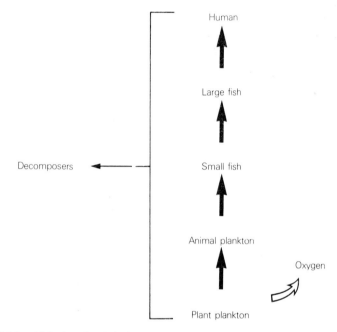

Figure 14.2   Links in a food chain

The sea contains a mass of tiny plants which we call *plant plankton*. If the sea became poisoned with chemicals which killed this plankton, the whole food chain would collapse. There would also be another problem. Plant plankton supply a great deal of oxygen when they photosynthesise, so the oxygen cycle would also be seriously disrupted. The number of organisms which feed on the dead remains of plankton and fish would be reduced. Essential chemicals would not be recycled. The effects of this might well be important for other sea plants.

Food chains and webs and recycling all depend on their being balanced numbers of organisms. If the balance is changed, the environment changes too. Our activities can, and do, change the balance in a very short time. Without understanding the balance completely we cannot predict what the effects will be. It is possible to cause large changes in the environment without actually realising it.

We must take care that the changes we make do not make the world a worse place to live in. This is where *ecology* can help us. Ecology is the study of the balance among living organisms. Through ecology we can check to see if the balance is changing. Also, as we understand more we will be able to predict more accurately the effects we might have.

Ecology – investigating the balance

In just a few years of education you cannot easily study the changing balance of organisms. To do this you need records that have been built up over many years. You can, however, learn about some of the ways in which ecology can be studied. Simple ecology involves finding out what organisms live in an area, and how many of each there are. You could just go out and identify and count all the organisms. However, if you think about this for a moment, you will realise that this is not as easy as it sounds.

Just to identify and count all the organisms in your school field or local park could take months, if not years (Figure 14.3). A simpler way is to take a *sample* of the area and identify and count the organisms in that. You choose your sample so that it fairly represents the whole area. Even this is not very easy and so there are aids to help you.

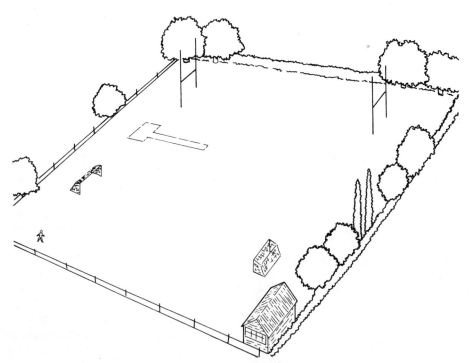

Figure 14.3   It is impossible to count all the organisms, even in a small area

Sampling plants

As plants do not move, sampling an area for them can be quite easy, using a basic piece of apparatus called a *quadrat*. This is a wood or metal frame which measures 0.5 m × 0.5 m. All you do is put it on the ground and identify the plants inside it (Figure 14.4).

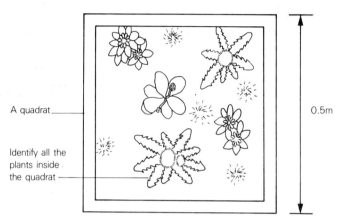

A quadrat

Identify all the plants inside the quadrat

0.5m

Figure 14.4   Using a quadrat

Very often you do not need to count the number of plants in the quadrat. You estimate how much of the area they cover and write this down as percentage cover (Figure 14.5).

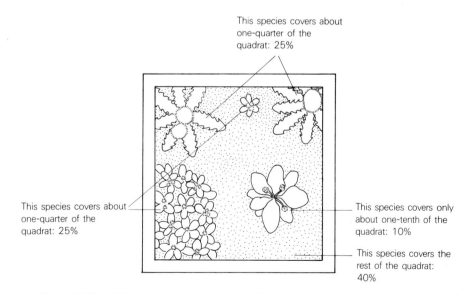

This species covers about one-quarter of the quadrat: 25%

This species covers about one-quarter of the quadrat: 25%

This species covers only about one-tenth of the quadrat: 10%

This species covers the rest of the quadrat: 40%

Figure 14.5   Estimating percentage cover with a quadrat

An even simpler way of sampling plants with a quadrat is just to mark down which plants are present. Take lots of quadrats in an area. Each different type of plant is given one tick for every quadrat you find it in. The plants with the most ticks are the most common. Experiment 14.1 uses this method.

Where to put the quadrat is the next problem. There are many ways of deciding this, but the idea is to use the quadrat to sample several different areas of the field. These areas should be chosen at random so that you do not influence the results. For example, if it is a sunny day and half the field is shaded by the tower block, then you would be influencing the results if you decided to sunbathe whilst doing the experiment (Figure 14.6).

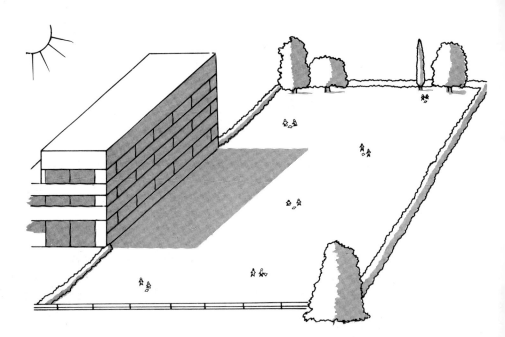

Figure 14.6   Quadrats must be used in random areas

A simple way of choosing random sites for your quadrats is this. Stand in the centre of your area with your eyes closed. You need an old gym shoe (or something similar that you can throw without causing damage). Close your eyes and let a friend spin you around. Then throw the gym shoe over your shoulder and place the quadrat where it lands. Do this ten times, each time in a different direction and changing how hard you throw. In this way you are likely to get ten fairly random samples. Remember though that the system is not foolproof, so guard against any cheating.

Experiment 14.1

Using a quadrat to sample a field

1. Choose the area you are going to sample. Draw a fairly accurate plan of the area and pick out the centre.

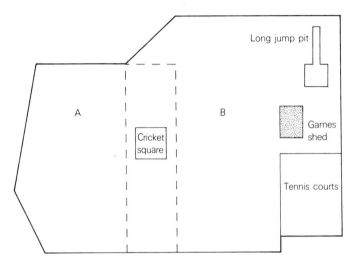

A or B would be suitable areas

Figure 14.7   Choosing an area

2. Choose the object you will be using to throw; it must be fairly heavy, but soft. Do not throw the quadrat; it will break.

3. Obtain a quadrat. If you have not got a wooden one then make one out of a couple of old wire coat hangers. Make sure it has sides 50 cm and that it is reasonably square when you use it.

4. Draw out a results chart like the one below before you start. For each quadrat, simply tick the column if the plant is present.

5. Sample ten quadrats randomly. Record each different plant you find. Do not forget to include bare ground if you find any. Make sure you can identify each different plant before you start.

Quadrat	1	2	3	4	5	6	7	8	9	10	Total
Plant name											

6. Treat the results as follows: add up the total number of ticks for each different plant and write it in the 'Total' column. Now draw a bar graph of the results like the one below. This will give an easy-to-follow picture of which plants are common and which are less so.

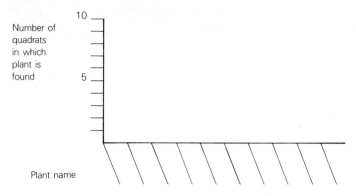

7. Was your sampling random?

8. Do your results agree with what you had expected to find?

Sampling animals

Animals are more difficult to sample since they usually move away when you want to count them. The only way to sample them is, therefore, to catch them. There are many ways of doing this. The simplest way of catching very small animals is to sweep a butterfly net through the area you are sampling (Figure 14.8).

Sweep the net through the vegetation

Figure 14.8   Sampling with a butterfly net

You can easily count the larger insects, and by using a pooter you can hold the smallest ones whilst you count them. You can compare what you catch in a single sweep in one area with what you catch in a single sweep in another.

A pitfall trap is a good way of catching the smaller ground animals (Figure 14.9). It is simply an old jamjar or yoghurt pot sunk into the ground. Animals fall in and cannot get out. You can bait the trap with meat or rotting vegetation, or you can leave it without bait to see what sort of animals fall in by chance. Put a piece of wood or stone over the trap to stop large animals or rain from getting in.

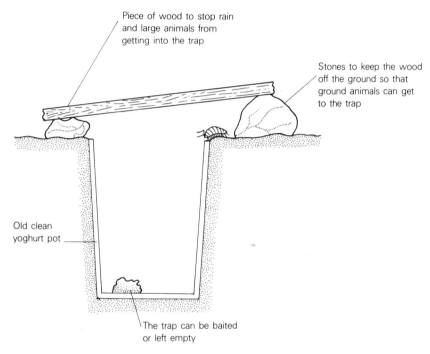

Figure 14.9   A pitfall trap

Experiment 14.2

Using a pitfall trap to compare two areas

1. Set up two identical pitfall traps, one in an open area and one under bushes or undergrowth (Figure 14.10 (overleaf)).

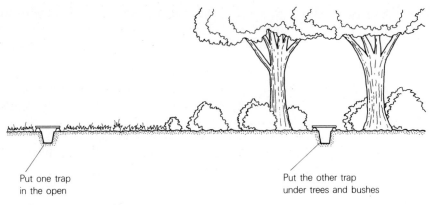

Put one trap
in the open

Put the other trap
under trees and bushes

Figure 14.10   Placing pitfall traps

2. Leave the traps for several days. Each morning inspect both traps. Identify and count all the organisms in them. Then remove the organisms.

3. Record your results in a chart like the one below.

Type of animal	Total number caught in open area	Total number caught in covered area

4. Was there any difference in the type and number of organisms found in the two areas?

A changing balance

Even though there is a balance between different organisms, this does not mean that the number of organisms always stays the same. As conditions change slightly from one year to another, so the numbers of organisms will rise and fall. The overall balance remains the same, however.

For example, rabbits feed a lot on grass. If the weather is warm and there is plenty of rain, grass grows well. There is plenty for rabbits to eat; they feed well and reproduce quickly. The rabbit population rises. If the warm summer is followed by a very cold winter, there will be less food. Many rabbits will die and the population will fall. Next year it may be a cold summer, meaning less grass grows. The population of rabbits will not rise so high.

If a group of foxes feeds only on the rabbits, then as the rabbit population rises there will be more for the foxes to eat. The fox population rises. More foxes means more rabbits will be eaten, and so the rabbit population might fall again. This, of course, means there is less for the foxes to eat and some of them will die. Thus the rabbit and fox population go up and down. Their numbers depend on the weather and on how many rabbits get eaten. Overall the balance remains but the numbers change (Figure 14.11).

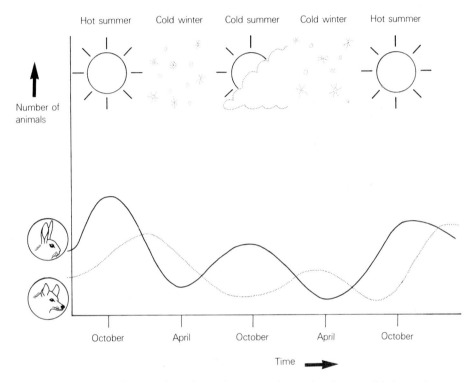

Figure 14.11   The number of organisms may change but the overall balance does not

14.2 Humans and the balanced environment

We have constantly tried to improve the quality of our own lives. We have tried to grow more and better food. Machines have been manufactured to make life easier and more enjoyable. By continually making progress many of us now have, at least in the Western world, a very comfortable life. We are rarely hungry and there are many different sorts of food available. Our shops are full of things we can buy. Our homes are solid. Most have gas and electricity, so we need never be cold. We have fridges and freezers to store our food, and microwave ovens to cook it. There is television and radio for our enjoyment, cars and motorbikes for our transport. We have computers to play with and to help organise our lives.

Much of this progress has taken place in the last 100 years. A lot of it has happened because we have made bigger, better and faster machines which do more than people alone could. Science and technology have allowed us to learn more about our world and how to get the best from it.

In this race into progress we have not always paid attention to the environment. We have often done damage and realised it only after it has happened. For example, damage was done by the chemical DDT. This is an insecticide used to protect crops against attack by insects. It was sprayed on to crops. Insects ate it, and birds ate the insects. Then birds, like the peregrine falcon in Scotland, ate the smaller birds. Eventually the falcons ate enough DDT to affect them. Many died. Some DDT got into the rivers and into the sea. It got into sea plants and into the fish that ate them. Other fish then ate those contaminated fish, and eventually the DDT ended up in penguins and other large animals. Some of it ended up in humans who ate the fish. (See Figure 14.12.)

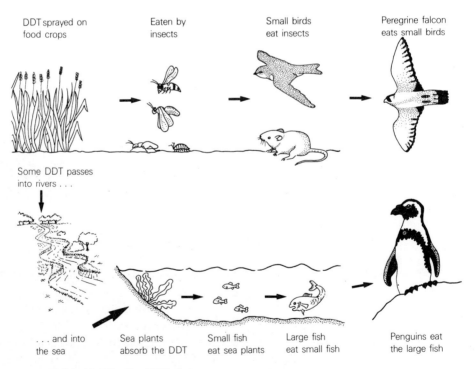

DDT sprayed on food crops

Eaten by insects

Small birds eat insects

Peregrine falcon eats small birds

Some DDT passes into rivers . . .

. . . and into the sea

Sea plants absorb the DDT

Small fish eat sea plants

Large fish eat small fish

Penguins eat the large fish

Figure 14.12   The DDT chain

DDT was discovered in peregrine falcons in the Highlands of Scotland and in penguins in the Antarctic. No DDT had ever been sprayed in the Antarctic and very little in the Highlands of Scotland. The chemical had travelled far from the crop it had originally been sprayed on. It had effects no one had dreamed of. As a result, DDT was banned in Europe and North America, but it is still used in some parts of the world.

Incidents like this have made us realise that we must study more carefully the effects of our activities. With care, we can continue to make progress without doing damage. This is where the study of ecology is so important, because it allows us to watch the environment closely. We can see small changes and take steps to prevent large ones. In this way we can maintain the balance in the environment.

Agriculture

As the population has increased, so farmers have had to produce more food. Growing more crops has meant greater use of land. Hedgerows and wasteland are disappearing. Fields have become larger. Chemicals, too, have become much more important. Very few crops in the United Kingdom are now grown without fertilisers, herbicides and pesticides.

Removing hedgerows and ploughing up wasteland has happened on a large scale. It has meant that many wild plants and animals have become rare as their homes are destroyed. We do not know whether this will have a large effect on the balance of the environment, but it does mean that there may be fewer organisms to enjoy in future.

Chemicals do have more serious effects. They can get into food chains like DDT did. DDT was particularly harmful because it is very long-lasting and remains active for many years. Modern pesticides are more short-lived and are destroyed in the soil or in organisms. Some of them are only effective for one or two weeks. They are sprayed on to a crop just at the time when the pests are active, thus killing many of them. If they should get into a food chain they break down before they can do much damage.

Fertilisers often cause more of a problem. These are leached from the soil and pass into streams and rivers. They are just as useful for water plants as for agricultural crops. They increase the growth of water plants and choke up rivers. The increase in plants can lead to increases in bacteria. This can disturb the balance in a river and can lead to the death of fish. Many fertilisers pass into the sea. Once again we do not yet know what effects this will have in the long-term. (See Figure 14.13 (overleaf).)

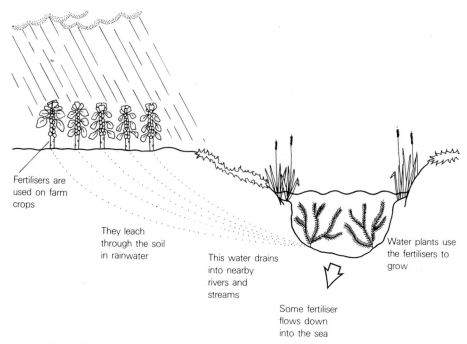

Fertilisers are
used on farm
crops

They leach
through the soil
in rainwater

This water drains
into nearby
rivers and
streams

Some fertiliser
flows down
into the sea

Water plants use
the fertilisers to
grow

Figure 14.13   Pollution by water-borne fertilisers

Industry

Some industries operate on a very large scale (Figure 14.14). They use up huge amounts of resources and produce lots of waste as well as useful products. We often think of industries as sources of pollution. This is not, however, the only way they can upset the balance.

Figure 14.14   A large earth mover

Think, for example, about the paper industry and look at Figure 14.15. The paper industry uses enormous numbers of trees. Just think about how much paper you will use in a day. There are books, newspapers, cardboard boxes, sweet wrappers, toilet paper and tissues. Much of this is thrown away and has to be replaced by more paper from more trees. Millions of tons of paper are used throughout the world every day.

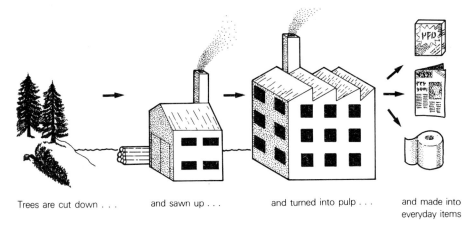

Trees are cut down . . .　　and sawn up . . .　　and turned into pulp . . .　　and made into everyday items

Figure 14.15　The paper industry

Trees, by photosynthesising, are an important part of the oxygen cycle. If too many are removed, this may be disrupted. The supply of oxygen may fall a little. It is essential, therefore, that new trees are planted to replace the ones cut down. Doing this will help maintain the balance and also mean there will be trees for paper in years to come.

Whenever substances are burned, carbon dioxide is released into the air. Power stations and heavy industries, like the steel industry, produce lots of carbon dioxide. We produce it, too, in our homes when we heat them, and from our cars. With more and more people in the world, more and more carbon dioxide is produced. Scientists have discovered that carbon dioxide tends to keep heat on the Earth. It forms a sort of 'blanket' in the atmosphere which lets the Sun's heat in but does not let it out again. This has been called the 'greenhouse' effect and it may make the Earth a little warmer.

What will happen if the Earth keeps warming up is not well understood. Some people believe that it will melt the ice at the North and South Poles. The water would flood many countries including much of the United Kingdom. Others think that warming the Earth would cause more water to evaporate from seas and lakes. This would form lots of cloud which itself would then stop the Sun's heat from getting to the Earth (Figure 14.16 (overleaf)).

Figure 14.16   Possible effect of a worldwide temperature rise?

Since we cannot predict what will happen, we need to follow very closely any changes in the environment.

Pollution   'Pollution' means adding substances to the environment which may harm it in some way. We are all polluters to some extent.

Litter (like that in Figure 14.17) is a form of pollution.

Figure 14.17   Litter

Litter is unsightly and can be dangerous. Some of it, like tin cans and old cars, takes years to decompose. Plastic litter does not decompose at all. Uncontrolled litter dumping can seriously harm the environment. Animals can die from trying to feed on thrown away food in bags. Plants may be covered and cannot photosynthesise.

Litter is a particular problem in towns and in leisure areas like picnic sites. It is an unnecessary form of pollution. It could easily be avoided if everybody disposed of litter correctly.

Other sources of pollution are not so easy to deal with. These include agricultural chemicals, like fertilisers and pesticides. They also include substances like sulphur dioxide, and nuclear radiation.

Sulphur dioxide

This gas is produced when coal and oil are burned. It is produced in particularly large amounts by power stations and also in car exhausts. One of its main effects is that it dissolves in rain water to produce 'acid rain'. The acid, when it gets into soil, stops plants from growing so well. Sulphur dioxide itself also attacks plants. It dissolves in the water layers inside the leaves, making the leaves go yellow and die.

Sulphur dioxide has changed the acid levels in lakes and rivers throughout Europe. We do not yet know what effect this will have on the microorganisms involved in the recycling processes.

Sulphur dioxide can be removed from smoke but this is costly. If it were removed from power station smoke, electricity prices would have to rise. In the end, however, it might be cheaper to do this than to clean up the damage caused by the gas.

Oil

It is easy to see the effects of oil pollution. Sea birds get covered in oil and cannot fly. Other animals and sea plants, too, get covered and killed. The oil often comes from tankers which leak oil when damaged. More often the tankers actually dump the oil when washing out their tanks.

Crude oil like this is messy but can be dealt with. Detergents are used to disperse the oil and make it sink. The oil is then naturally decomposed by bacteria. However, the effects of the detergents are not understood. It is possible that they may damage food chains much more than the oil. Once again, we know too little. Preventing the damage in the first place must be better than trying to clean it up.

Nuclear radiation

Nuclear radiation can kill. In much smaller doses it causes changes to genes or mutation. The long-term effects of such mutations cannot be predicted.

Nuclear radiation comes from atomic explosions and from nuclear power stations. Power stations use radioactive substances like uranium to make heat, which in turn is used to make electricity. After they have been used, the waste products are still radioactive. They are of no use, however, and are dumped. Usually they are sealed in concrete drums and dumped into the ocean or buried in deep mines.

What no one can be sure of, is how long the concrete drums will last before they leak. The wastes they contain will stay radioactive for several hundred years. The drums are carefully made and should last as long as the wastes. We will have to wait a long time to find out whether they do.

Nuclear power stations also use water for cooling and they are therefore often built near the sea. They draw in cold sea water and dump it back into the sea again. The heat is lost into the ocean waters. There is a risk that radioactive compounds can get into the sea water. Although great steps have been taken to prevent this, it has happened. Nuclear pollution of the sea is another form of pollution which could have serious long-term effects.

14.3 Conservation

Conservation is our attempt to keep the balance in the environment. With so many people in the world the environment has to change. We have to grow food and we must have industries. Through conservation we try to reduce the effects of these changes.

Some forms of conservation, such as limiting the number of whales caught and banning the hunting of fur animals, need the cooperation of many countries. Others, such as preventing damage and pollution to the environment, are the responsibility of each one of us.

The countryside

Uprooting wild flowers is illegal in England and Wales. Picking the flowers or fruit is not illegal, provided the plant as a whole is not damaged and provided enough flowers are left for seed. Some very rare plants are specially protected. For these it is illegal to pick them or harm them in any way at all. As more and more land is used for agriculture or industry, truly wild countryside becomes rarer. If some plants are to survive then they must be protected. (See Appendix.)

The same is true for wild animals. You may not take eggs from birds' nests, except for a few pest species of bird (see Appendix). You may not kill any wild birds except these pest species and a few species shot for sport or food. Many other animals, too, are protected and you may not do anything that could harm them.

You can get the lists of protected plants and animals from the Nature Conservancy Council. In general, you should try not to damage wild plants and animals at all. Accidents will happen, no matter how careful you are, but when you are out enjoying the countryside stick to footpaths. Try not to trample plants; leave animals alone; do not drop litter which could harm or kill them. 'Take nothing but photographs. Kill nothing but time. Leave nothing but footprints.' (See Figure 14.18.)

Never leave litter

Do not trample or otherwise damage wild flowers   Leave animals alone

Figure 14.18   Some rules for the countryside

National parks

These are areas of the countryside which have special rules to prevent their environment from being changed. People still live inside the parks, and farmers still farm the land. However, the land itself and the wildlife is protected. In this way, plants and animals will not die out. Future generations can visit the parks and enjoy nature undisturbed. (See Figure 14.19 (overleaf).)

Most countries of the world have National Parks. In Africa, the huge National Parks have been set up to try to stop wild animals like elephants and rhinos from dying out.

Figure 14.19   The National Parks, like Snowdonia, are one way of conserving the beauty and harmony of nature

Reclaiming wasteland

In parts of the United Kingdom large areas of land have become derelict or covered in waste. This is particularly true of the waste heaps and land around industry and mines. For many years huge mountains of spoil were dumped and left. Now, though, attempts are being made to reclaim certain areas. Soil has been brought in and plants encouraged to grow. There has been a lot of success and a lot of land has been returned to the wild again.

Managing fish

Sea fish form an important part of our food supply. We can, however, quite easily overfish our oceans. This reduces the number of fish left to breed, and thus the numbers which can be caught in the future. By reducing the number caught, we can make sure that there are enough left to breed.

Why is conservation necessary?

Conservation helps to prevent plants and animals from dying out. If they die, they are lost forever. We do not know what effect that might have.

Many plants supply useful drugs or other chemicals. We cannot say what chemicals we may need in the future, nor what plants we might get them from. We would, therefore, be unwise to allow plants to become extinct.

Genetic engineering is a new science. Genes from wild plants can be used to help breed better crops. If a plant becomes extinct its genes are lost.

Plants and animals all form part of food webs. We do not know what would happen if a food web is seriously disturbed.

Conservation is necessary because we must try to keep parts of our world intact. Sometimes we do great damage to the environment because we understand so little about the complex way it works. An example of this was the DDT poisoning of peregrine falcons referred to earlier. At other times we do damage in spite of knowing what harm can be caused. For instance, in many parts of the world large areas of forest are being chopped down even though many scientists say this will seriously affect the ecological balance. Until we can live in the world without causing such damage we must conserve certain areas. At least in this way we may be able to overcome any mistakes that may be made.

Summary

1. A balanced environment is necessary to maintain food webs and to allow recycling.

2. A balanced environment does not mean that the numbers of organisms always stay the same.

3. We influence the environment through agriculture, industry and by simply taking up living space.

4. Some of our activities harm the environment. Pollution is an example of this.

5. Pollution is the addition of harmful substances to the environment.

6. Conservation is the attempt (a) to preserve a balance in the environment and (b) to prevent plants and animals from becoming extinct.

Wordfinder on Chapter 14

(Teacher, please see special note in front of book.)

Copy or photocopy the wordfinder. Do not write on this page.

Find the question by starting somewhere on the *outside frame of letters* and going clockwise.

Find the appropriate words.

The leftover letters will give a number answer to the question.

I	N	T	H	I	S	Q	U	A	D	R
R	B	U	R	D	O	C	K	C	N	A
E	U	T	H	T	E	A	C	E	O	T
V	T	W	H	E	A	T	O	L	I	H
O	T	N	S	L	W	S	L	A	L	O
C	E	E	M	O	S	S	M	N	E	W
S	R	R	S	I	E	A	E	D	D	M
I	C	L	O	V	E	R	H	I	N	A
D	U	L	E	V	E	G	N	N	A	N
U	P	T	H	I	S	T	L	E	D	Y
O	Y	N	A	C	S	T	N	A	L	P

Appendix

'Pest' species of wild birds

Collared dove	House sparrow	Magpie
Crow	Jackdaw	Rook
Feral pigeon	Jay	Starling
Great black-backed gull	Lesser black-backed gull	Woodpigeon
Herring gull		

Wild birds specially protected at all times

Avocet
Barn owl
Bearded tit
Bee-eater
Bewick's swan
Bittern
Black-necked grebe
Black redstart
Black-tailed godwit
Black tern
Black-winged stilt
Bluethroat
Brambling
Cetti's warbler
Chough
Cirl bunting
Common quail
Common scoter
Corncrake
Crested tit
Crossbills (all species)
Dartford warbler
Divers (all species)
Dotterel
Fieldfare
Firecrest
Garganey

Golden eagle
Golden oriole
Goshawk
Green sandpiper
Greenshank
Gyr falcon
Harriers (all species)
Hobby
Honey buzzard
Hoopoe
Kentish plover
Kingfisher
Lapland bunting
Leach's petrel
Little bittern
Little gull
Little ringed plover
Little tern
Long-tailed duck
Marsh warbler
Mediterranean gull
Merlin
Osprey
Peregrine
Purple heron
Purple sandpiper

Red-backed shrike
Red kite
Red-necked phalarope
Redwing
Roseate tern
Ruff
Savi's warbler
Scarlet rosefinch
Scaup
Serin
Shorelark
Short-toed treecreeper
Slavonian grebe
Snow bunting
Snowy owl
Spoonbill
Spotted crake
Stone curlew
Temminck's stint
Velvet scoter
Whimbrel
White-tailed eagle
Whooper swan
Woodlark
Wood sandpiper
Wryneck

Wild birds specially protected during the close season

Goldeneye
Greylag goose (in Outer
  Hebrides, Caithness,
  Sutherland and Wester Ross only)
Pintail

Specially protected wild animals

Mammals
Bats (all 15 species)
Bottle-nosed dolphin
Common dolphin
Common otter
Harbour (or common)
 porpoise
Red squirrel

Reptiles
Sand lizard
Smooth snake

Amphibians
Great crested (or watry) newt
Natterjack toad

Fish
Burbot

Butterflies
Chequered skipper
Heath fritillary
Large blue
Swallowtail

Moths
Barberry carpet
Black-veined
Essex emerald
New Forest burnet
Reddish buff

Other insects
Field cricket
Mole cricket
Norfolk aeshna dragonfly
Rainbow leaf beetle
Wart-biter grasshopper

Spiders
Fen raft spider
Ladybird spider

Snails
Carthusian snail
Glutinous snail
Sandbowl snail

Specially protected wild plants

Adder's-tongue spearwort
Alpine catchfly
Alpine gentian
Alpine sow-thistle
Alpine Woodsia
Bedstraw broomrape
Blue heath
Brown galingale
Cheddar pink
Childling pink
Diapensia
Dickie's bladder-fern
Downy woundwort
Drooping saxifrage
Early spider-orchid
Fen orchid
Fen violet
Field cow-wheat
Field eryngo
Field wormwood
Ghost orchid
Greater yellow-rattle

Jersey cudweed
Killarney fern
Lady's-slipper
Late spider-orchid
Least lettuce
Limestone woundwort
Lizard orchid
Military orchid
Monkey orchid
Norwegian sandwort
Oblong Woodsia
Oxtongue broomrape
Perennial knawel
Plymouth pear
Purple spurge
Red helleborine
Ribbon-leaved water-
 plantain
Rock cinquefoil
Rock sea-lavender (two rare
 species)
Rough marsh-mallow

Round-headed leek
Sea knotgrass
Sickle-leaved hare's-ear
Small Alison
Small hare's-ear
Snowdon lily
Spiked speedwell
Spring gentian
Starfruit
Starved wood-sedge
Teesdale sandwort
Thistle broomrape
Triangular club-rush
Tufted saxifrage
Water germander
Whorled Solomon's-seal
Wild cotoneaster
Wild gladiolus
Wood calamint

Further information can be obtained from The Nature Conservancy Council
Headquarters: 19/20 Belgrave Square
                London
                SW1X 8PY
Publications: Athingham Park
                Shrewsbury
                SY4 4TW

Index